COGNAC

COGNAC

THE SEDUCTIVE SAGA
OF THE WORLD'S
MOST COVETED SPIRIT

KYLE JARRARD

WILEY

JOHN WILEY & SONS, INC.

Copyright © 2005 by Kyle Jarrard. All rights reserved

Published by John Wiley & Sons, Inc., Hoboken, New Jersey
Published simultaneously in Canada

Design and composition by Navta Associates, Inc.

For general information about our other products and services, please contact our Customer Care Department within the United States at (800) 762-2974, outside the United States at (317) 572-3993 or fax (317) 572-4002.

Wiley also publishes its books in a variety of electronic formats. Some content that appears in print may not be available in electronic books. For more information about Wiley products, visit our web site at www.wiley.com.

Library of Congress Cataloging-in-Publication Data:
Jarrard, Kyle, date.
  Cognac : the seductive saga of the world's most coveted spirit / Kyle Jarrard.
      p.   cm.
  Includes bibliographical references and index.
  ISBN 0-471-45944-5 (cloth)
  1.   Brandy.   I. Title.
  TP599.J37 2005
  641.2'53—dc22

                                                                        2004011819
Printed in the United States of America

10 9 8 7 6 5 4 3 2 1

For my belle-famille charentaise

In Cognac, we understand how to wait. It's the only way to make it good.

—Jean Monnet (1888–1979),
Cognac trader and European statesman

Cognac is born of exceptional circumstances. It is a natural prodigy, an accident, a miracle.

—Robert Delamain (1879–1949),
author of the 1935 classic *Histoire du Cognac*

Claret is the liquor for boys; port, for men; but he who aspires to be a hero must drink brandy.

—Samuel Johnson (1709–1784)

What a nice cup of tea!

—Queen Elizabeth the Queen Mother (1900–2002),
after tasting old Cognacs at Hennessy in 1980

CONTENTS

INTRODUCTION

*T*O HAVE A COGNAC IS TO BECOME A PLAYER in an old and rich story. People everywhere know about Cognac. They might not know just how it's made, but they like it. They might use it in a cocktail, or they might savor it for an hour. Either way, they'll remember it—that brandy from France.

Often expensive, Cognac is always classy. Pricey, because it takes so much work to take a mediocre white wine, distill it into crystalline firewater, and then age it in big oak barrels for years until, the miracle complete, it has become an amber-hued nectar. Seductive, because it satiates the senses with a fantastic range of fragrances, from white vine flowers to green apples, from apricots, peaches, and almonds to cloves, pepper, and the forest floor. Elegant, because it is an indisputable symbol of high refinement: a bottle of Cognac is the gift of gifts—the best of the best—to mark a grand success.

Cognac is the fruit of an incredible set of circumstances: the gentle climate of southwest France that makes grape growing the natural thing to do, easy access via the Charente River to the Atlantic for shipping Cognac to points north in Europe or to ports half a world away, and the proximity of great oak forests out of which to fashion venerable barrels without which Cognac wouldn't exist at all.

But these only begin to explain Cognac's raison d'être. Perfect geology has its fundamental place; Cretaceous oceans laid down the chalky basement upon which the house of Cognac has been built and into which the roots of the vineyard have grown deep. History has always been on Cognac's side, too, like a big brother, pushing it along or rescuing it from the abyss. More than once, this great drink stood at the edge of certain doom at the hands of despotic sovereigns, soft-headed politicians, and greedy businessmen—not to mention fickle and cruel Nature.

It's an epic tale. Just about everyone who ever had a part in the affairs of Cognac's ocean-facing motherland also had a hand, one way or another, in Cognac's destiny—be it Celts, Romans, Visigoths, Merovingians, Carolingians, Vikings, dukes of Aquitaine, kings and princes of England, barons of Poitou, counts of Angoulême, La Rochelle traders, French kings, Dutch distillers, Protestant exiles, Catholic zealots, English free traders, American horticulturists, German invaders, or European Union bureaucrats.

And just about anyone who ever lived in Cognac country or romped through it from the Bronze Age to the Internet Age has had a part, willing or not, in one conflict or another as France formed itself into a nation. People weren't fighting over brandy, of course; but again and again Cognac country found itself in the thick of various frays, whether during those long centuries when it was a premier wine-making region—its white wines were famous all over northern Europe—or since the late 1500s, when it began exporting the clear brandy called eau-de-vie and undertook its four-hundred-year march to markets the world over.

It was a rough journey made all the more difficult by the ups and downs of international trade: from war-halted commerce to staggering import duties, from contraband and fakery to usurpation of the Cognac name. Then there's the love-hate business feud fought across the Atlantic between the Americans and the French in the name of protecting chicken prices or soybean shipments, the bottle of Cognac with a duty hammer raised above it at each turn of the story. And don't forget the awful diseases that have cut through the vineyard, or the tiny louse that arrived on native American vines and wiped out the vines of Europe, or the solution to this Armageddon that came again from America, using old Texas vines. Not least should you forget the German lieutenant who rushed into France with the Nazis but, having been born and raised in Cognac himself, protected the stocks against his own thirsty armies. Doesn't this add up to a fine glass of luck?

Lovers of Cognac will tell you that of course it should have survived the grind of history. Because it unlocks the gastronomic soul of man and people crave it. Because it can't be copied. And because it's simply perfect.

Countless trading houses have watched over Cognac down through the years: *négociants* like Hennessy (no. 1), Rémy Martin (no. 2), Martell, and Courvoisier (tied for no. 3), the giants who rule the realm today. Hundreds of others have come and gone, and yet these now-lost names speak of Cognac's perennial power to remake itself, to get through bad years and come out shining again, even if under someone else's roof. Many were those who shuddered as this family-run industry came to the attention of spirits groups back in the 1960s. But no disasters have occurred, even though almost all of the leading Cognac houses are now owned by multinationals. In fact this industry is in excellent health despite its many far-flung godfathers making decisions in places like Bermuda and Japan.

In fine form but top-heavy, which may or may not be good; the top four houses control 74 percent of the market, the top ten run 84 percent. That leaves only a sliver of the pie for dozens of other traders who manage despite the odds, but almost nothing for the independents who sell their own Cognac themselves. These proportions matter greatly, if only because there's so much money involved, a megamarket worth €1.3 billion a year, or about $1.6 billion; 95 percent of that is exports. Put another way, more than 127 million bottles of Cognac were shipped in the 2003 calendar year, nearly 121 million of those heading abroad. America absorbs the lion's share at 41 percent of all exported Cognac. Some 153 countries import it. Hardly a spot on the planet remains out of reach.

And yet Cognac doesn't rule the spirits market. Indeed, it has to fight for its spot on the bar shelf. According to Impact International, the worldwide sales market for Cognac is at least 110 million bottles per year; add to this all other brandies that aren't Cognac, and you get 158 million bottles. Whiskey's worldwide market is 980 million bottles; vodka sales are about the same, and so are rum's; gin's sales are 460 million bottles, and tequila's 385 million; and then there are the world's various liqueurs, which add up to 375 million bottles a year, plus all the home brews, which adds another 1.3 billion bottles. That leaves Cognac with just under 2 percent of the global spirits market.

A drop in an ocean of 5.6 billion bottles of spirits. But a drop that might as well cover the world for all its depth, for all the twists of fate and miracles that, lined up, make for a saga peopled by a colorful cast of characters, well, straight out of history.

THE GRAPES ARE COMING

ABIKE RIDE UP BEHIND SAINT-SEVER-DE-Saintonge in the summer can be quite hot and the hills a struggle. But it's worth the climb. Up here, on these slopes, you can look back north and see everything: a long quiet stretch of the Charente River winding east to west, hills all around cascading into the valley, their sides covered with row after row of vines, a green multitude standing rigidly in the steamy air. Here and there the ranks are broken up by rectangles of sunflowers or wheat or corn that invite the eye to stay and rest. Small hawks ride the hot August breezes down and up, watching. Farmers ride little tractors between the vines, spraying treatments against mildew or trimming off leaves so the sun will fall more bountifully on the swelling grapes. Now and again a car will sail down one of the white-rock roads, heading south toward Pons or maybe west toward Saintes. You can also look east and see plumes from the smokestacks at the Saint-Gobain glass factory outside Cognac, a dozen kilometers away. Between here and the maiden city, the vines only get thicker, their ranks more numerous, until they cover just about everything in the heart of Cognac country.

If you have enough energy, it's good to pedal on higher, above Jarlac. There's a stub of a limestone windmill on the crest by the road. You can drop your bike into the wildflowers and climb over the bramble-draped rubble of the mill and scramble onto its base. The peace of the world lies spread out all around and a breeze comes in off the Atlantic.

Of course, you soon get up and walk out into the vineyards. The thick walls of leaves radiate coolness. The soil is dry and kicks up into dust. Down the slope, a jackrabbit freezes in its tracks, then bolts. You can't help but scour the stones beneath your feet, for this is very interesting ground.

It takes only a few minutes to find one—a big white limestone clam about the size of a dessert plate poking out of the topsoil. Pick up one of these clams—now just old rocks beat up by farming tools and the passage of tractors—and it sits heavy in your hand, inspiring thoughts of life's old lines stretching far back through deep time. A single one of these clams would have made an interesting meal, steamed and slathered with butter, accompanied by a local white wine, surely followed by a dose of Cognac.

Life in the warm, shallow ocean that once covered Cognac country
has left behind abundant limestone fossils.

Clams, oysters, gastropods—all these and more lie scattered on the ground wherever you go. Winegrowers will exclaim, "The ocean was here!" It's maybe fifty kilometers away today, due west. But it was here, all right.

The big clam rising out of the soil today lived on the bottom of the tropical Cretaceous sea 80 million years ago. Sea levels were high all around the world, and the Atlantic—formed as North America, Africa, and Eurasia pulled away from each other—was on its way to becoming a respectably sized ocean. Geologists call this time the Campanian, an eleven-million-year-long layering of rock that dominated the last half of the Cretaceous.

Also living in huge numbers in the warm, shallow sea on the western flank of Europe were sponges, rays, rudist bivalves, sharks, and turtles. It was a good time, biologically speaking. The water was full of nutrients pulsing from ocean rifts as the Atlantic widened. Things could only grow.

In this well-lighted park of evolution it is the teeming billions of creatures at the base of the food chain that open the story of Cognac. Without a doubt, they are the fundamental physical link between far-gone times and the glasses of Cognac enjoyed today. Collectively known as plankton, these life forms flourished all through the Cretaceous, which ran from about 135 million years ago to 65 million years ago, and still do today.

Among the most important plankton in regard to the rocks underlying the Cognac hills are the single-celled algae called coccolithophores. These plants have something special about them that produces a covering of tough, calcitic disks. This outer assembly measures only a few microns across and yet looks like an elaborate spaceship ready for interplanetary travel. Scientists aren't sure what purpose the hard shell serves the plant within, but some speculate that this layer protects it from sudden environmental change. One thing is sure: a coccolith, like everything else, doesn't live forever.

Once the tiny plants die, their shells sink to the bottom of the sea, by the billions upon billions. They are not alone, either. There are planktonic animals about the same size called foraminifers that have similar futuristic-looking shells that get shed when life comes to a close. And there are the slightly larger ostracods, crustaceans a few millimeters long whose coverings look like beans. It's not hard to imagine, then, a blizzard of calcitic debris blanketing the ocean floor. Add millions upon millions of years of such blizzards, press and pack it all tightly, and you eventually get beds of chalk hundreds of meters deep.

Deposits of this limestone are widespread around the world. Probably the most recognizable limestone locale is the White Cliffs of Dover. In France, limestone is common all around the Paris Basin from Normandy to Champagne, and in the southeast from the Ardèche to Marseille. Limestone also underlies the Aquitaine Basin, the giant low-lying region facing the Atlantic that runs from Poitou in the north to the Pyrenees in the south.

In the Charente River valley, a pocket of northern Aquitaine about half the size of Massachusetts, these broad and deep layers of white rock form the foundation of Cognac. And it is in this wide, sun-filled valley ripe for growing grapes that Cognac country was built—its many wealthy cities, innumerable distilleries, and ranks of stone warehouses—from its source down to the Atlantic, a stretch of 350 kilometers mainly through the Charente and Charente-Maritime Departments in southwestern France.

To Jean-François Tournepiche, who heads the archaeological section of the Musée des Beaux Arts in Angoulême, the shelves of white rock that form the basement of Cognac country are like a "stack of plates slipped over and lying one against the other," each one younger in age as you move northeast to southwest. Cutting through these plates of time is the Charente as it winds down from the uplands of the woodsy Limousin region to the east—home of oaks used to make barrels for Cognac—on its long journey to the Atlantic. The limestone-built cities strung east-to-west along its banks—Angoulême, Jarnac, Cognac, Saintes—will be forever associated with the world's most coveted brandy. The river meets the sea near Rochefort, with its glorious history of royal shipbuilding, just south of La Rochelle, the port from which so much salt and wine headed north in the Middle Ages and from which thousands of barrels of Cognac soon followed.

South of the Charente the white, chalky terrain rolls lightly; this is late Cretaceous country, prime terrain for the finest Cognac, with many a fossil underfoot, and it stretches down toward Bordeaux. North of the river the hills climb through early Cretaceous country and then into Jurassic lands; these older limestones, too, have had a role in the evolution of Cognac.

The Jurassic was the period of seventy million years before the Cretaceous and, like its descendant, a time of rising and falling oceans and expanding sea life. The Atlantic Ocean was just beginning to open up, and Europe was just a half-dozen islands off the newly formed North American continent. These close-set islands lay just north of the equator, and the climate was hot and humid. Imagine a shallow, translucent sea, with beaches, marshes, and lagoons. This was the time of the plesiosaurs, big sea reptiles with four paddles and snakelike heads, giant marine crocodiles, huge turtles, and ammonoids, mollusks that could fill their tightly curled shells with air to rise to the surface or sink like a submarine. Rounding out the busy sea life scene were oysters, clams, brachiopods, urchins, and gastropods.

As the Jurassic period ended, oceans were withdrawing and leaving behind gulfs and briny lagoons in low-lying areas of the Cognac region from La Rochelle to Angoulême. Scientists have found remains of numerous ancient animals from this time in thick gypsum and marl beds just north of Cognac. This early-Cretaceous site, in the Champblanc quarry near the village of Cherves-de-Cognac, has only begun to be uncovered; the first digs, in 2002 and 2003, have given scientists high hopes that the site will illuminate a dark period. Among the finds here are fish, turtles, amphibians, crocodiles, flying reptiles, dinosaurs, some early mammals, and birds.

Seawater sometimes invaded the ancient Cognac country depression, and freshwater washed down from rain-battered continental heights. Then the land became exposed for more than forty million years. When the ocean finally poured over the region again to begin another chalk-laying epoch for the rest of the Cretaceous, there was a botanical explosion under way along the shores, where flowering plants were putting on a color show that outshined the long years when the duller green conifers ruled the old plant world.

Just as the limestone varies in age from one side of the Charente valley to the other, so changes the soil—and the grapevines and Cognac produced.

The geological center of Cognac country lies in what is called the Grande Champagne, which is also the name of the best *cru*, or growth, where grapes for making Cognac are cultivated. In this zone, the Cretaceous limestone dates to the Campanian stage, which ran from eighty-three million years ago to seventy-two million years ago, and to the slightly older Santonian stage, which began eighty-six million years ago and lasted just three million years. Close by is the next-oldest stage of rock, a two-million-year slice called the Coniacian, named after Cognac, that lies in part under the town as well as along the Charente; a lot of this rock ended up being used in buildings and houses.

In the Campanian, the ocean was rather shallow and oysters were abundant; these ancient conditions created a soil that today is crumbly and chalky and mixed with clay that stores water and keeps vineyards in good shape even during the dry weather of high summer. In the Santonian, the sea was generally deeper, and the chalk laid down during these years has ended up in the twenty-first century being a little harder but still rather crumbly, clayey, and finely layered. Today's vineyards flourish in soft chalk since their roots can go deep without much impediment, absorbing numerous minerals along the way that help give Cognac its agreeable bouquet of aromas.

Grande Champagne, the premier *cru*, lies south of the city of Cognac on the left bank of the Charente and is centered on the town of Segonzac. (The name *Champagne* here does not refer to the bubbly known around the world today; rather, it is an old form of the word *campagne*, or countryside.) Comprising only a few thousand hectares of vines, this growth forms the innermost of a series of terrains reaching all the way to the Atlantic. Cognacs made in this zone are the world's best—for lightness, finesse, and floral and woody flavors that linger in the mouth a long time.

Grande Champagne's sister growth is Petite Champagne. It, too, has its roots planted in Campanian and Santonian chalk and hugs Grande Champagne to the east, south, and west. While the resulting Cognac is similar to that of Grande Champagne, it's a shade less exquisite, its fragrances a bit less lasting. Put Cognacs from the two Champagnes together, however, and you get an eau-de-vie known as Fine Champagne that has long pleased Cognac lovers for its delicate balance.

Next comes the Borderies, a small plot northwest of Cognac on the right bank of the Charente. Here the rock is less uniformly laid down, constituting a mixture of Cretaceous stone from the Turonian stage (ninety-one to eighty-eight million years ago) to the Santonian, a swath of time that makes it generally older than the Champagne areas. The clayey-sandy soil produces a sweet, very floral Cognac that some say imparts a distinct aroma of violets.

Surrounding all these zones in a fat circle, from east of Angoulême to slightly west of Saintes and encompassing Cognac and Jarnac, is the Fins Bois, followed in a wider ring by the Bons Bois. Last but not least is the Bois Ordinaires in the sandy country near Rochefort and La Rochelle by the sea. All three regions constitute a mixture of Jurassic and Cretaceous chalk of varying percentages and densities that produce quite different vineyards. Most of the Cognacs coming out of these areas are powerful,

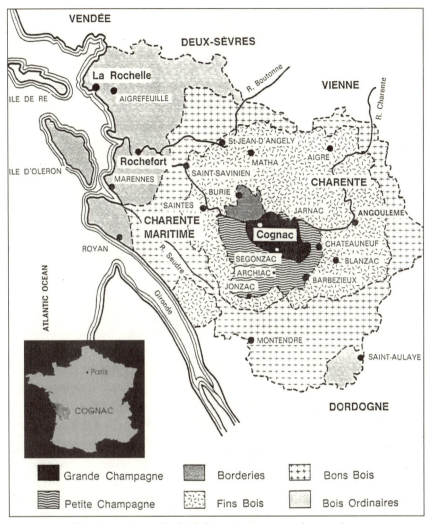

The Cognac vineyard is divided into six *crus*, or growths, spread out
like rings from the capital city.

making them best for use with lighter Cognacs from interior lands to
make blends.

The first scientifically accurate map of the region's geological foundations was drawn up by Henri Coquand, a geologist and teacher, and published in 1858. Tournepiche has one of Coquand's colorful maps hanging
in the offices at the Beaux Arts museum in Angoulême. It shows in rich
greens and reds and blues the ages of the rocks spilling down from the

northeast in younger and younger layers. One can imagine the thriving submarine environment, the chalky-clayey muds, the beds of sand and calcitic remains, the ocean currents mixing up the debris and preparing the long sleep that will result in the deep compression and formation of dozens of meters of limestone.

But all good things come to an end sooner or later, and it was no different in Cognac country. The quiet limestone-laying years were dealt a rude shock sixty-five million years ago. This is when many scientists believe an asteroid set off or abetted the second-largest extinction in geologic history. In the marine environment, 70 percent of all species were wiped out in a blink of time. Also hit hard were families of the coccoliths that form the basic substance in limestone and the bryozoans, marine creatures that lived by the millions in colonies and whose remains are another big part of Cognac's founding rock. As the dust settled, the survivors reorganized. Here then begins the Cenozoic era, known as the Age of the Mammals.

Sea levels stayed relatively high until just a few million years ago, and likewise the climate was mostly warm. Landmasses continued tacking this way and that, most spectacularly with India rushing toward Asia to knock the Himalayas into being, and with Africa crowding closer to Europe, giving birth to the Alps and throwing Iberia into a spin until it smacked into France and lifted the Pyrenees that form the French-Spanish border. Global temperatures declined in the latter part of the Cenozoic, then plunged in the next geological era, the Quaternary, or the last million and a half years or so. This was the Pleistocene Ice Age, when glaciers plowed over the Earth.

The very earliest people to live in Cognac country came out of Central Europe. Scientists say these people, most likely *Homo erectus*, arrived in Charente just over half a million years ago, in the early Paleolithic, or Old Stone Age. The climate was cool, if not frigid, and these peoples lived by hunting and gathering. No *Homo erectus* bones have been found hereabouts, but hundreds of their flint tools have turned up in gravel pits in the Charente valley between Cognac and Jarnac and also in caves in eastern Cognac country. The oldest human skeletal remains in the region are 200,000 years old, an archaic form of *Homo neanderthalensis*.

The Pleistocene Ice Age saw four big glacial expansions, the final one—which lasted about 60,000 years and is known in Europe as the Würm glaciation—ending a little less than 12,000 years ago. For most of this time it was the Neanderthals who were running the show. These humans lived in a space stretching from the Near East to western Europe for 170,000 years; the period from 100,000 years ago to 35,000 years ago was their heyday.

Toward the end of their long reign, the Neanderthals were joined in their seminomadic world by more anatomically modern *Homo sapiens*, the Cro-Magnons. What caused it is uncertain, but something extraordinary happened and the Neanderthals exited the scene; suddenly they had disappeared from France by 30,000 years ago, and vanished from all of Europe by 25,000 years ago.

Some scientists say that the Cro-Magnons rolled into Europe and took the place by storm. Other experts see a less warlike scenario, with interbreeding gradually eliminating the Neanderthals. What occurred—even a species-ending virus is not out of the question—is just not known.

The remains of a very late Neanderthal adult were found in Cognac country in 1979 near the village of Saint-Césaire, in the valley of the Coran, a clear stream running south into the Charente. A few tens of thousands of years ago this place was primeval forest, and limestone cliffs lining the valley stood even higher. Discovered buried in a rock shelter, the skeleton lay among artifacts associated with Cro-Magnons. Centuries upon centuries would pass before the Cognac country area became a booming agricultural center, but even 36,000 years ago human beings found the place to their liking and made their homes on bluffs. Such spots could be easily defended, as would be seen when Stone Age bands settled down in huge camps.

The Würm glaciation is known to have been quite cold in its final stages, especially about 18,000 years ago. Ice moved as far south as northern Germany and southern England, and it spread out from the Alps. Glaciers also advanced out of the Pyrenees and from the Massif Central in the heart of France. In Cognac, the countryside was less icy and more steppelike, as the Gulf Stream made the climate more habitable than the rest of Europe.

Because so much water is taken up by glaciers, sea levels in the late Würm were sixty to ninety meters lower than now and the coastline was two hundred kilometers farther west. The Atlantic beaches are where they are today because twelve thousand years ago the world warmed, glaciers shrank back, and ocean levels soared. That break in the weather allowed people all over Europe and elsewhere to make one of the most dramatic transitions in history.

The Neolithic period, or New Stone Age, opened in 5000 B.C. in the

Cognac basin. The hunting-and-gathering lifestyle gave way to settlement, herding, and agriculture. As people took up farming, they became producers, and populations rose. Evidence of big open-air Neolithic camps has been discovered up and down the Charente valley. Though you could walk right over them in the fields and not have a hint of their existence, a new breed of archaeologist is coaxing these locales out of the dirt.

Jacques Dassié, for one, has crisscrossed the skies of this region for years, snapping photos of the sprawling outlines of these camps, which are plainly visible from aloft. These etchings mark man's vast efforts over time, since whenever a trench or pit or hole was dug, the soil was changed. Today those cavities, long filled in with debris, retain more water than the surrounding land, allowing plants to turn brighter green and be seen by scientists in airplanes. Dassié's 130,000 photos have brought to light 2,200 sites. A few dozen have been dug up, leading to much discovery about the time from the Neolithic period to the Middle Ages.

The Neolithic produced a succession of sophisticated cultures. Many clues to this long, shadowy past have come from the camps these people built on hillsides or rock promontories; most lie in the western parts of Cognac country around Saintes. Dassié has spotted about 120 of them during his flyovers since 1962. Anywhere from one hundred to six hundred meters in diameter, the camps were protected by a single or multiple perimeter of trenches four to eight meters wide and three to four meters deep, above which rock or wooden ramparts were added for extra height. Entry to the camps was purposefully made difficult via narrow, pincerlike defiles. Postholes show that sizable structures were built within some of the camps.

The Diconche camp, atop a cliff on the outskirts of Saintes, is one of the finest Neolithic examples in Saintonge. Three different civilizations lived here for most of the third millennium B.C. Scientists have collected 400,000 artifacts from the site.

Throughout the middle of the Neolithic, these New Stone Age peoples built other big structures, too: the megalithic dolmens. Though today they look like giant stone tables among the vines, these were tombs covered by a mound of dirt and rock, with access to the central chamber through a tunnel. Dating to as early as 4500 to 4000 B.C., the dolmens of western Europe are among the oldest examples of human architecture in the world.

While the big camps and tumuli tell much about the Stone Age, it is the many single burial pits that distinguish the Bronze and Iron Ages of the last two millennia before Christ. Dassié has located two thousand or so of these sites, in which urns with ashes and human bones have been found. Other items include iron nails and bars, a sword bent in two, and the handhold of a shield.

Though the picture of Charente's early Iron Age remains fuzzy, scientists have a clearer idea of its final years. One example is the necropolis of Chenon, in north Charente, whose funeral urns contained incinerated bones, vases, clasps, and knives; these date from between 500 B.C. and 450 B.C. Other urns have turned up in the Quéroy cave east of Angoulême, but these were empty; burned human bones, oddly, lay next to the urns.

The Celts of central Europe, pressured by populations from the east, began moving across Europe and, by 400 B.C., had settled nearly all of France. They were a warrior people, with a talent for fashioning iron swords. They were also skilled farmers, who ignited an agricultural boom using iron plows.

The last half of the Iron Age winds the clock down to Roman times, when the Santons, a Celtic tribe, dominated Cognac country. Their homeland, today Saintonge, covered what is now the western half of the region, roughly that of the modern-day Charente-Maritime Department.

Not a lot is known about the early days of the Santons. One thing is fairly clear: they hadn't yet begun cultivating vines. It was the Romans who would import this art. On the other hand, it's certain that the Santons made salt and that they got even better at it once the Romans introduced the more efficient methods used on the shores of the Mediterranean. Soon, Saintonge salt and wines would set out on a voyage down through the centuries.

Excellent farmers, the Santons also raised animals in abundance and produced surpluses of grains; these would serve to keep Rome's army supplied and fed on its campaigns through Gaul, an area about the size of France today. Historians note that ultimately, Gaul did not fall because it was economically inferior. On the contrary, Gaul enjoyed many profitable links with the Roman Empire, especially along the route that brought wines and luxury goods from the Mediterranean Roman province of Narbonensis along the Garonne into Bordeaux country. Commercial routes across the Gaul countryside were initially developed by traders of Greek origin who, centuries earlier, established the colony of Massalia (Marseille) and a number of satellite towns along the Mediterranean and in the Rhône valley. Along these virtual highways moved vast quantities of goods that made Gaul into the trade platform for western Europe. Down from the north came tin, copper, iron, glassware, grain, and salt, while up from the south went wine and decorative wares. A great number of amphora shards from the last century before Christ have been found in Cognac country. This trading frenzy gave rise not only to more farming but to the development of big towns in Gaul.

As is well known, Julius Caesar's drive to conquer and subdue all resistance in Gaul was anything but simple, and the Santons generally didn't make things easy for him. When Vercingetorix, the Celtic warrior-king, and his forces were pinned down by Caesar in August of 52 B.C. at Alésia (Alise Sainte-Reine in Burgundy), the Santons answered the call by sending twelve thousand fighters to relieve their comrades. The Santons' neighbors to the north, the Pictons, sent eight thousand, and the Petrucores, who lived to the southeast, five thousand. Tens of thousands of other tribesmen from across Gaul hurried to try and save Vercingetorix. But it was all for naught as Caesar won the day, marking the beginning of half a millennium of robust Roman power in this woodsy land.

Like many of the tribes of Gaul, the Santons rapidly adopted the victors' customs. Conflict had been costly, but commerce was king under *Pax romana*. During this initial postwar heyday, the Santons apparently found themselves abruptly elevated to a prestigious spot on the empire's map.

Marcus Agrippa, right-hand man of Augustus, was charged by his emperor with making certain that Roman values were winning over hearts and minds in Gaul. Working from Lugdunum, capital of Gaul and known today as Lyon, Agrippa conceived a web of roads linking the region's centers. One line the governor drew went west from Lugdunum over the Massif Central and ended at the Santons' town, Mediolanum Santonum. Mediolanum was being built on the Carentonus (Charente) and is believed to have been named by Augustus as the first capital of Aquitania, a Roman province stretching from the Loire to the Pyrenees. The city may well have held that honor for well over a century, before power shifted north to Limonum (Poitiers) in the mid-second century. After Poitiers, it was Burdigala (Bordeaux) that ruled over the province in the third century. Mediolanum Santonum, as a result, found itself teetering at the historical abyss.

But first, and for about 150 years, Mediolanum, modern-day Saintes, was an important city in this part of the world. In just a few decades it grew in size from almost nothing to a fantastic 150 hectares. At its cultural apogee, it was home to as many as fifteen thousand people, and a busy trading center.

Its most spectacular monument is the Arch of Germanicus. For the modern visitor, the arch jumps out of the two-thousand-year-old past with a giant's strength. It first loomed near the head of a bridge that crossed the river west into Mediolanum and today stands not far from its original spot. The arch is the only significant monument in town that wasn't torn down to build a rampart around the city in the late third century. Germanic peoples were pressing the eastern frontiers of the empire, while Saxon and Frankish pirates were raiding the coasts of Gaul. Rome decided to erect defenses. Rampart builders took apart Saintes, seizing any materials they could find to protect the town. Parts of this rough rampart have been dug out below street level.

The other big Roman ruin in Saintes is the amphitheater, which lies in a bowl between hills west of the old city and could seat twenty thousand. Elsewhere in Mediolanum there were thermal baths, elaborate homes, and workshops for glassware and pottery. Highways also led north to Limonum, land of the sea-faring Pictons, and southward to Burdigala,

The two-thousand-year-old Arch of Germanicus used to stand on the bridge leading into the walled city of Saintes.

where the winegrowing Bituriges Vivisci lived between the Garonne and the Atlantic.

Upstream from Mediolanum there were many big farms scattered along the valley—but few sizable towns. If you go up the Charente today from Saintes, the next city you come to is Cognac, a journey of 30 kilometers or so. In Roman times, though, there wasn't even a place called Cognac, and certainly no signs that the world's premier eau-de-vie center would arise here. There was, however, a group of houses and farm buildings in an area corresponding to the western parts of the current city. If not yet a town, it was nevertheless a busy farming center, and there is clear evidence that Roman land owners introduced vineyards and made lots of wine.

Besides Mediolanum in the west, the other important Roman city in Cognac country lay 75 kilometers to the east: Iculisma, present-day Angoulême, perched on a limestone plateau. Evidence of human presence here, where today the old city towers above the Charente, dates from 4,000 years ago. While clues to villages here before the Romans are paltry, a town arose during the reign of Augustus that thrived on farm goods, pottery, shellfish, salt, and wine. The strongest marker of this period, however, is the chockablock wall that came to enclose the 25-hectare site. Like the one thrown up to protect Mediolanum, Iculisma's rampart was erected in great haste in the late 200s.

Nearly all the ramparts piled up around the cities of Cognac country were begun during the reign of Probus, who inspired a defensive frenzy across Gaul once he'd defeated the Germanic tribes that had pushed deep into empire and restored the borders at the Rhine and Danube. These works against incursions came first, but then Probus had another idea for restoring Gaul's prosperity—let them grow grapes. His decree lifting all restrictions on viticulture in the Gaul and Danube provinces was a historic moment for wine. With one order, a grand industry took up its long, fruitful march.

Vineyards had been established in Bordeaux country as early as the middle of the first century A.D. Bordeaux-area vintners produced lots of wine, so much that they exported it via the Atlantic. Grape growing and wine trading in Burgundy most likely began in the late second century, in Germany's Mosel valley in the late third century, in the Seine valley near Paris in the fifth century, and at the mouth of the Loire in the fifth century. Cognac country wouldn't get skipped over, and it appears that Bordeaux viticulture migrated the short distance north into the Charente valley as early as the second half of the first century, as evidenced by local manufacture of amphorae to transport wine.

The ruins of two farm buildings at La Haute-Sarrazine, in the western stretches of Cognac, include a collection of ground-level basins, walled with plaster. Many of these basins were linked by lead pipes or by canals, indicating that wine was made here as early as the second half of the second century and well into the third century. Christian Vernou, former curator of museums in Cognac and Saintes and now head of Dijon's archaeological museum, helped coax this early winemaking site out of its deep past. He figures that La Haute-Sarrazine probably produced several thousand hectoliters—maybe 100,000 gallons—of wine a year. This would have made the site very large for its time, he notes. "What's most interesting is the exceptional size of the *fouloir*, the largest found so far in Gaul, as well the surface area of the wine storehouses." The *fouloir* is the basin where the grapes had the juice stomped out of them. Scientists believe that there had to be a big vineyard close by, very likely owned by a wealthy person who invested a lot.

Numerous Roman-period wine facilities lie scattered across Charente, many near the coast, where the gigantic vineyards of the Middle Ages would develop. Given all these sites, Cognac country was a premier winemaking zone of southwestern Gaul during the first centuries of the first millennium A.D.

Aquitania's two and a half centuries of prosperity (31 B.C. to A.D. 235) are classified as the *Haut-Empire*, or Upper Empire. This happy period was followed by the *Bas-Empire*, or Lower Empire, running from 235 to 476, when things soured. The turning point came in 253, when Germanic peoples raided all the way to the Seine, before pulling back. A few years later, in 258, they pushed into Gaul again, breaking through to Spain. Another big land raid began in 275. Saxon and Frankish pirates struck along the coasts of northwestern Europe, bringing terror to oceanside Charente.

Mediolanum, urban star of western Cognac country, cowered behind its rampart, four-fifths of the city abandoned. Soon the site was not even Mediolanum anymore; now it was Civitas Santonum, or Santonas. This break with things Roman would occur across Gaul as cities changed names.

Even though everyone feared the "barbarians" would arrive at any moment, the big country villas of Charente continued to grow, some into sumptuous estates. Decimus Magnus Ausonius, a fourth-century poet and professor, describes one of his properties in the area as having big fields, woods, and vineyards, all worked by many farmers. When he got bored, Ausonius would leave his villa and head into town. The city might not have been so much fun, however, retrenched as it was, stripped of its finest buildings, its cemeteries pillaged for stone, and its people hunkered down in a long waiting game or watching nervously at the ramparts for raiders.

And ever more eastern tribesmen came in wilder and bigger waves. The biggest alarm sounded in 401, when the Visigoths living in Thrace decamped and raided northern Italy. Then, at the end of 406, an avalanche of Germanic peoples crashed over the winter-frozen Rhine: Vandals, Sueves, Alans, Burgundians, Franks, and others. The Roman garrisons did little to resist. The Vandals, making a long dash that would take them into North Africa, may have sacked Angoulême despite its stout rampart but spared Saintes in their sweep through Cognac lands. The invaders thoroughly ravaged the countryside along the way, destroying villa after villa.

The Vandals didn't stay long, but a decade later the Visigoths would arrive and remain for nearly a century. This tribe had come a long way from Thrace. By 418, the Visigoths ruled southwest Gaul and part of Spain. Their capital was Tolosa, today Toulouse. In Charente, the first fifty years of Visigoth rule were not heavy-handed, but it was just the calm before the storm. Visigoth soldiers, perhaps lacking enough to do, turned to raiding estates for food and sacking cities, tearing apart what centuries of Roman rule had wrought. Improbably, Charente's vineyards survived all this havoc. Some say this was because the barley-beer-drinking Visigoths acquired a taste for the local wine; they even accepted it as ransom for towns they held hostage. If so, they surely wouldn't have wanted to uproot the source of their favorite drink.

Soon enough, though, another batch of invaders—the Franks—were in northern Gaul and heading south. The Battle of Vouillé, believed to have been fought near Poitiers, was rapidly settled by the newly Catholic king of the Franks, Clovis. Some say Clovis himself struck the blow that felled Alaric, the Visigoth leader. Victorious, Clovis and his soldiers then liberated the cities of Aquitaine in the name of orthodoxy. Most of the Visigoths scurried over the Pyrenees. They would hang on for another two hundred years in Spain, until a Muslim army overran them. Aquitaine, meanwhile, would concentrate that much harder on its very profitable farming and winemaking.

Much Ado about Salt and Wine

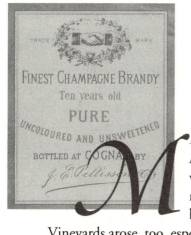

M AKING PARIS THE CAPITAL OF HIS MERO-vingian kingdom, Clovis left much of the realm's administration to bishops who were building churches across the countryside. Vineyards arose, too, especially around monasteries, as churches had heavy wine needs: to serve at communion and to dispense to pilgrims, travelers, and the sick. Wine was also exported. Some of the *vin* produced in the area around Paris was sold in England and Flanders.

But after Clovis's kingdom was divided among his descendants, bountiful Aquitaine quickly sank into a period of tumultuous violence. Angoulême, Saintes, and Poitiers, all thriving cities, suffered as they changed hands from one prince to another. Likewise, country people were at the mercy of Frankish raiders who wrecked their crops and vines. Plagues slashed through the population, too, and bad weather sparked famine.

Cycles of chaos followed by brief decades of peace were the fate of

the region until the close of the 600s, as the kingdom broke up into independence-minded regions and control shifted from the king to dukes or to
estate managers. One dynasty of these managers broke the back of
Merovingian power to become the next Frankish rulers, and a son of this
family, Charles Martel, turned out to be Aquitaine's first big hero, when he
countered an Arab force that surged out of Spain in 732. Martel's crush-
ing defeat of this Muslim army that had plundered outer Bordeaux and
burned Saintes remains one of Christian Aquitaine's defining moments.

It was Martel's grandson, Charlemagne, who became emperor of the
Frankish empire in 800. A well-educated man, he made it his goal to help
bring Europe out of its backwardness and pushed a program to build hundreds of churches and schools. But if knowledge was on the way up, farm
output wasn't, mainly because tools were primitive and scarce. Vineyards,
on the other hand, were spreading across Europe, especially along river
basins from which barrels could be transported rapidly to markets. It was
Charlemagne who gave the wine industry a major kick by ordering the
planting of vines in the Rhine area and expanding viticulture in Burgundy.
Champagne got a big boost when Reims became the site for crowning
kings of the empire, events that attracted many aficionados of its wines for
the long and lavish festivities. Charente's vineyards also expanded during
these years, in tandem with ever more churches and monasteries.

But then came more and more Norsemen out of Scandinavia, their
bounty raids becoming outright invasions by the 840s. Charlemagne
rushed to boost defenses and even had some success in stopping them.
Louis I le Pieux, who inherited the empire from his father, struggled to do
the same, but the Vikings' longships kept coming. To make matters worse,
quarrels among Charlemagne's descendants got so bad that the coasts
were often untended.

In 845 Vikings showed up in great force along the shores of Cognac
country. After establishing a base at Taillebourg, north of Saintes, they
sacked the Charente valley. Saintes was burned, and so was Angoulême;
every church they came across they destroyed. The same occurred up
north in Poitou, where the town of Poitiers was torched a couple of times;
Bordeaux, too, was burned.

Generation after generation of people in Cognac country, with no one
to save them, could only wait for the raids to taper off. In the meantime,
winegrowing, which takes years to achieve production, became a shaky
business, with the sudden destruction of one's livelihood a constant worry.

The weakness of the last Carolingians allowed powers in the northwest and the center to boost their support for the successors of Robert le Fort—a count who held sway between the Seine and Loire and whose two sons rose to the throne—and install Hugues Capet as king in 987. His hold on the nation was weak, however, limited to a few areas in the center-north, and rivalries among his many vassals, spread over vast areas, were nonstop.

The counts of Poitiers, Angoulême, and Anjou feuded over Aquitaine, which encompassed a belt from Saintes in the west to Clermont in the east, and from Poitiers in the north to the Dordogne in the south. Eventually, the Poitiers counts, styling themselves dukes of Aquitaine, got the upper hand. This turn-of-the-millennium contest saw many casualties. One was Saintonge, tossed back and forth from one warlord to another. Then, for strategic reasons, the count of Angoulême began working with the duke of Aquitaine to restore order. This partnership led to some victories for the Angoulême group and increased its area. That was a godsend, as market towns under the Angoulême wing flourished, Cognac among them.

The Angoulême counts belonged to a family called Taillefer, which means, roughly, "cut by the blade." According to legend, one of this clan's first leaders fought a Viking chief and not only smote him with his sword but succeeded in cleaving him in two, vertically. The Taillefers went on to expand their rule far beyond Angoulême. They would hold power for nearly three hundred years, popping up in various episodes of the saga of Cognac country.

The population rose for the first time in ages. Swaths of forest draping the southwest were felled, and winegrowing and grain growing swelled once more. Windmills and watermills were used widely. Slavery went into retreat. The peasant lived a serf's life, owning plots called *tenures*, but also doing forced labor on his lord's *domaines*. A serf swore allegiance to his master, paid taxes, and endured the lord's control over processes like winepressing.

As ever, however, such prosperity soon fell victim to greedy castle owners who frequently marched out with their armies to attack the next castle over or loot the countryside. The counts of Angoulême looked unkindly on all this. Enter another hero of the Angoulême clan: Guillaume IV, who around 1025 spent much time besieging castles of wayward vassals. Chroniclers list graphic recordings of eyes put out, tongues cut off, and all manner of brutal injury done in the name of maintaining order in the realm. Guillaume IV's successors had it even tougher when the dukes of Aquitaine, their erstwhile allies, grabbed at Saintonge again, one even winning over Cognac castle from the count of Angoulême.

While lords quarreled, the church underwent a grassroots revolution. It seems that the landowning, winegrowing abbots had become detached from their spiritual mission, some growing very rich. Clergymen at the bottom of the hierarchy had been forced into servility. This meant that there were few left in the church to guide the faithful at the dreaded end of the first millennium and the baleful dawn of the second. Out of this anxiety, Christian faith swelled and monasteries stepped in to guide where old church institutions could not. The Benedictine movement, erecting a vast power structure, had 1,500 houses by the end of the first century of the new millennium.

Witnessing the random violence racking the countryside, the monks made it their mission to rein it in. They ordered warriors to respect churches and church property and demanded an end to the pillaging of towns and farms. They also reshaped the countryside as monasteries, abbeys, and churches arose in great numbers in the eleventh and twelfth centuries, creating the blanket of Romanesque sanctuaries for which Cognac country is famous.

For the peasant of medieval times, the church was a wondrous repository of images, a fantastic realm of magic and mystery. From baptism to burial, his life passed again and again through this place. Countless pilgrims, too, gravitated to these sanctuaries as they walked trails south

Massive church building during the Middle Ages gave Cognac
country its blanket of Romanesque sanctuaries.

through Aquitaine to pray at the tomb of Saint James at Compostela in far-off Galicia.

A pilgrims' guide of the times recommended that the stroller coming down by way of Tours stop at the basilica built over the tomb of Saint Hilaire in Poitiers, or at the basilica in Saint-Jean-d'Angély, north of Saintes, where one hundred monks worshipped night and day, or at the basilica erected over Saint Eutrope's burial place in Saintes, site of numerous miracles.

Meanwhile, another very inspired body of Christian pilgrims was heading off to try to wrest Jerusalem from the Seljuk Turks following a call to arms by Pope Urban II in 1095. Those who stayed behind in Charente had a much freer hand to get on with the big businesses of the day: wine and salt.

The weather in 1100 was perfect for farming, and the nice spell was to last another couple of hundred years. These decades represented the high point of something called the Medieval Warm Period. Vineyards grew in England and produced so much wine that the French tried to shut out English wines. All across western and northern Europe, agriculture became very productive.

The winemaking area where the Cognac industry put down its roots is a region in northwest Aquitaine called Aunis. It was here, on a Jurassic plateau surrounded by marshes inland from the port of La Rochelle, that the first commercial vineyards flourished and from whence they would spread southeast until they arrived centuries later in the Cognac heartland. Aunis made great quantities of wines, mostly whites.

Robert Favreau, former professor of medieval history at the University of Poitiers and specialist on Cognac country in the Middle Ages, says the region was particularly well suited to large-scale winemaking. "Aunis was surrounded by marshlands, with just one road cutting through it. A sort of island. It was chosen for winegrowing because the sunshine was just right. And then there was easy access to La Rochelle on the west. Boats didn't have to go up estuaries to get to the port like they did when they went to Bordeaux or to Nantes. Boats arrived directly at La Rochelle."

Salt was the other hot item. The big abbeys of Charente owned many saltworks along the coasts of Aunis and Saintonge. Much of this production was exported from La Rochelle to northern Europe, but a lot was also shipped inland, up the Charente. The little river port of Cognac became the main salt-trading town of this interior market. Taxes levied there on boats heading upriver enriched the local lord as well as the bourgeois

Salt making along the Atlantic coast and on nearby islands
has been a thriving business for centuries.

merchant class, and families jockeyed for a piece of the enterprise. In salt, then, Cognac made its seed money for the future world-class vineyard.

Marcel Lachiver, leading light on the history of France's vineyards, says that without salt and wine Cognac certainly wouldn't have come along. And key to its birth was the surge of commerce with northern Europe and with the Mediterranean basin via boats plying the seas, a mode of transport that was "much easier on the wine compared with overland travel in carts along bad, bumpy roads, and also much cheaper." In Lachiver's view, Cognac's specialness arises from two factors: the region's "moderate climate, which allows the grapes to mature well, and the proximity of the ocean."

Despite the warm weather, winegrowers in northern Europe couldn't produce enough of their own wine to meet demand. Ships from England and other countries along the North Sea headed down the coast of France to La Rochelle, where they loaded up not only with many barrels of wine but also with tons of salt. Dozens of ships came and went. Vineyards hugged La Rochelle. More vineyards were planted around other centers of northwest Aquitaine, like Olonne, Surgères, Tonnay-Charente, and Saint-Jean-d'Angély, as well as out on the salt-marshy islands of Aix, Ré, and Oléron. The trade soared, and the "wines of La Rochelle" showed up all over northern Europe, in England, Scotland, Ireland, Flanders, Denmark, and elsewhere.

All levels of society had a part in this bonanza: lords, churchmen, peasants, and an emerging bourgeoisie. A corps of vineyard workers formed. Forest workers, barrel makers, and winepress makers also played big roles.

But if newly efficient vine-tending techniques were proving useful, vinification techniques in twelfth-century France hadn't advanced that much from age-old ways, and many wines, while much appreciated, were low in alcohol and so didn't always hold up. Winegrowers lived in fear of their stocks going bad before they could be sold. In fact, harvests were regularly done early, in September, so as to ship the wine by October in order to get it to market by Christmas. This didn't help the quality of the wine—a lot of the grapes that went into it were barely mature. If there was unsold wine around as late as the following spring, winegrowers were forced to dump it. Not only did the majority of wines not survive for long, they spoiled even more quickly when they were shipped long distances.

Some historians believe it was the Flemings and other northern customers who spurred the people of Aunis to grow ever more grapes. These traders had noticed that the wines made on the sunny Atlantic coast tended not to go bad en route to the North Sea market as often as wines made in the Paris and Reims areas. Playing their regional card, Aunis won a business jackpot, and La Rochelle rapidly became commercial queen of the seaboard.

Then, in the spring of 1137, Guillaume X, the duke of Aquitaine, completed his own pilgrimage to Compostela, though he was dying after having drunk foul water along the way. Drawing up his will, the duke had no choice but to leave Aquitaine to his fifteen-year-old daughter, Aliénor, known to many as Eleanor of Aquitaine.

Aliénor's was no small territory. It extended all the way from the Loire to the Pyrenees and far outsized the holdings to the north of the Capetian king of France, Louis VI. Three months into her reign, Aliénor married the king's sixteen-year-old son, Louis, at Bordeaux. A month later, traveling to Paris after the festivities, the couple learned that the king had died of dysentery. The duke and duchess of Aquitaine became king and queen of France.

Rescuing the Holy Land, meanwhile, was still the great imperative, and when Louis VII embarked on the Second Crusade, he took along his bride. Evidently, however, young Aliénor didn't behave herself in a chaste enough way on the trip to suit Louis, and so not too long after they returned home, he repudiated her for this and for not having produced a male heir. It was March 1152 when their marriage was annulled. Two months later, Aliénor married Henry Plantagenêt, duke of Normandy and grandson of King Henry I of England. Henry controlled Normandy, Anjou, Maine, and Touraine. Aliénor had Aquitaine, including Poitou and Gascony. When Henry II rose to the throne in 1154, Aliénor became queen of England. The couple ruled over lands that stretched from the Cheviots to the Pyrenees.

Aliénor's marriage to Henry bolstered trade between England and the Continent—most importantly in wine. English wines were notoriously thin and poor, and the English had long turned to sunnier France for pleasant-tasting alternatives. For years English traders had purchased much of their wine at the annual fair at Rouen, on the Seine, but after the marriage of Henry and Aliénor merchants headed farther south for better supplies, loading up at La Rochelle, and at Nantes and Bordeaux. Huge shipments from these ports also headed to Flanders and across northern Europe.

Henry reigned for thirty-five years, during which he spent much of his time quelling revolts in England and on the Continent. Aliénor, meantime, gave birth to five boys and three girls. Her favorite, Richard, rose to the throne in 1189, only to get himself killed a decade later in the Limousin while quarreling with a lord over a trove of Gallo-Roman gold coins found by a peasant. Aliénor then rallied round her last son, John, and went on a loyalty-affirming tour of Aquitaine. Among her many acts of largesse was the confirmation of independence charters for several towns, including Poitiers, Saintes, and La Rochelle, her wine-exporting favorite, and for the Ile d'Oléron at the mouth of the Charente. Other towns, though, would have to wait for this privilege. Angoulême didn't get its charter until 1204, granted by King John. Cognac got similar rights in 1215, for a further commercial boost. Nearby Jarnac wasn't granted a charter at the time. If it had, some wonder if we might not be drinking Jarnac today instead of Cognac.

Aquitaine's other big port, Bordeaux, had its charter reconfirmed during Aliénor's visit, but she did nothing to address the Gascons' big worry: heavy taxation on wine exports. Aliénor was still fiercely protective of her Aunis wines, and though the Gascons vaunted their wine as superior (a light red, almost a rosé, called *clairet*), she remained faithful to La Rochelle, which was still enjoying a boom in its wine business with England and elsewhere.

About this time, by the way, John put a ceiling on the price of wine in England. It is notable that his edict mentioned the wines of Poitou, as well as those of Anjou and the Seine basin, but not those of Bordeaux.

Evidently a lot of wine was going out of La Rochelle, carried in thirty-meter-long boats. These vessels transported maybe six dozen *tonneaux* of nine hundred liters each, which added up to tens of thousands of liters. Ships able to carry such amounts were often built by Flemings and manned by a couple of dozen sailors, usually from Oléron, Bayonne, and Cantabria. La Rochelle even made a new port to handle rising commerce and to accommodate ever-larger vessels. In coming decades the size of ships would explode as hundreds of wine boats circulated from Iberia to Scandinavia.

Though La Rochelle was the major wine-exporting port by the start of the 1200s, it hadn't yet moved much into the import business. Ships often arrived off La Rochelle loaded only with stones that served as ballast when there was no other cargo. Nearing La Rochelle, the ships would dump all their rock. Accumulations of this bulky discharge, mostly stones from England and Scandinavia, got so bad that shipping off Aunis became dangerous. Signs marked the submerged piles. Some of the rock got put to good use, though, to shore up the jetties of La Rochelle or to pave its streets.

Boats grew ever larger as thousands of liters of wine
headed to customers across northern Europe.

Inland river ports also got into the wine game, namely Saint-Jean-d'Angély on the Boutonne, a tributary of the Charente; Tonnay-Charente, upriver from present-day Rochefort; and Saint-Savinien, a little farther up the Charente. Over the years, more and more ports would be built along the Charente, making it a super-waterway of trade when Cognac came along.

Meanwhile, John didn't endear himself to his new English subjects by divorcing his first wife, Isabella of Gloucester. His standing on the Continent was no better, either, owing to the scandal he stirred up over a woman in the Taillefer clan, Isabelle, heiress of the count of Angoulême. It was the summer of 1200, and John had been attending a meeting in Lusignan, near Poitiers, where he intended to strike a peace deal with the count of La Marche, Hugues IX de Lusignan. The English king, thirty-three, spotted Isabelle, only thirteen, among the guests at the parley and fell in love. The problem was that she was engaged to Hugues. John arranged for Hugues to go to England on business, and while the count was away, the king married Isabelle.

The Lusignans were deeply offended and turned to the French sovereign for help. In 1202 Philippe II Auguste ordered John to appear in court in Paris. When the English king balked, Philippe ordered the confiscation of all of John's lands and invaded Normandy. Seeking help, John induced Bordeaux to provide him with ships and matériel by lowering taxes on its wines. La Rochelle cried foul but was soon granted the same privilege, the better to put the two wine centers on an equal commercial footing.

John found himself in an ever tougher position in the north, however, and then just as Normandy was about to fall to the French, his mother died on April 1, 1204. Within months, Brittany, Anjou, Maine, Touraine, and most of Poitou were won by Philippe Auguste. John found himself dispossessed of nearly all of his Continental holdings except for La Rochelle and a piece of Aquitaine from Saintonge to the Pyrenees.

The English king would strive for years to regain lost lands, at the same time living a lavish lifestyle. For an idea of what and how much went down the hatch at the royal table, sometime around 1215 John placed an order for 120 *tonneaux*, nearly 110,000 liters, of Gascony *clairet*. After that order, merchants from Bordeaux began appearing in English ports to sell their wine under the nervous stares of jealous La Rochelle traders.

When John died, his widow, Isabelle, decided to go home to Angoulême, where she married Hugues X de Lusignan, the son of the man

John had taken her away from in the first place. This couple would become strategic players of the center-west, beginning with the run-up to the French capture of La Rochelle in 1224, as Hugues de Lusignan and associates did much in the way of creating havoc to help pave the way for the French sovereign, Louis VIII, to seize the port and sever the wine trade with England. La Rochelle wine merchants in England, considered enemies, had their stocks seized. Their big market suddenly gone, La Rochelle winegrowers boosted shipments to Flanders, where the upper classes saw wine as a status symbol. Those Englishmen, by the way, who'd been hooked on La Rochelle wines, now managed to get their supplies via Bruges.

Wine was expensive and sometimes scarce in the north. Thus its value rose, enriching traders. When the Flemings, especially in cities like Saint-Omer, tried to profit by hiking taxes, the winegrowers of La Rochelle, Niort, and Saint-Jean-d'Angély cut off trade until the other side backed down.

In 1235, Louis IX came of age and took over as king. In 1241, his younger brother Alphonse also came of age and was given dominion over Poitou, Saintonge, and Auvergne. Alphonse's rise incensed Isabelle d'Angoulême, who couldn't abide seeing the lands of her dead husband and her former mother-in-law under Capetian rule. She even threatened to toss out her new husband Hugues if he didn't do something, which inspired him to launch a revolt against the Capetians. Lords across Poitou, Saintonge, and Gascony joined forces; Bordeaux and Bayonne were charged with grabbing La Rochelle to cut off trade and burn houses with winepresses or vineyards.

The English king, Henry III, getting wind of the insurgency, landed with his brother, Richard of Cornwall, and an army at Royan, south of La Rochelle, in May 1242. Louis IX reacted quickly, invading Poitou, razing strongholds. Henry did likewise as he moved inland, taking town after town until, in July, he came to Taillebourg, north of Saintes. Rather than fight there, Henry's brother pulled the English forces back to Saintes, where the two armies battled on July 22. The French rapidly got the upper hand. Desperate, the English made a dash outside the walls but were hit so hard in close-quarters fighting in the vineyards that they rushed back inside. Louis besieged the town. Henry realized he was outnumbered, lost control, and tried to have the city burned, then fled, leaving Saintes to the French.

Louis would have gone after Henry, but dysentery broke out among his soldiers and he himself fell ill. The king returned to Paris for rest and treatment, while Henry went home to England. In April 1243, France and England agreed to a truce. Louis took no pity on the rebels. Hugues de Lusignan and Isabelle d'Angoulême were made to beg forgiveness. This they did, though it didn't keep the king from transferring to Alphonse all the territories he had seized in the war. Hugues and Isabelle lost huge landholdings, marking the beginning of the end for this fabled family.

Louis remained ill and came close to death, whereupon he vowed to go on a crusade to the Holy Land if he got well. He did indeed recover, at which point he headed off with all the major players (notably his three brothers) to Egypt, where they were captured. The price of freedom for the king and his followers was a fortune in gold. His brother Robert d'Artois died fighting in Egypt, along with hundreds of noblemen, including Hugues de Lusignan and his son, whose destitute descendants would sink into historical oblivion.

It would take until 1259 for England and France to conclude the Treaty of Paris, in which Henry renounced his claims to Normandy, Anjou, Touraine, Maine, and Poitou and swore fealty and homage to Louis for Aquitaine, bringing to an end what is called the first Hundred Years' War. The treaty may have bought a few decades of peace, but it was really an "unworkable charade," argues Robert Fossier, a Middle Ages specialist who taught at the Sorbonne. It got a bad reception in France since it left Aquitaine to the enemy. Whether the English liked the deal or not was really less important, Fossier notes. After all, English thinking went, "We still have Bordeaux and its wine trade. What other Continental lands do we need?"

A clause in the treaty said that if Alphonse died without an heir, his lands in Saintonge south of the Charente would revert to England. Louis's brother did die childless, in 1271, but it was not until Edward I signed a treaty with Philippe IV le Bel in 1286 that this half of Cognac country actually came back to English rule. Saintes saw itself divided down the middle, with English troops stationed around the Saint Eutrope Cathedral on one side of the river and French soldiers staked out at the Arch of Germanicus on the other. The Charente valley became an uneasy borderland.

Along the seaboard, disputes simmered between sailors from Normandy, who were subjects of France, and sailors from England-allied Bayonne. For one reason or another anger between these leagues of sailors exploded. Norman sailors pillaged and burned Bayonnais boats at Royan, and they beat up Bayonnais citizens in La Rochelle. Bayonnais and English sailors then sacked La Rochelle.

Incensed, Philippe ordered the confiscation of all of Aquitaine from Edward, and both sides went onto war footing in 1294. French forces moved south and occupied Bordeaux. Gascon and English sailors prevailed at sea, but on land strong points changed hands over and over. In the end, both sides saw that neither could win, and a truce was signed, but French troops remained in Aquitaine until the duchy was returned to Edward in 1303.

Back in English hands, Bordeaux had a golden age, with wine exports growing into a gargantuan business. Total wine exports from all the ports of Gascony were 80,000 *tonneaux* a year in the 1310s, or about 72 million liters. England received half of that. Much of the rest of Bordeaux's exports went to France, Flanders, northern Germany, and Spain, which in turn led to the spread of Castilian and Basque wines in northern Europe and in England.

Under the French, La Rochelle managed not only to remain a serious exporter of wine but also to become a major importing center. Coming from the north were cloth from Flanders, tin from Cornwall, and lead from Ireland; Iberia in the south sent up wax, leather, iron, horses, and oak for barrels.

The vineyards of La Rochelle prospered, and tens of thousands of barrels of wine left its ports each year. Wine in the Aunis region was produced from two main grapes: *chimère*, which made a white wine, and *chauché noir*, which gave a red. Other grapes thought to have been cultivated at the time include *chauché gris* and *fromenteau*, both for white wine. Producers even mixed these to make wines that were held in high esteem for years.

Other nearby regions were also getting into the game. As a result, the verdant vistas of vineyards along the coast began creeping up the valley of the Charente. Winegrowers around Cognac were trying the *colombard* grape, which made a sweet white that they exported via the Charente and became, after salt, another of the region's big commercial successes.

But then it started to rain, and two hundred years of warm weather ended. The harvest of 1315 was miserable, and the prices of wheat, salt, and wine soared. It rained again in 1316, and harvests failed. The drenching weather lasted seven years, until the winter of 1322, when it got very cold and thousands starved. Thus began the Little Ice Age, an unsettled and trying epoch of alternating spikes of cold, rain, and brutal heat that would last until the 1850s.

A few years of mild weather, though, allowed a recovery from the first stretch of rain and cold. The vineyards of Bordeaux and La Rochelle got back in business, exports took off, and the world was once more awash in wine. But in 1324 some pro-Aquitaine partisans hanged a royal official of the court of Charles IV at Saint-Sardos, in the Agenais south of Périgord. Offended, the French king went to war, grabbing Saintonge and the Agenais, but he hit a wall in the Bordeaux heartland. The mother city used pikes driven into the Garonne to bar attack from upriver, and the English court of Edward II provided it with catapults. Other Gascon towns resisted, too. The conflict sputtered along until 1327 when a pact allowing the French to retain the Agenais was made. From there, they could control and tax wine traveling west to Bordeaux and bar its sale to those who would sell it to traders for England.

Charles died the next year, and because he didn't have an heir, the French turned to Philippe de Valois, a nephew of Philippe le Bel, for the succession. But by 1340, Philippe VI found himself pulled into a new conflagration when Edward III of England, a grandson of Philippe le Bel, declared Philippe VI a usurper and claimed the French crown. With that, the two nations were again blown into a conflict—fueled by a fervent desire to control Aquitaine, the treasured land of vineyards and wine—that would rumble on viciously for 113 years.

THE DIFFICULT BIRTH
OF AN EAU-DE-VIE

*T*HE HUNDRED YEARS' WAR WAS A DARK ERA in Cognac country, an apocalypse of ruin, famine, and death. Saintonge, Poitou, and Gascony paid heavily as the English and the French battled, ripping up the land, emptying the countryside, and fighting for sovereignty over towns like Cognac again and again.

The first region of France to suffer in this wrenching contest, however, was Normandy, where Edward III and his eldest son, Edward, prince of Wales, led an expedition ashore in July 1346 and sacked everything in sight. The army then bore down on Paris, coming within thirty kilometers of the city to burn and loot before heading north. At Crécy-en-Ponthieu, the forces of Philippe VI forced the English into a fight, only to lose disastrously. The English army then went north and laid siege to Calais. When it fell a year later, the English had a toehold through which to do even more commerce.

While Edward and his army battered the north, the king's lieutenant in Aquitaine, Henry of Lancaster, put together an army of

Englishmen and Gascons and launched a raid from Bordeaux north into Poitou. The French call this kind of dash a *chevauchée*, which Fossier says joined together a few thousand men but didn't always have a precise military objective. People in their path did the only thing they could—flee. The raiders would seize grain and animals and burn farm buildings. "The peasants could put up with all that, though," Fossier says. "But what really hit hard was when the raiders went out into the vineyards and cut the vines. If a grain mill was destroyed, it could be rebuilt in a year. But it takes five years to regrow a vine."

Henry of Lancaster cut into Saintonge and Poitou as into butter, pillaging and torching towns and installing garrisons at Lusignan, Saint-Jean-d'Angély, and Poitiers. Saintes remained in French hands, as did Cognac, Angoulême, and La Rochelle, and then Henry pulled back to Bordeaux.

Wine production in the Charente region all but ended, to the commercial benefit of other winegrowing regions closer to the Paris market, and forests, in retreat for centuries, sprawled anew. Raiders forced cities to pay colossal sums to be left alone, only to return months later and demand more money.

Then the Black Death marched in, reaching Bordeaux and Cognac by the summer of 1348, killing vast numbers of people and bringing war to a halt. In the first century of the bubonic plague's spread, France's population would fall by more than half, from twenty-two million in the 1340s to fewer than ten million in 1445. Citing these numbers, Emmanuel Le Roy Ladurie, France's leading medieval historian, notes that the burden of the plague fell on the peasants, who made up more than 85 percent of the population. The plague struck hardest in cities, which were packed with farmers and their families.

The people and economy of Charente were still reeling from this scourge when the flames of war ignited anew in 1351. Jean II le Bon, the new French king, sent an army into Poitou and Saintonge to retake towns captured by Henry of Lancaster. Lusignan and Saint-Jean-d'Angély fell in short order.

Enter the terrifying Black Prince: Edward, eldest son of the English king. Named lieutenant in Aquitaine like Henry of Lancaster before him, Edward landed in Gascony in the fall of 1355 and went on a *chevauchée* until his army numbered ten thousand. The next summer this band set out to link up with Lancaster's army, which had landed at Cherbourg and carried out brutal raids in Normandy. When Edward got to the Loire, however, he found it flooded and had to turn around and go back south.

Jean le Bon's more mobile forces gave chase, though, and caught up with Edward at Poitiers.

The English were outnumbered two to one, and the Black Prince wasn't eager for this fight. Still, the confrontation erupted on September 19, 1356. With the outcome still very much in doubt, the Black Prince perceived an opening and ordered a final charge into the melee. Other English forces struck at the French rear. In the tumultuous finale the French royal guards were decimated and *le roi* Jean himself was captured.

The Black Prince pulled back to Bordeaux with his prize, and the next spring took Jean to London. Victorious, the English pressed their advantage, demanding sovereignty over all of northern and western France and a fantastic ransom for Jean. Under the 1360 Treaty of Brétiny, France ceded less than Edward had demanded but still a colossal amount of territory: all of Aquitaine from the Loire to the Pyrenees, including La Rochelle, plus Calais and environs, giving England oceanfront supremacy that would greatly benefit its economy for years. Jean was released upon payment of part of the ransom—though, in a curious twist of history, he would subsequently turn himself back over to the English when certain treaty arrangements concerning royal hostages were breached, and then die in London only a few months later.

The plague lumbered through Europe again in 1361. Across an ever more desolate landscape roamed lawless bands of discharged soldiers who went to work for whichever baron would pay them, and they would attack towns and castles for loot. These *routiers* had most of France under their thumb for years. Anarchy and disease combined to keep France mired in hopelessness. Little if any farming or winegrowing was done, and starvation raged.

The Black Prince, meantime, took power as duke of Aquitaine. His favorite residences were at Cognac and Angoulême, where he presided over grand fetes. With their own interests in mind, the Angoulême and Poitou barons collaborated with the viceroy and his administrators during the 1360s.

But Aquitaine was not a happy place. When the prince demanded more taxes, the Aquitainians sought redress from Charles V, the new French king, who was, in their book, still the overlord. Charles ordered the duke of Aquitaine to appear in Paris. The Black Prince replied that he would—but with sixty thousand soldiers. Charles declined to back down and war broke out yet again.

The first big blow to the English came in 1370, when Sir John Chandos, their leading captain, was killed not far from Poitiers in a skirmish with the French. Other English-held places soon made deals with the French and changed sides. When Limoges agreed to rejoin the French camp, the Black Prince grabbed back the city and massacred its people. It was his final exploit before dysentery forced him to return to England in January 1371.

The next year brought Charles a major victory at sea, when a Castilian naval force allied with the French decimated an English fleet off La Rochelle. Suddenly, the sea lanes between Bordeaux and London were under threat. English wine merchants could only have shuddered at the prospect of losing this lifeline. On land, the new French constable, Bertrand du Guesclin, moved north to south, winning over town after town in Poitou and Saintonge. Poitiers, La Rochelle, Angoulême, Saint-Jean-d'Angély, and Saintes all surrendered by the fall of 1372. (A few other towns along the Charente took their time giving up; Cognac, for one, wasn't back in French hands until 1375.) Suddenly the English realized they had no means of countering the French. English-controlled Aquitaine had again been reduced to a smaller space, its northern edge pushed south to the Charente.

The countryside suffered immensely. No one could work the farms, and vineyards were either destroyed or died from neglect. Wine shipments from Bordeaux, which had risen sharply in the 1360s, plunged again by half to ten thousand *tonneaux* a year. The price of wine in Cognac country also crashed in the 1370s and 1380s, causing much distress for growers and traders alike.

Things on the economic front didn't significantly improve for some time, despite periods of calm under successive truces. A civil war at the start of the 1400s only made matters worse. It began when Jean sans Peur (the Fearless), duke of Burgundy, hired thugs to hack to death the brother of the king, Louis d'Orléans, on a Paris street in 1407. On one side were the backers of the slain Louis, known as the Armagnacs and led by Bernard d'Armagnac, father-in-law of Charles d'Orléans, one of Louis's sons. On the other side were the Burgundians, supporters of Jean sans Peur. Wild clashes between the two erupted in Paris and elsewhere, including, of course, restive Aquitaine, where both sides eagerly sought English assistance.

Charles d'Orléans himself was one of those who cozied up to the English, but unfortunately got himself into heavy debt after agreeing to pay them to help him fight the Burgundians. That deal, signed in 1412, allowed the English to move north across the Charente and enter the thickening fray. And cross quickly they did—the locals served them much wine produced there in the river valley, which they evidently liked a lot, the better to lubricate them to march onward and leave the region in relative peace.

But the price was high, maybe ten thousand *écus*, which Charles was unable to pay. Forced into a corner, he sent his younger brother Jean, only eight years old, as a hostage to England until he could come up with the money. But Charles himself would be captured three years later and end up a prisoner in England. All told, Charles would remain there for twenty-five years, while his brother would stay thirty-three years, not coming home until age forty-one.

In the brothers' absence, the county of Angoulême, which Jean had inherited and which Charles had helped him rule, spiraled into chaos. Agriculture lay idle while the plague reaped human lives. Even the brothers' agents in the county joined up with the *routiers*. Towns like Cognac lost much of their population. Commerce was moribund, and the economic gloom was thick.

By the 1420s and 1430s, bandits had made life in Aquitaine a nightmare as they robbed, raped, and murdered their way back and forth across the countryside. Combat between English and French partisans erupted over and over again in Poitou, Saintonge, Périgord, and the lands upriver from Bordeaux. And the plague kept coming back, forcing the peasants to surge into the cities for safety all over again and abandon their barely functioning farms and vineyards. The countryside became a no-man's-land.

At last, Charles VII went on the offensive in the late 1440s to try to end the war for good. By 1450, all that England still held in the north was Calais. The French army then turned on Aquitaine and rolled up city after city until Bordeaux fell in June 1451. One of the French lieutenants in this reconquest was none other than Jean d'Angoulême, who had returned from England.

Shocked by the severing of the wine lifeline with England, the Bordeaux bourgeoisie appealed to Henry VI for relief. Christopher Allmand, former professor of medieval history at the University of Liverpool, explains: "This is where the wine trade comes in. The economic links with England were very considerable and the prospect of the loss of English trade was something which meant a very great deal to the people of Bordeaux."

Henry VI replied by sending John Talbot, earl of Shrewsbury, who

retook the city. But the foothold wouldn't last for long. In the final battle
of the Hundred Years' War, on July 17, 1453, at Castillon, east of Bordeaux, the French prevailed easily, using newfangled artillery. Two months
later Bordeaux capitulated, and the curtain fell on three centuries of
nearly uninterrupted English rule. But the nation that won lay devastated,
swept by a plague that claimed the lives of half its people, its fields barren,
its ports and towns shattered. As the biographer of Jean d'Angoulême
wrote, France was "so ruined and depopulated that she more resembled a
desert than a flourishing kingdom."

And yet, soon enough, life improved dramatically in the absence of
war, so much so that in the last half of the 1400s confidence came roar-
ing back. One person who felt this way was Jean d'Angoulême, leader of
the rebirth around Angoulême and Cognac. The job was daunting. Arable
tracts were choked with trees and brush (as the saying went, "The woods
came to France with the English") and had to be cleared. Jean also paid for
reconstruction of churches, had fortresses rebuilt, and modernized castles
at Angoulême, Cognac, Bouteville, and Châteauneuf. He was called Le
Bon Comte Jean and was revered for leading Cognac country back to
prosperity.

Farmers and winegrowers had it good again during the last years of the
fifteenth century. Big markets and fairs in the newly bustling cities were
either started up again or created by official order, and goods traded hands
in ever greater quantities. Tolls exacted on wine, salt, grain, fish, and other
commodities moving along trade routes testify to a thriving economy.

The Charente valley was no exception to this rebirth, as goods moved
up and down the river. Taxes levied along the way spurred development
and spread wealth out into the countryside, giving the winegrowing
industry, for one, a vital leg up after untold generations of strife.

Wine, of course, was still the most prized business, and everyone
rushed to get the vineyards working at top speed. This wasn't so easy
down in Bordeaux, seized by France at the end of the war. First, the wine
trade with England crashed. Then there was the problem of replanting
vines. Laborers and winegrowers were scarce, so concessions were offered
to draw people in. It would be decades, however, before life settled back
into normal patterns.

In the interim, Bordeaux merchants had to look to places other than
England for new outlets. Markets within France weren't promising, what
with Brittany, Normandy, and the Paris area already well supplied with
wine from elsewhere. So Bordeaux traders turned to the Hanseatic League

in northern Germany for new customers, which turned out to be quite profitable. Business got another big boost when France avoided another war with England and concluded a treaty that eased relations and reinvigorated trade. English traders were even allowed to return to Bordeaux and pick up wine. Not that the Bordeaux merchants entirely trusted them. For years they had required wine ships coming from England to land downriver at the port of Blaye and unload their guns there before sailing into the city. Only on the way back out, loaded with hundreds of casks, were they allowed to pick up their arms.

Wine exports from Bordeaux to England rose briskly through the close of the 1400s and the start of the 1500s. Connoisseurs even began placing specific orders for wines from certain domains, eschewing common *clairets* and whites of the old days for higher-quality wines with distinctive tastes.

La Rochelle, too, reestablished its place in the world wine market. Louis XI smoothed the way in 1472 by declaring that the Rochelais could trade with any country they wished, even nations quarreling with France. Trade with England, Scotland, Ireland, Flanders, and Spain took off. Ships from the alliance of Hanseatic cities arrived in great numbers to load up with the region's wine at this premier port, and to get salt along the coast. Portuguese and Italian traders were everywhere. Merchants from Brittany, Picardy, and Normandy were also busy at La Rochelle. Ships roamed far inland, too, to trade goods at Charente river ports like Saint-Savinien, Taillebourg, and Cognac.

Times were good. All across southwestern France a first "renaissance" was well under way. Culture was making great leaps forward, helped by the advent of printing. Paper mills began to fill the country around Angoulême in the 1490s, where the waters of the upper Charente were pristine and good for making the new product. This industry would prosper for centuries.

Perhaps the most fateful event of the last decade of the 1500s occurred right in Cognac: the birth in 1494 of François, France's future king, grandson of Le Bon Comte Jean. François grew up surrounded by talented artists and adventurers. One traveler he surely heard about was Jean Fonteneau, known as the Saintonge Captain, a Cognac country native who sailed along the coasts of Africa and the eastern shore of North America when the earth was barely unflat. Another adventurer François had to have known of was André Thévet, an Angoumois who visited not only much of the Levant but also Brazil, from which he brought back a plant the locals smoked called *petun*, which he rechristened Angoumois

François I, born in Cognac, surrounded himself
with artists and adventurers—and maybe knew
an apothecary or two dabbling in distillation.

Weed, grew in his garden, and smoked. If true, this was the very tobacco
that the world knows today and that found its way into cigars enjoyed
with Cognac. Thévet also noted that when a person smoked too much, it
went straight to the head, like a strong wine.

And there was another breed of specialist that couldn't have been far
from the Cognac court: the apothecary. These explorers of the chemical
and physical worlds spent much time contemplating nature's secrets.
One process that riveted their attention was distillation, the technique
(probably developed by the Greeks and Romans and then elaborated
by the Arabs) of extracting the essence of liquids via evaporation and
condensation in an alembic (*al-anbiq* in Arabic). Apothecaries were able
to draw forth the "soul" of plants to use as perfumes or remedies. One
fruit that lent itself well to distillation was the grape, whose juices

emerged from the still as a powerful alcohol (*al-kuhul*) that came to be called aqua vitae, water of life, or in French, eau-de-vie.

This refining process is believed to have made its entrance into France in the last half of the 1200s, when two scholars living in Montpellier revealed their knowledge of texts on Arabic alchemy and praised the virtues of eau-de-vie. One of these explorers of essences, the doctor Arnaldo de Villanova, called aqua vitae the "universal medicine" and claimed that it prolonged life. Another, the theologian Ramón Lull, gave advice on how best to fine-tune distillation to get optimum results.

Two early recommendations were to use a slow-burning, moderate fire in heating the fermented grape juice and to avoid running the elixir back through the still too many times—both helping to retain more of the original spirit of the grapes in the final drink. These instructions would later prove essential in the evolution of the making of Cognac.

Eau-de-vie as a drink caught on rather slowly, however. The complicated process of distillation, which was expensive anyway, was often the jealously guarded secret of apothecaries. Even so, as Le Roy Ladurie notes, more and more experimenters were testing these processes, not only in Flanders but in parts of France as well. "People at this time were generally familiar with the ways of distillation," he says, "and there were many artisans trying it out."

People who drank eau-de-vie liked it—a lot. A doctor complained in 1493 that Nuremberg had given itself over to drinking aqua vitae. But there are also signs that this early eau-de-vie might not have been tasty. There are even reports that it could provoke one to vomit. To get around this problem, people spiced it up like they did bad wine, adding aromatic plants. In any event, this was strong stuff, and it convinced anyone trying it that it could perform life-enhancing miracles. Anything that warm going down just had to!

No one knows if this kind of firewater was slung back during the many fetes and dinners at the Cognac castle or at François's other residences to the north along the Loire, but that there was much revelry is certain. Anybody who was anyone was there, basking in the radiance of the cultivated new king, who was only twenty-one when he rose to the throne in 1515. This was a rich world of cultural grandeur—sophisticated, intellectual, refined—steeped in Italian styles and thought and in the intense study of antiquity. It was also a court of manly pursuits, of raucous hunts and tournaments.

First in line to be in the shadow of the king were men with grand military talents like Pedro Navarro and Anne de Montmorency. Reform-minded clergymen joined the entourage, as did lawyers, doctors, professors, statesmen, explorers, architects, poets, and artists. And then there were the many women who flocked to the handsome, though married, king. It was an innovative assembly whose humanistic thinking spread all across France.

The power of the royal family eventually came to be centered on the Loire, though Cognac country wasn't abandoned. The move northward was typical of François's ways, as he became a major choreographer of change, according to Jacques Péret, specialist at the University of Poitiers on the sixteenth, seventeenth, and eighteenth centuries. "In the general context of the Renaissance," Péret says, "François I played a very important role, all the more because he personally gave the movement a powerful boost. The Angoumois, Saintonge and especially the Poitou region, closest to the Loire valley, all benefited very well from his actions. For a time, at least. Because it wasn't too long before this intellectual and artistic movement was submerged by the rising tensions of the Reformation and the long wars that came out of that."

Though France's undisputed champion of culture, François was also a man of action—within months of his accession he elected to go to war in Italy, in an effort to assert French authority there. A decade later, however, he got himself captured at the siege of Pavia in 1525. All over again, France endured a big fiasco and saw another crop of its military chiefs fall. "All is lost, save my honor and my life," he wrote to his mother. The king of France then got sent off to Spain, where he was held prisoner by the Holy Roman emperor–elect, Charles V.

Meanwhile, a new wind was blowing—the first stirrings of a challenge to papal authority by Martin Luther. This reform movement had many early partisans in France, especially in intellectual circles in Paris and Meaux. When François emerged from captivity in Spain in 1526, having agreed to a treaty by which he would cede certain territories to Charles and having handed over two of his sons as hostages in case he reneged, one of the first things he did was to intercede in the trial of a scholar facing heresy charges for possessing books by Luther, ordering him freed. François then allowed adherents of the Meaux circle to return from exile. As a result, many believed that the French king fully supported the goals of the Reformation.

But national concerns arose again when François repudiated his deal with Charles within months of his return to France. To induce the emperor to give him back his sons, he cobbled together the Holy League of Cognac, comprising France, Venice, Florence, Milan, and the papal states. Charles was not impressed and declined to give up his valuable hostages. François then turned to England for help, forming an alliance with Henry VIII to increase the pressure. When France and England declared war on Charles in 1528, the emperor challenged François to a duel. The French king accepted, but the fight never occurred. The next year their argument came to a head, and François agreed to pay a great ransom for his sons and to marry Charles's sister. Though everything went according to plan—the money was paid, the sons were returned, and the French king got a new queen despite his hankering for mistresses— François and Charles would clash repeatedly in coming years, emptying their coffers.

Gold was the currency of the day, and for years Spanish and Portuguese explorers had been scouring western seas for riches and a route to the Far East. A Florentine navigator, Giovanni da Verrazzano, with the blessing of François, joined the rush to find a passage to China. Sailing on the *Dauphine*, Verrazzano arrived along the North American coast in 1524. Working his way up the seaboard, he claimed everything in sight. At one place, he later wrote, "We saw in this country many vines growing naturally, which growing up, took hold of the trees as they do in Lombardy, which if by husbandmen they were dressed in good order without all doubt they would yield excellent wines." Farther northeast, Verrazzano entered a bay that he named Nouvelle Angoulême, known today as New York Harbor.

Verrazzano's exploration of the North American coast found it to be contiguous, disappointing his king's hopes. Still, the Florentine, who has a bridge from Brooklyn to Staten Island named after him, undertook two more voyages: one to Brazil, from which he brought back exotic lumber, and the last to the Caribbean, where he was captured by a tribe and eaten.

The Frenchman Jacques Cartier took up the search for riches, claimed Canada for François, explored its coast and rivers, and yet found neither a route to Asia nor gold. A participant in the Canadian enterprise was a Protestant nobleman, Jean-François de la Roque, lord of Roberval. While his attempt to colonize these lands failed due to hardship, it laid down markers of ownership in Nouvelle France. François's friend Jean Fonteneau, the Saintonge Captain, was among those asked to go along as navigator for the lord of Roberval; back from that expedition, he later made other attempts to find the Northwest Passage and wrote about how to navigate these waters. His career ended in 1544, when he made the mistake of stealing a dozen Basque cargo ships off Portugal, only to be pursued by a Spanish captain, Pedro Menéndez de Avilés, all the way to La Rochelle. There, Menéndez engaged the Saintongeais in battle and recovered some ships and cargoes. A few years later Menéndez would found, for Spain, the first permanent settlement in North America—at St. Augustine in Florida—but only after massacring a nearby community of French Protestants at La Caroline.

For François, the Protestants had become a concern, especially after zealots put up broadsides criticizing Mass all over Paris on a Saturday night in October 1534. One of them had even been affixed to the door of the king's bedroom at Amboise castle. Reaction was swift, *Parlement* ordered a crackdown, culprits were burned—and François went along with it all.

When the king wasn't caught up in this question, he was busy dealing with Charles. Their warm-cold relationship never quite settled into stability, meaning that armies were constantly being deployed—to great expense. One way to raise money was via the *gabelle*, or salt tax. Several regions of France (collectively known as the *grande gabelle*) had already been paying it, and in 1541 François decided to apply the same rules to the salt-making zones along the southwestern coast, including Cognac country shores, which paid much less. Resistance among the salters was stiff, riots broke out in La Rochelle, and the governor of the town only just got the situation back under control before François showed up and sat in judgment of the rebels. To everyone's surprise, he yielded to arguments that the salters should be pardoned. As for the tax plan, it was shelved but not abandoned.

The fortunes of another big Cognac country commodity—the excellent white wines being made along the coast—were also just starting to change in the middle-to-late 1500s. The old vineyards around La Rochelle that were given such a big push by Aliénor d'Aquitaine had long made a white wine that was still very popular in northern Europe. But with the slowly rising popularity of eau-de-vie, Flemish traders were beginning to entice the winegrowers of Aunis to switch to grapes that were especially suitable for the still. Eventually, these *cépages* would replace the old "noble" grapes—and bring on a definitive decline in wine made along the coast.

If Aliénor's old *vignes* were going to the dogs, the vineyards around the city of Cognac, much farther inland, didn't give in to commercial pressures so fast. Winegrowers in this area continued to grow *colombard* grapes

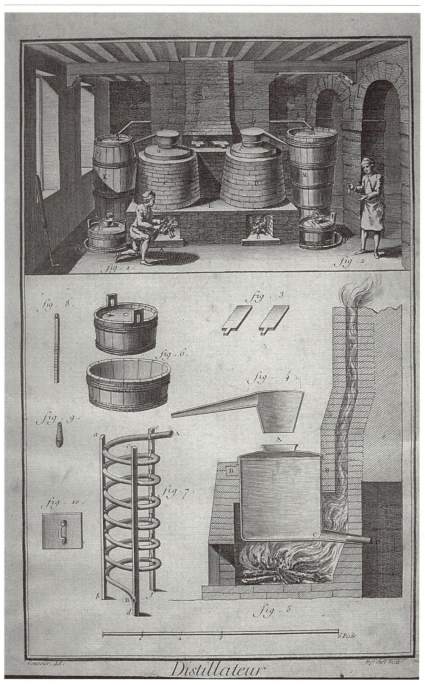

Distillateur

As eau-de-vie grew more popular, the Flemings pushed the Aunis winegrowers
to grow grapes whose wine distilled nicely.

for an aromatic white (apparently much like Sauternes) that in the last half of the 1500s went by the name of Vin de Cognac and even Champagne—and that suffered little when transported long distances by boat.

More than the Champagne growth, however, it's the Borderies area, just northwest of Cognac, that is most commonly associated with the *colombard* wines of yore. Records of shipments of wine from the Cognac region include 119 *tonneaux* heading to Anvers in 1556 and 54 *tonneaux* bound for Middelbourg in 1563. Slightly earlier, in 1551, boats from Hamburg carried 170 *tonneaux* of this wine. These whites were less bitter and higher in alcohol than the inferior wines being churned out along the coast—and more to the liking of customers in the Low Countries, who bought the lion's share. (If wine from *colombard* grapes was distilled, however, it produced an alcohol that was less aromatic than if it had been made from common *cépages*. That is because *colombard* grapes usually made a wine of ten or more degrees alcohol—the common way to express the percentage of alcohol by volume—whereas the common white wine climbed to only eight degrees. Distillers will tell you that the lower the alcohol content of the wine going into the still, the tastier the eau-de-vie it will become.)

Heading out with these sweet wines was much eau-de-vie. Never aged, never blended, this colorless stuff would come to be known as *brandewijn*, a Dutch word for "burned wine," meaning that it had been distilled. And from *brandewijn* came the word *brandy* (also *brandywine*, a corruption).

For sailors on ships carrying it to England, the Low Countries, and lands farther north, eau-de-vie from Charente became the drink of choice, especially because their drinking water would go bad while the alcohol wouldn't. Eau-de-vie not only wouldn't make them sick, it kept them going. Marcel Lachiver gives a good idea of how eau-de-vie was viewed at the time: "Today, when you drink a great Bordeaux, you look for something almost like an aesthetic emotion, you look for the exceptional. When you drink an old Cognac, you also seek something special, its many aromas. But back in the sixteenth century, you just wanted pure alcohol. The sailor on his boat working on the ropes fifteen hours a day every day was looking for the fortifying kick of alcohol, and it didn't matter too much which kind."

By tradition, the Dutch were highly skilled distillers. They often took imported wines that had gone sour or had arrived in miserable shape, or were simply mediocre to begin with, and turned them into passable eaux-de-vie. These were then shipped to inland markets, where drinkers often mixed them with water to make something they believed resembled wine.

But if locally made brandies mixed with water were one thing, straight eau-de-vie from Charente was another, and the latter soon got the upper hand in the north. These regions, especially Scandinavia, often had just enough grain to feed their people but not always enough to distill alcohol and meet demand. Charente eau-de-vie filled the bill nicely.

While this kind of commerce bubbled along, making some people quite rich, the state was always seeking more funds, especially when François's need for money jumped again in 1544 after Henry VIII and Charles V invaded France. François rethought the explosive issue of the *gabelle* and decided to extend the salt-tax administration to the Atlantic zones. This moneymaking move, however, turned out to be less urgent than François had believed, and so it wasn't put into effect right away. That bought him a final few years of peace with the tough salters of Cognac country.

MAYHEM ON THE
CHARENTE

FRANÇOIS, THE COGNAC-BORN KING, WAS succeeded by Henri II. Pressed like his father for money, Henri soon put the salt tax reforms into motion. The result was a rebellion that dwarfed the first one of 1541–1542, erupting in Cognac country in the spring of 1548, when thousands of peasants (*pitaux*) led by noblemen and clerics began hunting down salt tax officials (*gableurs*) in the countryside and cities: Saintes, Cognac, Ruffec, Pons, and even Bordeaux. Salt tax collectors, many of whom were Protestant, were stripped, tied to boards, and beaten to death with batons and small hammers. Such brutal scenes were played out in high style in Cognac, as crowds sent their victims off with, "Go, then, evil taxmen, and salt the fishes of the Charente!" Other officials suffered similar fates, as did the rich. Looting of towns and farms was rampant. Maybe twenty thousand *pitaux* joined the insurrection.

"Because they were the biggest salt makers of all, the Saintongeais found it very hard to accept the idea of being included in the *grande gabelle*," Jacques Péret explains. "That meant lumping them with everyone else under that tax regime. And yet here they were the biggest producers of all."

After a summer of madness, Henri sent in troops, who struck hard. Hundreds of rebels were hanged or broken on the wheel, the population was disarmed, cities were slapped with big fines, and church bells that had sounded the rebellion were taken down. Amazingly, however, just one year later Henri changed his mind about extending the *grande gabelle* to the southwest and allowed the region to revert to its previous tax regime—in effect, going full circle on this very explosive issue. Shortly thereafter the king, seeking civil peace, went even further and abolished the *gabelle* in exchange for a big onetime payment. This tax exemption would last until 1789. Henri also amnestied the surviving rebels, so that in the end *La Révolte des Pitaux* had achieved what it had set out to do—and then some. People power had struck a blow against the Valois dream of mass taxation.

The suppression of the *pitaux* had been so heavy-handed, however, that it fed enormous resentment that would favor Calvinism's spread. Henri was even less tolerant of the Protestants than his father, and so as the number of Protestants rose through the late 1540s and 1550s, the king reacted firmly.

One act was to order the establishment of a heresy tribunal in the Paris *Parlement*, which became known as the *Chambre Ardente* (Burning Chamber); dozens of heretics were sentenced to death, though only a few were executed. *Parlements* in other cities, like Bordeaux, had similar courts, with higher rates of execution. Thousands of Protestants were on the run, and many ended up in Geneva, where John Calvin was enlarging his flock.

The nascent eau-de-vie commerce of these years is difficult to track in detail, but some rare documents about shipments indicate that the business was truly swelling. In 1559, for instance, a boat bound for London left La Rochelle with 20 *tonneaux* of wine and 12 *barriques* (225 liters each) of eau-de-vie. As it turns out, this was one of the earliest recorded shipments of eau-de-vie from the Charente region and a clear signal that the new spirit was being exported alongside wine, the region's longtime staple.

And yet the eau-de-vie trade couldn't have been vigorous. On top of that, the coming Wars of Religion would make it very hard to conduct

Heading out of La Rochelle in the late 1500s were vast amounts of
wine and the earliest shipments of Charente eau-de-vie.

business, all the more because Cognac country would be in the thick
of this conflict in which no one was spared suffering and the major
commercial activities of the day—winemaking and eau-de-vie distillation—suffered immeasurably.

Henri didn't live to see the Wars of Religion actually begin, however.
Three months after signing a grand peace with Spain and England that
same year of 1559, he was hit on the head in a jousting accident while celebrating the treaty and died. His fifteen-year-old son became François II.
The boy's mother, Catherine de' Medici, ran the government as regent.
She was joined, and quickly dominated, however, by two Guise brothers—François and Charles (cardinal of Lorraine)—who took control of
the royal machinery.

Tradition states that it was François de Guise who lit the fuse of war, in
1562. Passing by the town of Vassy on his way to Paris, he caught sight of
Protestants worshipping, and an altercation broke out. When it was over,
Guise's men had shot more than thirty unarmed people and wounded
scores. The Protestant Huguenots cried massacre. There was no turning
back as violence spread rapidly across France. In Cognac country, more
and more towns joined the Protestant cause. Huguenots vandalized
Catholic churches. Catholic forces replied vigorously, taking back towns
and either murdering rebels or forcing them back into the fold. Many

atrocities were committed by both sides, with people being hanged, bludgeoned to death, and tossed down wells.

Cognac country became a much-fought-over patchwork of territories. One anchor for the Protestants was La Rochelle, whose citizens took control in January 1568. Key cities in Aunis and farther inland across Saintonge were also Protestant-held: Saint-Jean-d'Angély, Saintes, and Cognac. The Catholics kept a firm grip on Pons and Angoulême.

Anxious to secure as much of the southwest as possible for the Protestants, the prince of Condé, their hero, made his way to La Rochelle, assembled a force, and moved through the countryside in the fall of 1568, determined to mop up the Catholics and seize everything in sight. With him was another military star, Gaspard de Coligny. Other troops joined the movement, mostly importantly those under Jeanne d'Albret, queen of Navarre, who was accompanied by her son, the future Henri IV. The army pushed into Saintonge and on to Angoulême, which capitulated. Protestant soldiers then ran amok. The priest of Saint Ausone church was doused with boiling oil. A group of thirty Catholics was locked in a house and either tortured or starved to death. Every religious edifice in town was sacked. The body of Jean d'Angoulême was removed and chopped to pieces.

Winter halted the fighting, but when spring came, Catholic forces moved south into Charente and caught the Protestant army near Jarnac. There, in a battle beside the river that people still talk about today, the Protestants were smashed and their commander, the prince of Condé, was killed.

Yet even after this and other victories, the Catholics still weren't able to claim the key centers of the southwest—La Rochelle, Angoulême, and Cognac—and so Catherine de' Medici, weary of the war, sought out peace. An edict in 1570 granted new rights to the Protestants, increasing the number of cities in which they would be allowed to worship. The Huguenots were also granted the right to keep four towns for two years: La Rochelle, Cognac, Montauban (near Toulouse), and La Charité (on the upper Loire).

From the following year—1571—comes one of the earliest mentions of a local distiller in Charente. A Rochelais named Jehan Serazin, he is referred to in an official document as a *marchand et faizeur d'eau-de-vie*— trader and producer of eau-de-vie. Historians believe that there were only a limited number of distillers in the region, as much of the distilling was being done in ports in northern Europe, especially by the Dutch, when Charente wine arrived from Cognac country. This would change, however, in the 1600s as more and more people set up their stills along the Charente, priming the pump of an industry to work ever faster through the next four centuries.

A wedding in Paris in 1572 set off the worst spate of killing in the Wars of Religion. Tensions between the two communities in the city had been high, and after Charles IX's sister, Marguerite, a Catholic, married Henri de Navarre, a Protestant, all hell broke loose. Of those who survived the massacre of Protestants on August 24, none was more important than Henri de Navarre, who converted to Catholicism but remained a prisoner of the court.

The next year the emboldened Catholics decided to go after La Rochelle. A siege lasted all spring, leading to thousands of casualties among the attackers, many from disease. By summer the Catholics lifted the siege, handing the Protestants of La Rochelle one of the biggest moral victories of the wars. Protestant resistance rose to ever more challenging heights when Huguenot leaders founded a federation of Protestant provinces—the United Provinces of the Midi—covering the area south of a line from Grenoble west to Saint-Jean-d'Angély. This move toward independence took a page out of the book of the rebellion in the Netherlands. The outcomes of both defiant struggles would further bond the two like-minded communities, whose numerous business and family links would quickly transform a fledgling eau-de-vie trade into a grand commercial success under the name of Cognac.

When Charles IX died in 1574, one of his brothers became Henri III. Two years later, Henri de Navarre escaped from the court and reverted to Protestantism. Navarre's doings were critical because Henri III had no heir at all when his brother died, which made Navarre next in line for the throne, a prospect that horrified Catholics. Extremists among them, led by the duke and cardinal of Guise, formed the Catholic League to block Navarre. When Henri III, faced with a League-led revolution that took over Paris, had the Guise brothers murdered at Blois in 1588, the League called outright for the king's murder. Henri turned to Navarre for help, and they marched on Paris.

But in the summer of 1589, just outside the city in Saint-Cloud, a League-inspired monk stabbed and killed the king, ending the Valois dynasty. Navarre took the title of Henri IV and fought for months to try to take back Paris, but ultimately gave up. Finally, Henri dropped the bombshell: in July 1593 he abjured Protestantism (again) and recognized Catholicism. The next year Henri entered Paris to much Catholic acclaim.

It wasn't until April 1598, however, that Henri brought forth his compromise: the Edict of Nantes. This affirmed earlier liberties granted to the Protestants and extended their civil rights, but it didn't settle the issue of how competing faiths could coexist. It also left the Huguenots with much of their military power. At best, the Edict of Nantes was a truce. Although both sides laid down their arms, in no way was the war nearly over.

At the close of the 1500s, then, Cognac country was a largely Protestant domain with strongholds at La Rochelle and cities up and down the Charente. But it was once more a wrecked region, its economy ripped up by nearly forty years of war. Replanting of its vineyards got under way once the fighting stopped, however, and soon exports of wine and eau-de-vie took off again, especially in the direction of independence-minded Netherlands.

In the north, the consumption of eau-de-vie from Charente was becoming wildly popular in taverns and bars, where it vied only with drinking beer and smoking as a favorite pastime. Demand for eau-de-vie was so strong that the Charente practice of distilling began expanding inland to today's Cognac lands.

It was all about making money, and the Dutch were the experts of the day. They knew more than anyone about distillation. They had long used stills of Scandinavian copper, which made the finest apparatuses. Now they sold more and more of these devices to aspiring Charentais distillers and then bought all the eau-de-vie they could produce.

A key to Dutch success was their close relationship with producers of the goods that they then resold at huge profit in far-off markets. Numerous Dutch agents settled in Charente in the first half of the 1600s, marrying into local families. Dangling prospects of riches in front of winegrowers anxious to get back on their feet, the Dutch traders had no trouble convincing much of the countryside to throw themselves into the eau-de-vie game.

The territory devoted to vineyards producing white wine expanded dramatically, most notably south of Cognac, so that the city became ringed with vines.

"Distillation in Charente was born of a massive vineyard making so much wine that they didn't know what to do with it all," Lachiver says. "Elsewhere in France, on the other hand, the vineyards were less dense, more spread out. Wine was destined for the urban market, above all, but there were few cities. Bordeaux was one, but there were no other big cities in the center-west of France. Thus it was the abundance of all this wine that, thanks to the Dutch, gave such a great push to distillation."

In short, the Dutch did what they do best: shaping the product to fit the market. The Dutch agents not only advanced money to winegrowers to buy more land and to plant more vines, they paid them quickly when the crop was in. Peasants became well-off. Distillers sprang up everywhere.

No one was left out of the rush, as barrel after barrel of Charente eau-de-vie took distant markets by storm. Eau-de-vie from the Bordeaux backcountry and from the area up the Loire from Nantes also took off. Eau-de-vie from southeast of Bordeaux became the famous Armagnacs.

Among the chief Charentais beneficiaries of the trading frenzy were the Protestants of La Rochelle, a city of twenty-five thousand during the reign of Henri IV. The port, midway between the markets of Holland and England in the north and those of Iberia in the south, bustled with activity, and merchants made great sums of money. A La Rochelle fleet was built in the early 1600s that plied the eastern Atlantic and ventured to the New World for trade.

The fleet had its competitors, however, as ships from the Basque country, Brittany, Normandy, England, and Holland rode in and out of La Rochelle. Activity was constant. Exports of wine, salt, and grain led the economy. Each winter fleets of up to a hundred ships were outfitted at La Rochelle for expeditions to rich fishing zones off Canada. Imported spices were another big ticket—pepper, cinnamon, nutmeg, cloves, and ginger—coming via Portugal, Holland, and England. Sugar arrived from the Caribbean to be refined and then shipped to the French interior. Textiles came from the north to be shipped southward or inland. The renaissance of La Rochelle echoed up the Charente valley in numerous foundries and paper mills.

But just as hopes were riding high, hatreds resurfaced when an arch-Catholic, François Ravaillac, stabbed Henri IV to death in Paris in 1610. The extremist from eastern Cognac country was found to have plotted alone. For his crime, he was tied to horses and torn apart on a square in Paris.

Henri's son, Louis XIII, reopened the war in Cognac country, his prime target being La Rochelle, centerpiece of the Protestant "state." It would hold out for six years. Starvation and disease killed half the population, the diehards eating anything they could find as the dead piled up. By the time the city surrendered, twelve thousand people had perished; another five thousand had escaped. When royal troops finally entered in 1628, only eight thousand people remained.

Even while this was playing itself out, the eau-de-vie industry somehow kept rolling. At Tonnay-Charente in 1624 two Dutchmen formed a company to build a distillery. The year after that, a trader at Tonnay-Charente purchased 124 *tonneaux* of Vin de Cognac and 61 *barriques* of eau-de-vie.

And yet with the fall of La Rochelle, the Protestants were routed. Another edict stripped them of military and political rights but left them the right to worship. This "peace" would turn the Protestants once more into heretics.

The king decided to make common cause, however, with the Protestant princes of Germany during the Thirty Years' War. Pushing hardest for a French role in this was the man who directed the final siege of La Rochelle, Armand Duplessis, cardinal de Richelieu. As in the past, however, such enterprises required lots of money, and taxation soared. This inspired a peasant revolt in southwestern France in the 1630s and 1640s. Armies of peasants called *croquants* swept across the countryside. Their favorite target was the taxman imposing levies on wine and salt. Wherever they were found, these officials were put to death in time-honored, spectacular fashion.

In the middle of the riots were winegrowers from Cognac, Jarnac, and Châteauneuf who were angered that the Aunis winegrowers were driving down prices by excessive production. Taxes were lower downstream, and transport to ports far less costly, both of which combined to heavily favor coastal vineyards.

Richelieu died in 1642, and Louis XIII the next year. Though neither lived to see the Treaty of Westphalia, which ended the war in 1648, both knew that France had won. The treaty was a turning point in the rise of Cognac: Spain's recognition of the independence of the Netherlands, capping the Hollanders' seventy-year struggle, gave the Dutch the freedom to pursue their course and become the globe's premier traders.

The Charente region caught a ride on those coattails as its brandies were clearly the best of all those being made in France. One secret to its success: distillers had to run it through the apparatus only twice before it was done. Just about everywhere else in France, distillers were running their alcohols back through the still again and again. This scouring, however, eliminated the tones of the original wine and the eau-de-vie wasn't very inviting. No wonder, then, that Charente brandy got noticed. Here was an eau-de-vie that emerged in great shape after two runs through the still.

The Charentais decided not to leave this promising business to Dutch

The Augier trading house was one of the first such
négociants in the heart of Cognac country.

traders alone. In 1643, Philippe Augier de Châteauneuf founded the
Augier trading house, one of the first such *négociants* in the heart of
Cognac country. It bought and sold not only eau-de-vie but also wine and
other products; it also imported popular items from Holland, like cheese.
More than 350 years later, the Augier brand is still around.

The Ranson family was also in the eau-de-vie business around this
time. It would later join forces with the Delamain family in the 1760s and
go on to make one of the finest Cognacs around today. Other early trading houses included Martineau, Marie-Séraphin, Prévot, Robicquet,
Pelluchon, Rouhaud, Richard, Guérinet, Riget, Brunet, and Lallemand.
Intermarriage between the families was common, these links creating a
core of traders in the Cognac-Jarnac area that dealt directly with foreign
markets—especially in Holland—bypassing middlemen in La Rochelle.
Sons of these families often went to live in Amsterdam to learn about
marketing eau-de-vie.

Such international links would be key to the successful development of
Cognac as a drink of choice known and sought after all over the world.

France's gains in the Thirty Years' War fed further desires for glory.
Richelieu's successor as First Minister was Jules Mazarin, who served Louis
XIV. Wishing to pursue the war against Spain, Mazarin sought more state

monies, but the Paris *Parlement* balked. Their rebellion was taken up by the Parisians, and by the end of 1648 Louis XIV and Mazarin were run out of town. Called the *Fronde*, the revolt lasted nearly five years, ravaging the Paris area and sparking famine. As the rebellion spread outward, there were many battles in Charente, though most towns joined the antiroyalist cause.

The one major exception was the city of Cognac, which came under cannon fire for ten days in 1651 by republican forces under Louis II de Bourbon, great-grandson of the prince of Condé who had perished at Jarnac in 1569, but the town held out in the end. Louis XIV would later reward Cognac, exempting it from direct taxes and from duties on its wine and eau-de-vie, which benefited certain families and greatly spurred the brandy trade.

Generally, however, rioting and conflict swept away many of the fragile gains of the short-lived golden age launched by Henri IV. It would take much effort by Louis XIV to turn the situation around, which he began to do as soon as he reentered Paris in 1652. The *Fronde* had been put down, but quarrels between the crown and *Parlement* and tax revolts rumbled. When the First Minister died in 1661, Louis did what no king had done in a long time: he declared that he would govern alone. His policies were implemented through a council of ministers, chief among whom was Jean-Baptiste Colbert, who ran the finances. Colbert believed in mercantilism, the idea being to create industries of high-quality products whose export would enrich France. Colbert erected a network of royal factories; established export companies to rival those of the Dutch and to spearhead commerce in North America, the Caribbean, West Africa, and India; and pushed the construction of a merchant marine.

Soon Colbert's machine was making France an economic powerhouse. To stay that way, it would need a navy to protect its shipping. To build and keep up such a force, Colbert needed places where it could be outfitted. Starting in 1665, he began construction of an *arsenal*, or shipbuilding facility, at Rochefort, at the mouth of the Charente and within sight of the quays where so many barrels of eau-de-vie were being loaded on trading ships heading to foreign ports. Other navy yards and ports were built at Toulon and Brest.

Another military engineering giant helping to direct all this was Sébastien le Prestre de Vauban. Among other things, he made sure France's coasts were protected. Off Charente, he secured close-lying islands with strong fortifications. La Rochelle was allowed to rebuild its walls.

It took maybe a million trees to build the navy. To Colbert and Louis XIV's great credit, oak forests were planted in the Limousin and in the Tronçais, in central France. Cognac lovers should know that the barrels in which their drink was aged were built from the descendants of those oaks, a line that goes back three hundred years. Cognac likely would not be the world-famous product it is today if not for those particular trees. Their unique components give Cognac its special flavors and allow it to age and breathe comfortably for decades, the better to transform a rough alcohol into a velvety elixir.

France's new fleet required armaments, and here the iron-rich country around Angoulême got into a lucrative game. Foundries cranked out thousands of cannons, cannonballs, and other ironwork needed for ships, and handily sent the matériel down the Charente to the Rochefort *arsenal*. Yet another set of families became rich handling all this business.

These were very good economic times for Cognac country. The flow of goods on the Charente was formidable. Many barrels of eau-de-vie were packed in the boats with everything else—from paper and tanned hides to pottery and textiles. The city of Cognac, enjoying its economic helping hand from the king, began to play the role of leading city in the region, to the long-term detriment of other jealous towns, like Jarnac.

Managing much of this trade were Protestant businessmen. Protestants concentrated in towns and had the top jobs. Farmers were largely Catholic. Tensions between the two groups simmered just beneath the surface.

Louis XIV aggravated this fragile situation as he became bent on marginalizing the Protestants. Even at the start of his solo rule, he insisted that the Edict of Nantes be followed to the letter and sent royal commissioners to work with judges in heavily Protestant areas—like Saintonge, Poitou, and the Angoumois—to determine where right-to-worship violations were occurring. More than two thousand Protestants were declared illegal residents and forced to leave La Rochelle. Then royal officials started tearing down Protestant churches and razing Huguenot cemeteries.

As the 1660s and 1670s progressed, Huguenots were barred from many professions. At the same time they were offered bribes to convert to Catholicism, including big tax breaks. Some converted, but most didn't. Encouraging Louis XIV to be firm was François-Michel Le Tellier, marquis de Louvois, who for years had been working alongside his father, Michel Le Tellier, state secretary of war. The two of them had reorganized, equipped, and enlarged the French army. Louvois's zealousness for reform was matched only by his intolerance of Protestants. Confident of the armed force he and his father had created, Louvois pressed the king to strike at another Protestant community—the Dutch—and their commercial empire.

Colbert was cool to a war, but he gave in and began gathering the money. Louis secured an alliance with the English, and went into action in 1672. The Dutch quickly collapsed before the onslaught of French soldiers. Desperate, the young republic offered France concessions, but Louis wanted more. As France upped the pressure, the people of the United Provinces handed the government to William of Orange, who saved Amsterdam and the republic by opening dikes to flood the country and stop the invaders.

The war with Holland accomplished little for the French, however. France even agreed to cut tariffs on shipping through its waters in ways that favored the Dutch. Trade would not only get back into motion but would fuel profits like never before. In no way was the Protestant republic a loser.

All the same, the Sun King was at the height of his glory. As if to celebrate, the king installed himself at his new digs at Versailles. Did Louis and the court, amid all the pleasure making in his new castle, ever toss back a Charente eau-de-vie? The king did enjoy liqueurs. One of his favorites was from Italy and called *rosoglio* or *rossoli*—it even sounds like *Roi Soleil*, the Sun King—an alcohol flavored with sundew, rose petals, orange and jasmine flowers, cinnamon, ginger, nutmeg, cloves, and more.

It was during these years that references to the eau-de-vie made in the Cognac heartland first showed up in the *London Gazette*, a semipublic newspaper of record. In 1678 there is a reference in the paper to "Cogniacke Brandy." In 1687 "76 pieces of Conyack Brandy" were for sale. A "piece" (from *pièce* in French) was the equivalent of three *barriques*, or 675 liters, so this lot amounted to more than 50,000 liters. (By 1700, one finds mentions of "Old Cognac Brandies," which were aged in oak barrels and which sold for a pretty price to upscale customers in London.)

The rare mentions of the name *Cognac*, by whatever spelling, in the late 1600s show that the Borderies and Champagne growths were only beginning the transition from the *colombard* grape to *folle blanche*, the *cépage* that would come to dominate since it made a weak white wine perfect for distillation. In just another generation, however, Champagne made the switch, closing the door on a long history of top-notch whites; the Borderies would hold out longer—persisting in specializing in sweet whites that still fetched high prices in London and Amsterdam—before succumbing to pressure from other sweet white wines (like Bergerac) and from the Cognac eau-de-vie industry, until by the 1750s and 1760s it, too, moved to mass *folle blanche* production and joined the distillation craze.

Protestant families running the eau-de-vie industry would face great stress in the 1680s. Louis, his foreign wars concluded, turned to domestic affairs. Unhappy with the low number of conversions to Catholicism, he dispatched troops to get the job done. Protestant homes were forced to lodge soldiers, who abused their hosts until they abjured their faith. These *missionnaires bottés* (booted missionaries) sparked mass conversions via atrocities called *dragonnades* (after the cavalrymen involved, the *Dragons*).

Inspired by the seeming success of these efforts, Louis revoked the Edict of Nantes in 1685. Protestantism was outlawed; its preachers were exiled. Any Protestant caught trying to flee the kingdom risked imprisonment or the galleys. Living in France were maybe a million Huguenots; over the next five years, as many as 250,000 escaped. Most went to Holland, England, and Germany; many headed to North America. Of the 30,000 who fled Cognac country, most were merchants, artisans, and skilled workers in the marine industries. Poorer Huguenots, especially farmers, weren't able to flee.

With the departing Protestants went much money and vast expertise. Protestants who had had business ties with people in the countries where they took refuge weathered the transition best. Many Huguenots in the eau-de-vie business, for example, settled in their former markets: Holland, England, and Ireland. There, they shared their knowledge of the industry with local traders and spread the fame of Charente brandy. These exiled traders kept in touch with family members who stayed behind, maintaining ties that kept the eau-de-vie business alive. Many immigrants or their descendants would return to Charente in the 1700s as the persecutions eased and help to revive or found trading houses that rose to commercial glory in the 1800s.

Amid all this, Louis found himself under threat again from abroad. William of Orange had replaced James II as king of England, and the power of two nations came to bear against France. War soon followed, with French forces racking up a number of victories. At sea, however, Louis's navy was crippled after losing to an Anglo-Dutch fleet.

Some of the worst weather of the Little Ice Age occurred in the thick of the fighting. The bitter winters and cold wet summers of 1692 and

1693 ruined crops and brought famine. Between 1691 and 1695 France's population fell by 1.7 million people, to 20.7 million. Loss of life was staggering in many regions, Cognac country included; there, as in other zones thickly draped with vineyards, the wine industry was left reeling.

A rebound soon followed, however, and as agriculture got back on its feet the population soared anew, so that by 1708 it exceeded its 1691 levels. Even so, people were terribly poor and misery was everywhere. No one was pleased when the king got involved in the War of the Spanish Succession. On top of that, the bogeyman of ice and cold returned with a vengeance in early 1709. Everything froze: rivers, the sea, and vineyards. The summer's harvest had been awful, and now the cold killed the next crops, sparking famine. Once more the population dropped, this time by 800,000. Making matters worse, France lost valuable toeholds in North America to the British and was left with a war-wounded economy that no one knew how to remedy. When illness took Louis XIV to his grave in 1715, many Frenchmen were not unhappy. Under Louis XV, whose rule would last until 1774, France would somehow pick itself up out of its difficulties to become an exporting giant. Cognac, one of the finest specialized products that the nation could offer to the world, would be right in the middle of it all.

RISING HOUSES, RISING FORTUNES

LOUIS XIV'S WARS HAD DRAINED THE STATE, and so much borrowing had gone to pay for armies and navies that the government was ready for almost any solution. Enter John Law, a Scottish financier, who established a bank in Paris in 1716 to issue banknotes. The idea was that by putting lots of money into circulation, commerce would rise and debts would decline.

At first, the plan went well, and thousands of French businesses profited. In Cognac country, the dominant Augier trading house rose even higher to become the star of a booming trade with Holland, Hamburg, and Guernsey, the Channel isle that served as a hub for commerce with Britain. Augier's fortunes soared as a speculative mood seized the eau-de-vie business.

It was also about this time that a young trader on Guernsey struck out on his own. Jean Martell was twenty-one when he came to France in 1715 and went to work in the Charente region trading in eau-de-vie. A decade or so later, Martell married Jeanne Brunet,

Jean Martell came to France in 1715 to work in the eau-
de-vie trade and left behind a company that remains a
market leader nearly three hundred years later.

daughter of a Cognac trader. When she died soon after, the Protestant
trader married Rachel Lallemand, the daughter of another rich Cognac
family. Martell used his wives' wealth to expand his company in Cognac.
Besides eau-de-vie, Martell dealt in leather, wheat, tallow, butter, coal,
indigo, wood, flower bulbs, and wool stockings. The house abandoned this
other merchandise by the early 1800s to deal only in eau-de-vie. Today,
Martell is nearly three hundred years old and tied for the position of the
world's number three Cognac company with its closest rival, Courvoisier.

In 1720 Cognac exports hit a peak that would not be surpassed for the
rest of the century. But then Law's financial schemes, especially sales of shares
in the Louisiana Company, collapsed, and the house of cards came down.
From its stellar heights as the leading agent for Cognac, Augier fell into
bankruptcy early in 1722 as the Dutch pulled back from business with the
unstable French market. Augier would slowly get back into the game in the
mid-1720s when favorable exchange rates lit a new fire under the market.
Martell, too, sank into difficulties as Law's bubble burst, but then bounced
back by building up a steady trade in Cognac eau-de-vie via Guernsey.

The irony of the Law experiments was that while thousands of companies went under, a great number of debtors—and especially the government—had been able to pay off their loans with the Scotsman's ultimately worthless paper money. For many people, this was a perfect opportunity to wipe their slates clean. As the historian François Pairault, expert on Charente and Poitou at the University of Limoges, notes: "A number of noblemen and ministers got rich by exchanging John Law's paper money for gold just before the collapse of the scheme. There'd been hints that the system was falling apart, and so they cashed in just in time." Thus liberated from financial burdens, businesses and the state set off an economic boom.

One of the architects of this renaissance was André-Hercule de Fleury, who ran the government for Louis XV. Fleury embarked on a reform of the monetary system, introducing the *livre tournois*, based on silver. The currency's value would remain stable until the French Revolution. Most prices, meantime, would rise through the 1700s as commerce spread.

Then another soon-to-be giant of the Cognac world came into the picture, but he was no foreigner like Martell. Rémy Martin was a Charentais winegrower who is said to have gotten into the eau-de-vie business as early as 1724. It wouldn't be long before his eau-de-vie became a favorite of the king. In fact, after Louis XV barred further planting of vines in France in 1731—to lift wine prices, sinking because of massive overproduction, and to stave off possible shortages of grain—an exception was allowed for the Rémy Martin house in 1738. (The edict against planting new vines would last until 1759, though it was never very well enforced in its nearly thirty years on the books.) Like Martell, Rémy Martin is another of the great Cognac houses still around nearly three centuries later. It towers as the number two powerhouse of the market.

By the 1720s, Cognac had a well-established reputation as the most flavorful eau-de-vie around. Almost overnight, it had become the big business on which the region staked its fortunes. Nearly the entire Charente valley joined in the craze, as every farmer, nobleman, or priest worth his salt planted the *folle blanche* vine. Eau-de-vie production soared wildly.

Hardly any exportable wine was made any longer. Nearly everything went into distillation. More and more trading houses opened, and their agents crisscrossed the countryside buying all the eau-de-vie they could find.

But not all the eau-de-vie of Charente was created equal. Those made within about fifteen kilometers of the city of Cognac got the highest marks and included the finest of the region's brandies—Champagne eau-de-vie from just south of town was noted for its light sweetness. Eau-de-vie from areas slightly farther out was often referred to as simply Cognac—and was slightly less delicious. This region corresponds to the area that surrounds Champagne and the Borderies enclave and that today is called Fins Bois. It is the largest of all the *crus*, reaching from Saintes to beyond Angoulême.

In the 1720s, Cognacs from around Saint-Jean-d'Angély, in the northwest corner of Fins Bois, went by the name of Best Cognac. A third area—of lesser quality—lay west and south of Fins Bois, closer to the Atlantic, in the region that now goes by the name of Bons Bois.

A fourth type of eau-de-vie was produced around La Rochelle and Rochefort, and on the islands, a zone designated as Bois Ordinaires. This winemaking heartland of the Middle Ages had thus completed its long decline from the heights of commercial fame to the pits of mediocrity, from making one of the finest wines of western Europe to producing one of its poorest eaux-de-vie. Only rarely did Cognac houses buy any of it for export and almost all of it ended up on the domestic market. It was considered so inferior that it wasn't even called Cognac, for that matter, though it is today.

In the early 1700s houses like Rémy Martin, Augier, and Martell further capitalized on their eau-de-vie by aging some of it in oak barrels. This process turned a clear alcohol to gold, enriched by the wood. Augier, for one, sold two types of Cognac in 1724: Young, which was colorless (*blanche*), and Old, which had a reddish tint (*rousse*).

Traders most liked to age eau-de-vie from Champagne, which they would keep in the barrel for at least two years. Champagne Cognacs, then, naturally got pricier. (Even in the mid-to-late 1700s, however, aged Cognacs amounted to only a small proportion of those sold.) Cognacs from areas outside the central zone were exported within a year of distillation, barely aged or not at all, but still enjoyed commercial success. It was about this time that the term *Cognac*, first applied only to the eau-de-vie made right around the city, came to be associated with all brandy shipped out of Tonnay-Charente and then with all brandies made in Charente. At last, Cognac had become the name of the brandy that would conquer the world.

Heavy traffic up and down the Charente made it the lifeline. Flat boats called *gabarres*, loaded with barrels of Cognac, plied the winding waterway. The Charente runs low in summer, but in winter it often

Flat boats called *gabarres* carried Cognac down the Charente River to
Atlantic seaports, from which it headed to foreign markets.

rises so high boats can't pass under bridges. Cognac traders have long
called it *la rivière de patience*. Numerous locks along the way make it slow
going at best.

Roads were not yet an economical substitute for moving large amounts
of merchandise, though the government had begun building networks of
them. It also embarked on canal building and other river improvements.
Transport costs dropped, and the export-driven economy grew even
stronger.

Mass consumption by a newly moneyed middle class became not only
the vogue in France but all across Europe. Exotic products from the West
Indies, Africa, and India struck consumers' fancies. Cocoa, sugar, tea, and
coffee were the curiosities of the day. West Indies trade was based on a
traffic triangle: French slave traders, often fitting out their boats at La
Rochelle, hauled cargoes—guns, textiles, metals—to Africa, exchanged
these for slaves, took their captives to the Americas where they were sold,
then used the profits to buy sugar, tobacco, rum, and indigo that they
brought back and sold handsomely on the French market. "It was a very
risky business," Jacques Péret says. "But when it worked you won the
jackpot. La Rochelle made its grand fortune this way, from the 1720s to
the Revolution. Other ports were heavily involved, too: Nantes, Le Havre,
Bordeaux."

Imported rum took off in a big way in the 1730s, especially in Britain and Ireland, and gave eau-de-vie from France a run for its money. The rum boom was part of a craze for spirits—including gin and whiskey—that seized the soul of Europe. As the thirst for distilled alcohols spread, the English distilled more gin and the Irish more whiskey, while the Dutch bought big cargoes of sugar from the West Indies to make even more rum.

So much alcohol was being poured down European hatches during these years that a backlash against the perceived evils of spirits arose. But not much of that venom was directed against wine drinking, which was seen as a minor affair. Perhaps this was because wine, especially from France, was getting much better. Wines made north of Bordeaux in the Médoc region were becoming hits abroad as well as on the domestic market. Growers were now aging these wines, thus making big investments in them. Even producers of "new" first-year wine could make quick cash. Top-notch wines from all over France adorned tables of the well-to-do, while lesser wines were a staple among lower classes. Production took off to fill demand.

The absence of big wars at home and a long spell of good weather brought high hopes for agriculture in an already optimistic age of Enlightenment. Cognac had its spot in the firmament recognized when Denis Diderot, great philosophe of the century, mentioned the city in his *Encyclopédie* as being "famous" for its brandies. Diderot believed strongly in economic progress. So did a lot of thinkers whose liberal market formulas were coming to the fore. Their *laissez faire, laissez passer* credo called on the government to stay out of the game, especially tax-wise, and give entrepreneurs a free hand to make money. Applied to agriculture, these ideas would help France to make a stab at ending food shortages. They would also put in motion new growth in the farming sector as a whole, especially after 1750, though not without price hikes that set the stage for the Revolution.

Most of the Cognac heading out of Charente in the first half of the 1700s went to Holland, England, Ireland, and the Hanseatic towns (especially Hamburg). The Dutch market fell off by the 1720s amid a gin and rum rage; instead, Londoners and Parisians became big Cognac consumers.

Louis Cullen, history professor at Trinity College in Dublin, who has written extensively on Cognac's difficult-to-track early years, says of the first half of the 1700s: "The pattern of consumption in the north is driven increasingly by a diversified and complex market. That puts brandy at a slight disadvantage. It also helps Cognac become a niche product. The London merchant and certainly the London consumers are now becoming the rich, stable buyers. And they have a characteristic that doesn't apply to other consumers of spirits: They're very well-off, and very interested in quality."

He adds: "The other great market that is prepared to pay the price is Paris. It's less quality-driven than London. What happens is that Parisians find that they can't live without their tipple, and so if the grape vintage is poor in the north of France, which it often is because of the harsh winter, local brandy becomes scarce and dear. And so they start buying in the Cognac hinterland in larger quantities, and they're prepared to pay over the odds for it. Outsiders like the Irish, who are buying regularly, stop buying altogether. The only people who continue to buy from abroad are merchants supplying the rich London market. And so the pattern in Cognac is that you have an unstable Paris demand, a small but stable London market, and a totally fickle market in Ireland, which can at times be the largest single market but at other times when prices are too high virtually disappears."

Some Cognac also traveled across the Atlantic to New France, Louisiana, and Santo Domingo in the Caribbean. Cognac's reach to the west was the natural outgrowth of France's ambitions in the New World. Wars of conquest for land and markets on the European Continent were becoming ruinous. While Louis XV could congratulate himself on victory in the War of the Austrian Succession in the 1740s, it was not in Europe that he was going to secure France's financial health. After Fleury's death in 1743, the king decided to rule on his own. While Louis XV proved mostly equal to the task, he was inconsistent and the country's debts kept climbing.

Louis eventually took on a finance minister to help bring order to the state's coffers—Jean-Baptiste de Machault d'Arnouville. Machault proposed a new 5 percent tax called the *vingtième* to be levied on all landowners—and in peacetime. First to balk was the clergy, which owned vast tracts. The king backed down. The magistrates of the Paris *Parlement* also balked, but then the king used his legal powers to force them to approve the edict.

Louis only made matters worse when, in 1756, he forced *Parlement* to approve a second, additional 5 percent tax to fund the war against Britain that had broken out in North America the year before and the conflict with the Prussians and the British that had just erupted in Europe. But no matter how much money the king raised, French strategic fortunes did not improve.

While France suffered military setbacks on the Continent, the British battered the French navy and kept it from aiding the colonists. In the end, France lost almost everything it had spent years developing in the Americas. New France was ceded, as were Louisiana and profitable Caribbean islands.

Cognac's fortunes had only climbed, however, in the run-up to the Seven Years' War and then especially during the conflict. Frenchmen, Englishmen, Irishmen—Catholics or Protestants—took up residence in the region to buy and sell eau-de-vie in great quantities. Traders like Guy Gautier came onto the scene in 1755, followed by James Delamain in 1759 and Richard Hennessy in 1765, along with many others who either survived famously or soon flopped.

Augier, Cognac's oldest house, sank into the doldrums for various reasons—poor management and family problems—while Martell became the strongest player of all by using its superior business acumen. When Jean Martell died in 1753, his widow's brother, Louis-Gabriel Lallemand, took over the company. It was Lallemand who consolidated the firm's dominance, especially in the London market but also in other British cities, like Bristol and Leeds. Lallemand also built up a big clientele in Ireland.

Most of the Cognac export trade was concentrated in the cities of Cognac, Jarnac, Saint-Jean-d'Angély, and Pons, while the center of the domestic trade was edging eastward to Angoulême and thence northward to Ruffec and Aigre (in the direction of Paris) as demand for Cognac eau-de-vie exploded in the capital. While all this was going on, the venerable trading houses of La Rochelle went into decline as that port got less and less of the commercial pie. Tonnay-Charente, on the other hand, took up the slack and became a principal transit point for Cognac heading abroad.

War helped Cognac in the late 1750s and 1760s because the fighting in the Caribbean reduced the flow of rum to European customers. Drinkers in northern Europe were also deprived of much whiskey and gin in these years because of poor grain harvests. As customers pounded the table for spirits, Cognac rushed in to slake their thirsts. Ireland was probably the biggest market, the shortage of spirits there being the most acute.

James Delamain, a Dubliner and a Protestant, figured among the many Irishmen who wanted to get in on the Cognac boom by doing business directly in Charente. His first deals were successful and assured him a toehold. Helping him was a major trader, Jean-Isaac Ranson, who was also attracted by the profits to be made in the Irish market. Their relationship got another boost when Delamain married Ranson's only daughter in

1762. That same year the two men formed Ranson & Delamain in Jarnac. In practically no time, this duo gave the Martell company real competition, as they outdid the dominant Cognac family in trade with Ireland, where Delamain's close contacts with his countrymen made all the difference in securing deals.

Martell's hold on the London market also weakened in the 1760s, largely because it couldn't deliver the quantities desired, especially when the Irish market was siphoning off so much eau-de-vie. Orders of Cognac for London had a tendency to arrive late (barrel making could be slow) and often showed up after rivals' goods had arrived. Competition from other Irish-led firms kept up the pressure. It was only because of the deaths in the late 1760s of some of these traders—Laurence Saule, John Jennings, Antoine Galwey—that Martell managed to hold on. The house not only survived, it flourished during the late 1700s under Lallemand and Jean Martell's sons, and then expanded to become the dominant trader of the golden 1800s.

Richard Hennessy, whose descendants would create Cognac's biggest name of all, showed up in Charente in 1765, hoping to get into the business. Past forty, Hennessy was a man of some experience, while his top competitors were much younger. Imbued with Catholic fervor, Hennessy had enlisted in an Irish brigade that fought for Louis XV. He is also said to have been wounded in the Battle of Fontenoy in Flanders in 1745 and to have discovered the charms of Charente after a sojourn on the Ile de Ré.

The story goes that Hennessy left the army in 1753 and lived for a time in Oostende in Flanders (today on the Belgian coast), where he learned the basics of the eau-de-vie trade as barrels of the brandy transited this neutral port for the Irish and English markets. In late 1765 he headed to Cognac country. After pondering for a few months the idea of settling in Tonnay-Charente and then choosing the city of Cognac

After a stint in an Irish brigade that fought for Louis XV, Richard Hennessy arrived in Charente in 1765 and ran a thriving eau-de-vie trade.

instead, he set up and managed a trade in eau-de-vie under the names Hennessy-Connelly & Cie, Hennessy & Cie, and Hennessy & Saule before leaving the business in the hands of his associate, John Saule, nephew of Laurence Saule, and decamping in 1776 for Bordeaux, where the outlook for the eau-de-vie trade, especially with the Americas, was better. In all, Hennessy stayed there for twelve years before returning to Cognac when Saule died to take over the business and form a new company in association with his son James—Hennessy & Fils—with the intention of developing the North American market.

The late 1760s also marked the beginning of a series of climatic swings that would plague the last quarter of the century. Prices fluctuated wildly according to crop yields. Yet Cognac exports stayed steady—and sometimes rose strongly—all the way until the dawn of the First Republic in 1792.

When Louis XV died in 1774, France's financial situation was still poor. Louis XVI sought to tackle the nation's debts by putting various tinkerers in charge of the finances, only to be forced to dismiss them one after another as they failed to resolve the problems. The only one who appeared to make any headway was the Protestant Jacques Necker, who stayed in power until 1781, when he made the error of publishing a glowing accounting of the state's financial health without mentioning the staggering cost of French loans to the Americans fighting the British in North America. Two more men tried to fix the economy through taxation, but they lost their jobs when opponents in the Council of Notables claimed that radical matters like land taxes, for instance, ought to be decided by the Estates-General—the representative assembly of the clergy, nobility, and commoners—which hadn't met since way back in 1614. The king had no desire to go that route and instead demanded that the Paris *Parlement* approve the tax. It declined, its powers were stripped away, and revolts broke out in the provincial *Parlements*. Cornered by all these troubles, Louis XVI reluctantly agreed that the Estates-General would convene in May 1789.

Nature was next to join this revolutionary drama, with a great hailstorm in July 1788 that raked the north of France and beat down the wheat. Bread prices skyrocketed. That winter the weather was very cold, and by spring hungry people were rioting. The malcontents also had the nation's political future in mind, as the Estates-General was due to air the many grievances of the people. The majority of their complaints concerned taxation. They also directed their anger at local officials and anyone thought to be hoarding grain. In Cognac country in the spring of

1789, bands of peasants attacked grain convoys, markets, and bakeries as desperation soared.

The Estates-General began deliberations in May at Versailles and by late June had transformed itself into a National Assembly. One delegate elected in Charente to attend was the eminent Cognac trader Etienne Augier, who sat in the Third Estate. Ending taxes on eau-de-vie and its transport topped his list. A key player trying to find a middle ground between the representatives and the monarchy was Necker, who'd been recalled. But his suggestion for a British-style legislature and a constitutional monarchy led the king to eject him once more, three days before the seizure of the Bastille.

July 14, 1789, was born of the hunger of Parisians. Many people also wanted to rush to Versailles and grab the king; others shouted for Necker's return, a plea that Louis XVI evidently heard since he restored him to power, to much acclaim. But the finance chief could do little to stem the crisis, especially when loans issued in August failed and money began pouring out of the country. France would avoid bankruptcy only when the revolutionary powers nationalized and sold off the very valuable properties of the church.

The bread crisis of 1789, however, didn't go away, and rioting resumed in the provinces. Symbols of the ancien régime were assaulted, manors invaded, and nobles' property seized. The National Assembly, in August, tore down the feudal system under which France had operated for centuries. Two years later, a constitution was adopted, followed by elections that put into office legislators unsympathetic to the king. That new assembly was swept away a year later by radicals who ousted the monarch altogether.

Throughout all this drama, the winegrowers and Cognac traders of Charente had a wild ride. In the years before the Revolution broke out, they'd made much money, especially after 1784, when Louis XVI cut export taxes on wine and alcohol, and after 1786, when England lowered its import taxes and allowed direct imports of Cognac. Charente's vineyards had sprawled ever wider until by 1788 there were more than 150,000 hectares in production; that compares with about 74,000 hectares today.

Cullen explains: "Some Cognac families did well. The Martells did the best in the eighteenth century. The Hennessys came abreast of them through speculation in selling to the revolutionaries in the 1790s. These are the actions of houses led by young men prepared to take what seemed at the time to be risks. The houses are becoming quite rich, and it's setting the basis for the famous nineteenth-century families: Hennessy, Martell, and so on."

Cognac exports doubled between 1775 and 1792, but toward the end of this period the wholesale price of Cognac began to take off. It also rose on the backs of poor wine crops in 1787, 1788, and 1789—and a Cognac shortage developed. Thirsty consumers turned to cheaper sources of eau-de-vie, especially from Spain and Armagnac country. Cognac makers themselves often bought these eaux-de-vie and mixed them with their Cognac to increase volume. This practice alarmed the powers that be, who published a decree in May 1791 in which they vowed to buy and sell Cognac only from Saintonge and the Angoumois. A declaration of independence was signed by Augier Frères, Hennessy & Turner, Veuve Martell, Lallemand & Co., Ranson & Delamain, Arbouin & Zimmerman, and Guérinet & Robin. This was Cognac's revolution, a fight for its name. The industry had long claimed its place in the market—and its creators fully intended to keep it that way.

With the declaration of the Republic in September 1792, however, Cognac prices dropped, and the industry retreated. The execution of the king in January 1793 sent things rushing down an ugly path as the British prime minister, William Pitt, expelled the French envoy to London. The National Convention in Paris replied with a declaration of war against Britain, Holland, and then Spain. Pitt put together a coalition that struck France's armies. Warfare and blockades slowed French exports, Cognac included.

When the Convention declared a mobilization of three hundred thousand men to protect France, an uprising broke out in the Vendée, the area of Poitou north of Aunis. This conflict would leave as many as a quarter million people dead as armies of royalist "whites" fought armies of republican "blues." The Convention responded with brute force and with the Terror. Mass executions of rebels, royalists, priests, and other suspected enemies took place across France. Hundreds of thousands of people died in this bloodbath.

The Terror also took its toll in the new department of Charente-Inférieure (today Charente-Maritime) and in Haute-Charente (now Charente). Charente-Inférieure, comprising Saintonge and Aunis, lay south of the Vendée, and Convention officials worried about its allegiance—and about Rochefort. Two Convention henchmen, Joseph Marie Lequinio and Joseph François Laignelot, charged with keeping the locals from delivering that port to the British, created a tribunal there, hired an executioner, and went to work. Between November 1793 and April 1794 scores of people appeared before this court, and dozens were executed: Vendée rebels, priests, naval officers, parents of emigrants, and partisans of one faction or another.

A similar court in La Rochelle executed scores of Vendée royalists. In Haute-Charente, a tribunal at Angoulême condemned to death many suspects, including Jean Fauveau, a barrel maker whose crime had been to refuse to let his son go fight the "whites" in the Vendée.

The economy reeled. The Convention tried to hold the nation's finances together, but the value of paper money tumbled and few wine-growers would take it as payment. The Cognac business crawled along, as shipments dropped from ninety thousand hectoliters in 1792 to thirty thousand hectoliters the next year (from 2.4 million gallons to 800,000 gallons).

With the English market closed off because of war, the big Cognac houses made shipments to other ports in the Channel engaging in contraband and to North Sea outlets. Houses also diversified, with Hennessy trading in a variety of goods via Hamburg, and Martell doing the same via Bordeaux.

International trade in goods like Cognac during the 1790s was an uneasy wartime business that involved much wheeling and dealing. Cognac traders like Hennessy got their product to London via Hamburg, a free port and reexport center for goods from Europe and North America. U.S. traders, their ships enjoying neutrality, arrived at Tonnay-Charente (and down at Bordeaux) with North American goods—tobacco, sugar, coffee—that they sold before loading up with Cognac and taking it to Hamburg.

The Americans also bought much Cognac to take to the United States, marking the beginnings of a serious transatlantic trade. One buyer was John Trumbull, revolutionary army officer and renowned painter, who came to London and traded in Cognac, buying from Hennessy and Augier in 1795 and 1796. Hennessy also supplied eau-de-vie to the revolutionary armed forces. Martell, too, landed big Cognac contracts with the state.

Business was good enough that another important trader came onto the scene: a partnership of Jean-Baptiste Antoine Otard, said to be the descendant of an old Scottish family, and Jean and Léon Dupuy, Charentais distillers. Otard, son of a longtime Cognac wholesaler who'd sold eau-de-vie for years to Augier, Hennessy, and others, was still a young man when the Revolution broke out, and as an outspoken Catholic royalist, he ended up in prison in Saintes. On the day before his execution, so the story goes, the inhabitants of his village broke him out of the jail. Otard fled to England but returned two years later, and in 1795, with his family's three decades' worth of Cognac stocks intact, he helped to found Otard-Dupuy. Needing more space for its stocks when Léon Dupuy began to land contracts with the Americans, the house bought for its headquarters François I's old Cognac castle and discovered that its humid cellars were perfect for aging Cognac. In just a decade Otard would join Martell and Hennessy as the top traders.

By the spring of 1794 French armed forces had run all foreign invaders out of the country, and the Terror dissipated. What remained was a nation in economic misery. Another bitter winter sent prices soaring and put basic items out of the reach of most people. Bands of brigands called *chauffeurs* roamed, murdering and pillaging. Discontent boiled over into demonstrations in Paris by crowds demanding bread in the spring of 1795, all of which were put down violently. The Convention devised a new constitution in the hopes of restoring liberal values to the Revolution, and though the document with its provision for a two-chamber legislature overseen by an executive Directory was approved in a plebiscite, opposition was intense. Royalists led an insurrection in Paris in October. One man the Convention turned to was a Corsican general named Napoleon Bonaparte, who directed cannon fire against the rebels and helped save the day.

The Directory persisted in trying to fix the economy. And then the royalists surged forward again, only to be halted by an army-backed coup d'état in September 1797. France once more fell into a Terror, as the Directory sought out enemies and censored the press. With the credibility of the state slipping fast, an inspired Napoleon returned to Paris to "drive out the lawyers" of the Directory. Revolution-weary people welcomed the coup of November 1799, and for the first time in many years hopes were high.

An "Ode to the Nineteenth Century" that appeared in a La Rochelle newspaper in December 1800 proclaimed, "The century about to end brought you, for so long, unhappiness and adversity; let the new century about to begin be the forerunner and the dawn of sweet happiness."

A DISTILLATE
TURNS GOLDEN

NAPOLEON, BEING ABSTEMIOUS, PROBABLY didn't down much Cognac, and certainly not like his foreign minister, Charles-Maurice de Talleyrand, a connoisseur of the great drink. Noting how a participant at a diplomatic dinner had gulped his Cognac, Talleyrand approached the guilty party and pointed out that brandy of this quality deserved more respect. The embarrassed guzzler asked Talleyrand to instruct him on drinking Cognac, to which the minister, serving the man another dose, replied: "Hold your glass in your hands to warm it up, give it a light circular motion, then bring it to your nose and inhale its aroma." And then? the diplomat asked. "And then? When we're done drinking, we put down our glasses and . . . talk!"

One thing Talleyrand surely discussed with his counterparts was the sale of the Louisiana Territory (which France had just recovered from Spain) to the Americans for eighty million francs. That was a formidable sum, which Napoleon used to help cover the costs of a scheme to invade England. Thousands of ships were built and plans of conquest readied, but then in 1805 the English fleet under Lord Nelson won the day off Cape Trafalgar, and the French navy was knocked out of existence for years.

French businessmen frowned. They'd only just begun to enjoy the fruits of a break in a decade of hostilities with Britain. Now French merchant shipping came under pressure from the British fleet. Only a few boats were able to export, and La Rochelle, Rochefort, and Bordeaux went into decline. In May 1806, England declared a blockade of French ports. In November, Napoleon, who had taken his army east intent on conquering Europe, put a blockade on Britain. No ship coming from England or its colonies could enter French ports or those of its allies. The next year the British imposed a further blockade on France and its allies, allowing through only neutral ships inspected to be sure they carried no matériel for Napoleon's armies.

Luckily for a number of French entrepreneurs, however, the emperor's Continental System leaked like a sieve—at least in the beginning. Cognac was among the merchandise getting through, thanks in large part to American shippers who, under neutral flag, entered the Charente River, loaded up with brandy, and took it to North Sea ports like Emden (on the Dutch-German border) and Tonning (north of Hamburg), from which it was reexported to European customers—especially the English. British grain crops weren't good during these years, which hurt whiskey production, and so the government hardly opposed imports of French brandy to make up for an alcohol shortage. Soon enough, American ships quit going to Emden and Tonning but would declare those North Sea ports as their destination while delivering the Cognac directly to English ports or hauling it to America.

Cognac shipments took off, rising from 32,000 hectoliters in 1800 to 100,000 hectoliters in 1807. Cognac traders, most notably the Martells, traveled to England to secure licenses to import their Cognac. The French government, despite its concerns, mostly winked at such dealings.

After a while, however, officials began enforcing the regulations, and matters grew complicated as the mutual blockades started to truly hurt. French customs inspectors refused to certify outbound shipments and even impounded ships. New rules said that no cargo would be cleared for export unless it contained some manufactured products, items that the British wouldn't allow in anyway. Some shippers got around this restriction by buying cheap manufactured goods and then dumping them at sea.

Apparently, tons of French crockery lie on the bottom of the Atlantic.

To make matters even more difficult, the British continued to raise import taxes on brandy. Cognac traders saw the miniboom melt away as shipments in 1808 dropped by half, to 55,000 hectoliters, and by half again, to 23,000 hectoliters in 1809 and 16,500 in 1812, the worst year.

The intensity of the trade war was matched by the great battles raging in Europe. Some Cognac houses kept afloat by supplying brandy to Napoleon's armies. But the emperor's warmaking and the Continental System weighed on the rural Charentais. To them the biggest burden was conscription; demands for horses, fodder, and food also inspired resistance. Whenever there was refusal of service, however, Napoleon was quick to use repression: sixteen thousand conscientious objectors rounded up in several departments were imprisoned on Ile de Ré. Hundreds died there or were executed.

By the time of Napoleon's ultimate defeat in 1815, the cost of his grand campaigns had risen so high that many people—especially Cognac traders and other members of the business class—were glad to see him go. Even

Napoleon's wars weighed heavily on businesses, and many Cognac traders weren't saddened by the emperor's ultimate demise.

the weather had been awful for some time, especially in 1811 and 1813, and grain prices were soaring. Perhaps the most frightening turn of events had been the British military advance through the southwest in 1814, during which the enemy occupied Bordeaux and then marched toward Rochefort with the intention of destroying the *arsenal*. It was only with Napoleon's final abdication in June 1815 after Waterloo that the British forces halted.

The emperor's coach ride to exile passed through northern Cognac country. All along the way—via Poitiers and Niort—diehard supporters lined the roads to hail him with cries of "Vive l'Empereur!" Arriving at Rochefort on July 3, he was acclaimed by supporters who stood shouting for hours outside the *Préfecture* where he was staying until he emerged to salute them. After a few days, Napoleon headed to the Ile d'Aix, where he continued to ponder whether to rally the sailors of Bordeaux and La Rochelle to fight on, or to try to breach the wall of British battleships blocking the shore and flee to the United States. Local officials of the new government, meantime, decided to block Napoleon's departure and arrest him. To avoid falling into their hands, or being delivered by them to the English as a prisoner, Napoleon chose on July 15 to hand himself over to the captain of the British ship *Bellerophon*, hoping for asylum.

Cognac seems to have had an interesting role in this final drama. One story has it that while Napoleon was contemplating his choices just off the Ile d'Aix aboard the French frigate *La Saale*, a cargo of Cognac was delivered to the ship on the orders of his official supplier of spirits—the better to make the presumed crossing to America more agreeable. The tale goes on to say that once Napoleon turned himself over to the British, they happily confiscated his trove of elixir and thoroughly enjoyed it.

Napoleon's drinks supplier is said to have been Emmanuel Courvoisier, who with a partner, Louis Gallois, had a very successful wine and spirits warehouse near Paris that the emperor visited in 1811. The Courvoisier family took this brief association with the emperor to the bank. Félix Courvoisier, son of Emmanuel, set up in Jarnac in 1835 and made the town Courvoisier's headquarters in 1843. Later on, in 1869, Courvoisier became the official supplier of Cognac to the imperial court of Napoleon III, if only for a short while before that Bonaparte, too, fell from power. Today, Napoleon's telltale silhouette appears on bottles of Courvoisier; the company has even bought some of what are said to be the emperor's personal effects (a hat, a coat, even a lock of hair) and put them on display at its Jarnac headquarters. Courvoisier also led the way in creating a class of Cognac called Napoleon; the name gives the nice but historically unfounded impression that the brandy is as old as the empire, when by law it only has to be at least six and a half years old.

But even as the Bourbon dynasty took power again, with Louis XVIII rising to the throne, recovery from the economic troubles of Napoleon's years didn't come quickly. The harvest of 1816 was a disaster, owing to the eruption in April 1815 of the Mount Tambora volcano in the Dutch East Indies, whose ash fallout turned 1816 in Europe into "the year without a summer." Floods, torrential rain, and deep cold ruined crops from one country to the next, and the whole Continent experienced food shortages. The poor weather lasted until 1820, the last of a run of about fifteen years that stands as the chilliest of the Little Ice Age in Europe. Commerce bobbed along slowly, with British protectionism stymying commerce with stiff duties. This mattered to Cognac traders since most of their exports went to Britain—83 percent in 1819. By comparison, Germany and the United States took in 5 percent that year; the other 12 percent went to the French domestic market.

In the absence of war, however, farmhands were plentiful once more, and much planting of new vines got under way all over France, putting into motion an extended expansion of the nation's vineyards and subsequent growth in the production of wine. Capital poured into the industry as trade began to take off again.

During the Napoleonic blockade, a lot of unsold Cognac had languished in cellars and warehouses, aging away—and becoming exquisite. Now, as it emerged to fill the glasses of aficionados in Britain, it was often humorously referred to as "Napoleon's brandy." The British had every reason to drink up, too, given how well things were going for them. With the industrial revolution, Britain had become the leading exporter of manufactured goods.

France lagged in this industrial remake. Still, it was a big producer of handmade goods and exported more of these than any other Continental nation. Silk, gloves, and porcelain were joined by goods like Cognac, which was becoming popular at the low end of Anglo-Saxon society. Cognac shipments tripled from 33,000 hectoliters in 1815 to 100,000 hectoliters by 1823, when Louis XVIII's reign was coming to an end.

Many Cognac houses set up shop in the first third of the 1800s, including most famously Exshaw (1805), Croizet (1805), Salignac (1809), Ménard (1815), Marange (1815), Hine (1817), Chabasse (1818), Bisquit (1819), Marnier (1827), Renault (1835), and Godet (1838). There were many others that didn't survive these years, however, as the British after 1826 levied even higher taxes on French brandy while keeping duties on grain-based domestic alcohol much lower. With that kind of pressure, it became extremely hard for Cognac producers to make money in their most important market.

By the end of the 1820s, Cognac makers were up against a wall after a series of bad harvests and bankruptcies. Protests against the government of Charles X exploded, and the king was forced to step down. He was replaced by Louis-Philippe, who looked kindly upon business and whose eighteen-year rule ramped up the fortunes of Cognac country. But the British protectionist wall showed no signs of cracking, and Cognac makers turned up the volume of their appeals to Louis-Philippe for urgent action. An 1838 report by Cognac winegrowers and traders warned the government that if it didn't do something to get British duties lowered, Cognac consumption would cease and force winegrowers to tear out their vines. Still, Louis-Philippe didn't act. François Pairault says this was most probably because he was also being pressed by industrialists in the north of France who didn't want to see certain products from Britain—like coal, wool, or textile machines—pouring into France under an open trade accord and putting them out of business.

Fortunately for the Cognac houses, however, liberal economic theories were coming to the fore in Britain. One voice for free trade was Richard Cobden, who bent the ear of the prime minister, Robert Peel, who in the 1840s forced through Parliament sharp cuts in import tariffs, a stance that ultimately cost him his job. Cognac tariffs fell by 30 percent, and Cognac exports shot above 200,000 hectoliters; by 1849, French eau-de-vie amounted to 8 percent of all spirits consumed in Britain, after just 4 percent in 1845. Peel and Cobden had saved a French industry.

While all this was happening, the French had been shedding restraints on their own economy by building rail lines, canals, and roads. The rail mania began in the 1840s, driven by British capital. Rail didn't penetrate Cognac country until the next decade, so the Charente River remained the lifeline of the brandy business. The river was kept in tiptop shape for navigation. Masons designed stone quays for Tonnay-Charente to handle the shipping boom. Rochefort and La Rochelle were similarly enlarged to handle bigger ships.

France's wider economic picture darkened in the mid-1840s with another run of poor harvests, high food prices, falling demand, bankruptcies, and unemployment. The rail boom went bust practically overnight, and thousands lost their investments. A backlash arose among workers, and a political demonstration in Paris brought down the government in February 1848.

Elections in December brought to power Louis Napoleon Bonaparte, nephew of the emperor. He was lifted to office largely on the votes of the recently enfranchised peasants, who looked kindly upon the days of his uncle. But Louis Napoleon didn't like a mandate of only four years, so he staged a coup at the end of 1851 to make himself president for life. The political left of the Second Republic cried foul, and Louis Napoleon replied by imposing martial law and deporting thousands. The press was put under strict controls, political meetings were outlawed, and figures like Victor Hugo and the Charentais winegrower-songwriter Claude Durand went into exile.

Cognac country didn't figure among the hotbeds of resistance, however. When Louis Napoleon went on a victory tour in 1852, shortly before a plebiscite confirmed him as emperor, thousands of people lined the road from Jarnac to Saintes shouting, "Vive l'Empereur! Vive Napoleon III!"

The Second Empire was a law-and-order regime, but also a probusiness one. From 1852 on, and despite mediocre grape crops for the next few years in Cognac country, financial momentum grew. The government favored the creation of investment banks that led to the establishment of many new companies. State aid gave the rail business a new lease on life.

In the transition to the Cognac boom of the 1860s, Charentais winegrowers planted more vines. Often now they would arrange them in rows, instead of letting them sprawl, and strung them on wires. A vineyard of hundreds of thousands of hectares arose. "It was a very going affair," Pairault says. "You could make back 25 to 30 percent of your investment in land in just one year, meaning that within four years your land was paid off. Small winegrowers, with just two hectares, could make a good living."

Never had so many hectoliters of Cognac been distilled. The process was simple, and the equipment easily within the reach of thousands.

It was at this juncture in the mid-1800s that practitioners of the tried-and-true technique of running the alcohol back through the pot-still a second time, in a process known as *la bonne chauffe*, resisted the methods of a kind of distillation perfected by Aeneas Coffey, an Irishman. Coffey stills worked very differently from pot-stills, using steam to extract the alcohol continuously in one "go." (Most Armagnac makers still use a type of these stills, while a few producers use a double-distillation method.)

ENVIRONS DE COGNAC — Distillerie d'un domaine

The mid-1800s saw a grand explosion in Cognac production as thousands
of people got into this affordable and easy game.

To this day, Cognac's primary secret lies in the *bonne chauffe*. Here's
how it works: grapes harvested usually in October are pressed and the
juice is left to ferment, without adding sugar to help it along, or sulfur to
preserve it. Some Cognac makers like to leave the lees (the yeasts that succumb after doing their alcohol-making job) in the wine heading into the
still, since they are known to enhance the flavors endemic to a growth.
(Grande Champagne is the *cru* most likely to distill on the lees, the better to capture its floral foundations.) Other Cognac makers will want little or no lees in their wine, to produce the very light eau-de-vie some
clients prefer.

The wine is loaded into the bulbous copper heart of the still. Copper
is de rigueur: it eliminates most of the fatty acids that would diminish the
Cognac. Copper is also a great heat conductor and resists corrosion by fire
or by liquids. The faucets and handles on the apparatus are made of
bronze, while the valves are stainless steel. Distillation should start not too
long after harvest—usually in November—and must be finished by the
end of March.

For the first pass through the still, a maximum of 2,500 liters of wine
goes into the main pot (*cucurbite*), which sits almost entirely within a brick

oven (*chaudière*), and is heated. Since alcohol's boiling point is 78.3 degrees centigrade and water's is 100, alcohol fumes rise first, into a squat, olive-shaped head (*chapiteau*) atop the main pot. As the soup below gets hotter, the fumes move along through the next piece, an elegant "swan's neck" (*col de cygne*). This duct leads through a towering, oval vessel (*réchauffe-vin*) full of the starter wine being fed down into the main pot. As the fumes are piped through this wine, they are cooled slightly; the hot pipe also serves to begin heating the wine before it goes into the main pot. The last ride for the fumes is via a coil (*serpentin*) spiraling down through a tall vat of top-warm, bottom-cold water. As the fumes cool, they recondense into an alcohol that flows forth and is captured in various receptacles.

About 750 to 800 liters of distillate emerge, an alcohol of 27 to 32 degrees called *brouillis*, with a smell like stewed prunes. The main pot is then loaded up again with the majority of this first *passe*, and the process is started anew. This second distillation, which will last twelve hours, is called the *bonne chauffe* (or *repasse*) and requires careful monitoring to eliminate the highly alcoholic heads (*têtes*, which smell like they could feed an alcohol lamp) which come out first, as well as the slightly lower-strength seconds (*secondes*, with a sweet smell like fresh butter or crepe batter) which come out in the back half of the process, and the final tails (*queues*, with an odor of rancid butter or bouillon cubes), which come out last. These parts—the *têtes*, the *secondes*, and the *queues*—from the front and the back of the process are redistilled: some put the *secondes* back into the *brouillis* or into the next starter wine; the *têtes* and *queues* are often put into the starter wine. But, again, each house has its own methods, leading to very different Cognacs.

What has been left behind after all this elimination is the very heart of the matter, *le coeur*. It has been excised from the middle of the long flow of condensed liquid using an alcoholometer. Exactly where a distiller "cuts off" the upstream *têtes* and the downstream *secondes* and *queues* from the heart is a calculated choice. Letting more *secondes* into the *coeur*, for instance, lowers its alcohol level slightly, and some houses prefer to make that kind of fruity Cognac. In any case, the much-coveted heart ends up with an alcohol content of 68 to 72 percent. If it's over 72 percent it can't be called Cognac.

The marvelous liquid has a pleasant, round, well-balanced aroma, but it's far too powerful to drink—and it certainly isn't Cognac yet. Now this carefully nurtured *coeur* goes into oak barrels—ideally 350 to 450 liters each—for aging, first in new barrels for a time, then in older ones

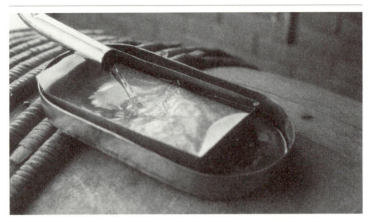

The very heart of the matter is called *le coeur,* excised from the middle
of the long flow of condensed liquid using an alcoholometer.

for years. Here it will incorporate aromas from the wood and begin
to become what Hugo, from his Guernsey exile, called the "liqueur of
the gods."

In each year of aging, 2 to 3 percent of the total volume of a barrel
evaporates, usually lowering its overall alcohol content by about 1 percent. This alcohol drop can sometimes be as high as 2 percent, or lower
than 1, depending on whether the *chai,* or storage place, is humid or not.
A sister Cognac is added to each barrel then and again by the cellar master, or *maître de chais,* to keep the cask topped up. The evaporated stuff is
la part des anges, the angels' share; millions of bottles of Cognac are "lost"
every year, a fact of life that Cognac makers know is part of the long
refinement. A visitor to a Cognac *chai* can't help but notice blackened
walls and joists; this is the home of *Torula compniacensis richon,* a fungus
feeding on alcohol vapors, which, from the grimy look of Cognac country buildings, must be fairly thick.

Since drinkers like Cognac best when it is about 40 degrees alcohol,
they would have to wait many years for nature to take its course. Clearly,
the world can't wait half a lifetime for every glass of Cognac. So its makers lower the alcohol level by adding demineralized water at least six
months before bottling, though this step-by-step process of cutting the
percentage of alcohol often begins just after distillation. Sometimes the
réduction elixir is made with an old Cognac mixed with water; or a few
liters of water can be poured into a newly emptied barrel to mix with the

last of the aged liquid, making another weak Cognac to use as a diluter. Some houses add sugar syrup to round off the taste of the Cognac; some use caramel to adjust its color; others soak oak chips in aged Cognac or hot water to make a tannin-charged additive that will give a young Cognac a distinctly "older" taste. By law, Cognac can be sold as soon as thirty months after its distillation.

Not only did these methods work well time after time, they put Cognac on a course to be the finest of all eaux-de-vie. But as Cognac's star burned brighter, its makers had to rally around their product to protect it from imitations. One way to do that was to bring order to one's own house.

Thus begins the story of Henri Coquand, a Charentais and a geology professor. He was asked by the government to do a survey of the natural resources of the Charente region, with an eye on their use in industry, building, and agriculture. In carrying out his task in the 1850s, Coquand rode horseback across the countryside picking up fossils, especially in cuts for rail lines, and getting an idea of the lay of the land across millions of years. He even defined several geological stages, including the Coniacian (88 to 86 million years ago) and the Santonian and Campanian (the next youngest slices of a few million years each), recognized by geologists everywhere.

Most important for the Cognac industry, Coquand was accompanied by an official taster whose role was to assess the quality of the eau-de-vie of any given vineyard. Evidently Coquand and the *dégustateur* worked hard at their enviable job 150 years ago. What they found was that the geology of an area—the nature of its rock, subsoil, and topsoil—would manifest itself in the unique qualities of its Cognac, a conclusion long recognized by producers and traders.

It worked this way: after Coquand had had a good look, scientifically speaking, at any given piece of land, he made a prediction as to the kind of Cognac the *terroir* should produce, and then sent the taster to test the eau-de-vie in that property's cellars to make sure. "It's very much worth noting," Coquand wrote in 1862, that "taster and geologist never once differed."

Jean-François Tournepiche, the archaeologist in Angoulême who so admires Coquand's 1858 map, lauds the scientist's work. "It's amazing that he could get out there on his horse and go all over the place and precisely pick out and define all the geological layers of the land in the whole region. He started the project with almost nothing, almost no information. And yet he figured it all out, that long ago, riding around. He remains a very remarkable individual in the history of Cognac."

Coquand reported that around 1855 there were nearly 100,000 hectares of vines planted in the Charente Department, nearly half of these in the Angoulême district, and about one-quarter in the Cognac district. Add in the vineyards of departments of Charente-Inférieure and Deux-Sèvres (to the north), and you get well over 200,000 hectares. As noted by Gilles Bernard, history teacher and expert on Cognac in the 1800s, there were only 140,000 hectares of vines in Bordeaux. Meaning that in the mid-1850s Cognac country had one of the highest concentrations of vineyards in France.

Coquand's rock work was complemented by the mapmaking of a civil engineer from Saintes named E. Lacroix, whose 1854 *carte* appears to have been the first to outline the different Cognac *crus*. With Saintes at its center, it showed four growths: Grande Champagne, Petite Champagne, Premiers Bois, and Deuxièmes Bois. His second, revised map in 1861 again showed the same four basic *crus*, and this time it was close to the modern map of growths. (Gradually, these four growths turned into seven, and even sixteen by some counts, before settling down in the twentieth century at six.) Thus rocks and brandy were correlated, setting in motion a process of revision that would last into the next century. Traders used the maps to set Cognac prices.

While Coquand and Lacroix were doing their thing, Cognac producers and traders were making their mark in another way—by shipping their liquid gold in bottles labeled with the house's name.

The city of Cognac got its first glass factory around 1860, but the facility used old methods—glass was blown. To boost production as glass bottling became the vogue, Claude Boucher, a self-made man, set up shop in 1878 on the edge of Cognac, taking over a traditional glassmaking firm. There, he invented a semiautomatic bottle-making machine in which compressed air did the work of the blower. Soon the factory was making fifty thousand bottles a day, far outpacing traditional firms and giving a boost to the sale and export not only of Cognac but of the wines of Bordeaux, Burgundy, and Champagne, as well as liqueurs and mineral water.

As bottling costs declined, Cognac houses shipped less and less of their brandy in barrels, though a lot of them still did. Instead, many shipped a finished product, whose aging was over once it was out of the barrel, in glass. By the 1890s, the use of bottles for shipping Cognac was practically universal as Boucher perfected his manufacturing method and launched mass production.

With bottles, the client could actually see the product: amber, inviting, warm. "Now Cognac had a distinct identity," Bernard notes. The customer also could depend on the age of the brandy in the bottle. Where Cognac houses had had trouble guaranteeing the age of their product, now they could better attest to its years. The client-supplier relationship grew more trusting.

Many of the early bottles were large, squat receptacles wrapped in wicker or straw called *dames-jeannes*, or demijohns. These vessels hold twenty to fifty liters and are often used by cellar masters to store Cognac they deem "finished" and don't want to age further. The use of single bottles (of seventy centiliters) soon followed, with shipments going out in wooden cases. More and more cork makers got into the act, too, to stopper the demijohns and bottles.

Bottle labels sporting the Cognac name appeared in the late 1840s and 1850s. Protected by patent law in 1857, *étiquettes* first helped to guard against fraud; imitations became much more recognizable. Most important, however, they redefined Cognac, dressing it up as a luxury product.

Cognac labels became high art and featured everything from elephants and tigers to bunches of bright golden grapes and deep green grape leaves, from uplifted medieval axes and javelins, to heralds, flags, crowns, and castles, not to mention figures like Louis XIV, Napoleon I, Empress Josephine, Napoleon III, and even Queen Victoria of England. (It's said that after the death in 1861 of her husband Prince Albert, the queen had a Cognac left each evening on his nightstand, a ritual that went on for forty years.)

Cognac country liked Victoria and it liked the liberal economic ideas percolating among British leaders in the late 1850s, all the more because this decade had for the most part been an economic stinker. Auguste Hennessy, looking back on these years in a speech in Saintes in 1869, recalled how the poor grape harvests of the mid-1850s (largely due to the spread of a powdery mildew called *oïdium* in France, which chopped output by 80 percent in 1854 alone) had made Cognac much more expensive and sent demand plunging, especially in England. Fraud had also hurt the business, he noted. British distillers, helped by duties on their products only half as high as those on imports, had had their hands free to dump imitations of French brandy onto the market, cutting British consumption of true French eau-de-vie by 40 percent from 1849 to 1859. Farmers and distillers in northern France also profited during these years and into the 1860s as they pumped out hundreds of thousands of hectoliters of sugar-beet alcohol that managed to catch on.

Secret negotiations between France and Britain on a trade treaty began in the fall of 1859 when Michel Chevalier, economist at the Collège de France, went to England to meet with Richard Cobden, hero of tariff reduction in the 1840s. Cobden had been drafted into the talks by William Gladstone, free-trade chancellor of the Exchequer. Chevalier, Cobden, and Gladstone held their first conversations on liberalizing commerce and planned for Cobden to visit Paris. The British negotiator did, and even had a meeting with Napoleon III.

Hard results came in 1860, when France and Britain signed the most important trade accord in the history of Cognac. The Cobden-Chevalier pact cut tariffs on Cognac by half, while raising taxes on British spirits by a quarter, so that the two duties were nearly equal. English and French distillers could compete on an equal footing. Compared with any other product covered by the deal, Cognac profited the most. The accord also applied to French wines and luxury items; French tariffs on many British goods were lowered, too. It wasn't truly a free-trade deal, but it did light a big fire.

Joy in Cognac country knew no bounds—Cobden even had a street named after him in Cognac—as the sun rose on the industry's golden era. From 140,000 hectoliters just after the treaty, shipments shot up to 420,000 liters by 1866. The story goes that Cognac traders doing deals at the Place du Canton were making so much money that they didn't even deign to recount the gold coins paid to them. Much of those profits went into the business, as the area planted in vines took off again, rising sharply from 1860 to 1870, when it hit 243,000 hectares (the size of Luxembourg). Land prices soared.

Vines took up so much space that hardly anything else was grown. Wheat production was nearly abandoned as King Cognac ruled. The years from 1861 to 1866 saw the Cognac country wine crop explode from 2.3 million hectoliters, about half of which was distilled into 166,000 hectoliters of eau-de-vie, to 11.2 million hectoliters of wine and 957,000 hectoliters of eau-de-vie. Untold thousands got rich. The city of Cognac filled with sumptuous limestone buildings. People worshipped Napoleon III: busts and portraits of the emperor reigned all over town. Trading houses sprang up one after another as speculators vied for a piece of the pie.

At the heart of feast was the British market, in which French eau-de-vie amounted to 11 percent of spirits sold in 1867; that's a lot, given competition from whiskey and rum. Britain was also a big reexporter of Cognac, shipping it as far away as New Zealand.

Meanwhile, civil war in the United States and high tariffs put a damper on many Cognac houses' hopes for that market. U.S. protectionism would grow even stronger: in the 1880s, France would get tough and bar salted meat and pork from the United States, angering a congressman and future president, William McKinley, who got tariffs increased further.

In France, the movement of Cognac got much easier during these glory years as rail lines spread. A line connected La Rochelle and Rochefort to Poitiers in 1857, and in 1867 service began between Rochefort, Saintes, and Angoulême, bringing on the decline of the Charente for shipping eau-de-vie.

Another victim of these years was the salt trade. Laws in the 1840s allowing the free trade of salt and the use of foreign salt in salting cod signaled the retreat. And Saintonge salters were ruined when dealers began to cater to customers' preference for the white salt of the Mediterranean, whereas Charente salt is often light gray. Easier transport by rail and lower tariffs turned the flow of salt from the Midi into a flood. Thousands of Charente salters emigrated, abandoning their ponds to the ocean.

While sectors like Atlantic salt—but not Cognac—were waning, pressure was brought to bear on Napoleon III to reenergize the economy. After bowing to the demands, the emperor found that the opposition wanted even more concessions. His foes won two-fifths of the vote in 1869, and the next year the yes votes for a parliamentary system were overwhelming.

But 1870 was not to be a good year—not for France, and not for Cognac. Eau-de-vie prices fell 20 percent as a result of overproduction. Then Napoleon III made the mistake of declaring war on Prussia. France was not only left reeling, but saw its emperor taken prisoner. In September, politicians in Paris declared the Second Empire over and formed a republic.

A truce followed early the next year, but France lost Alsace and part of iron-rich Lorraine, and was ordered to pay a huge indemnity to the Prussians. A leftist Commune arose in Paris, with workers taking over the heart of the city. The government of Adolphe Thiers, then at Versailles, sent an army into the capital that killed thousands of insurrectionists.

The Third Republic immediately faced an economic mess. Thiers, elected president in August 1871, was forced to seek public loans to help pay the indemnity to the Prussians. The government wielded the tax tool on consumer items. Excise taxes on wine and eau-de-vie shot up 66 percent. Domestic sales of Cognac fell by half from 1870 to 1871.

But these problems were almost insignificant compared with the appearance in Cognac country in 1872 of *Phylloxera vastatrix*, a tiny root louse that killed vineyards with stunning efficiency. The scourge apparently had come from the United States, hitching a ride on vines brought to Europe for study by botanists seeking a definitive cure for *oïdium*. The root louse showed up in France in the early 1860s and had done dark deeds in the Rhône valley and around Bordeaux. Now phylloxera was ravaging Cognac's vineyards.

To the geographer Victor-Eugène Ardouin-Dumazet, who traveled widely, phylloxera's effects were apocalyptic: "Nothing but empty houses! Ruin has knocked at many a door and misery is everywhere. How sad it is to visit these once-flourishing towns. Now the vineyards are gone, and the shock is to see that the region's commercial spirit is gone, too. Barren land comes into view with every step. It's a vista that breaks the heart."

PHYLLOXERA AND
THE TEXAS CURE

PHYLLOXERA IS A DARK AND DIRTY WORD in Cognac country. Legions of winegrowers became paupers as their vines died under the onslaught of a yellow insect barely visible to the eye. Thousands of new houses sat abandoned as people fled to the cities or abroad to count their losses. When it was all tallied up, the phylloxera disaster and recovery cost France 12 billion francs, nearly three times the indemnity it paid the Prussians.

This plague didn't strike Cognac's vines with a hammer blow, but rather whittled them away. In 1872 the vineyard stretched from the Atlantic shore east through the Charente valley all the way down to Périgord and totaled 246,000 hectares. Even after the first signs of phylloxera (in Crouin, near Cognac), the vineyard kept swelling as if it just wouldn't be stopped, reaching its apogee of 283,000 hectares in 1877. But phylloxera then went to work in earnest. By 1893 there were only 41,000 hectares of vines left.

The identifier of the culprit was Jules-Emile Planchon, a botany professor in Montpellier who in 1868 dubbed the insect he found on dead rootstocks *Phylloxera vastatrix*. The louse is especially active, producing a half-dozen generations each summer. The beast most likes the roots, from which it sucks out life-giving sap, provoking the formation of nodules that cut off the plant's circulation. As the root is slowly asphyxiated, the entire vine soon turns yellow, its leaves drop, and death follows.

Phylloxera moves through the soil if it is loose or cracked, and spreads easily on the wind, water, clothing, shoes, or farm equipment. After striking a vineyard, it might not invade the one next door, but attack at a distance. With the explosion of billions of these insects from each point of infection, phylloxera spread to annihilate vineyards draping vast regions.

Planchon also noted the connection between the arrival of the insect and the introduction of vines from America that, unbeknownst to the Midi winegrowers trying them out, carried the louse on their roots. The American vines were resistant to phylloxera and so remained healthy even as they disseminated the insect. Even though wine from these vines was poor, winegrowers kept experimenting with them. A nursery full of American vines was even opened in the Vaucluse Department in the southeast, from which many a vine emerged to multiply phylloxera's effects.

The American connection also explained why Europe's dominant *Vitis vinifera* succumbed to phylloxera when planted in the United States. Having no resistance to the insect, the vines soon died. Phylloxera hit America, too, by the way, when it ravaged California's vineyards in the 1870s and 1880s.

Incredibly, a number of French winegrowers who had lost their vines continued to replant the same European varieties that had just died, either out of desperation or ignorance of what was going on. Of course, phylloxera didn't spare the new vines, and thousands of people were ruined again.

Jacques Fauré, who from 1988 to 1996 directed the Bureau National Interprofessionnel du Cognac (BNIC), the professional body that oversees the Cognac industry, explains: "Phylloxera was endemic in America and at first caused no problems over there. But in Europe, the newcomer insect found tender, nonresistant plants to attack. It was like when the Conquistadors carried smallpox to America, massacring the Incas and the Aztecs."

The ugly invader from America conquered the southern half of France by the early 1880s, moving most quickly in the southeast. It advanced north up the Rhône valley and also west to join forces with another army of the insects spreading forth from Bordeaux. The combined forces then

Untold numbers of winegrowers became paupers
as their vines died under the onslaught of a
yellow insect barely visible to the eye.

marched to the Loire valley and points north. From 2.4 million hectares of
vines in 1875, France had only 1.7 million hectares by 1900. The center-
west suffered the most. In 1875 the two Charente departments had 11
percent of the nation's vineyards, but just 4 percent in 1900.

Amazingly, production of wine and Cognac continued to rise during
the early 1870s. Cognac country produced 14 million hectoliters of
wine in 1875, 8 million of which were distilled, three years into the phylloxera attacks. Shipments of eau-de-vie, despite some poor-weather years,
shot up to an all-time high of 478,000 hectoliters in 1879. These nice
numbers probably explain why the French government was slow to react
to the crisis.

The first offer of a government reward for a solution to the problem, in
1870, amounted to 20,000 francs. By 1874, however, as phylloxera's dev-
astations became clearer, the reward was raised to 300,000 francs. The
Montpellier Agriculture School went to work testing remedies. Something

like seven hundred solutions were proposed, including crazy ideas like toad venom, arsenic, or even a thumping device to scare off the critters. Three hundred or so of the notions were tried and a couple worked rather well: flooding vineyards for a time each winter or injecting carbon disulfide into the soil around the roots. Both were used to slow the killer. (If a vineyard was in a sandy area, it often survived, since the insect couldn't thrive in that terrain.)

For flooding to work, a vineyard had to be immersed in 20 to 25 centimeters of water for six weeks during the winter to kill the insects. Big efforts were made in various regions to this end, but if your property wasn't flat or near a water source, or if it lay on a hillside, this treatment was unworkable. Use of carbon disulfide, however, was the answer for a larger number of winegrowers. Working with big syringe-type injectors, they pumped the foul-smelling, oily liquid into the ground. This labor was hard but amounted to a radical asphyxiation of the insects.

Even so, the phylloxera epidemic hardly slowed, but pursued its course, blighting an ever wider swath of France's vineyards.

Ordinary people in the Cognac business were at a loss. Public prayers and processions for the salvation of the vineyards took place all over, though the clergy couldn't have been too pleased when all this fervor turned to anger and the wavering faithful began seizing statues of the local patron saint—often Saint Eutrope—and trundling them outdoors to whip them.

Then, in 1881, an International Phylloxera Congress took place in Bordeaux that weighed the ideas of a Frenchman who believed the best solution lay at the source of the crisis: vines from America. Gaston Bazille, president of the Agricultural Society of Hérault, in the south of France, was among the first to suggest grafting European vines onto American rootstocks, in the late 1860s. The idea was that the root (*porte-greffe*) would hold its own against phylloxera, while the vine growing above would make the grapes. Bazille's initial experiments didn't work so well, and it wasn't until 1872 that he had vine shoots shipped to him from St. Louis with which he produced thriving grafts. Now all the experts had to do was to find the right U.S. varieties to be the roots of a new vineyard for France.

To this end, Planchon, long a leader in the search for a way out of the crisis, sailed to New York in 1873, where he met up with Charles Valentine Riley, an entomologist who knew a lot about phylloxera. As the two scientists toured America together—through New Jersey, Pennsylvania,

Delaware, North Carolina, Ohio, Missouri, and Massachusetts—Riley introduced Planchon to grape species resistant to the insect. The professor used the voyage to draw up a list of nurseries in America where French winegrowers could order phylloxera-resistant plants. These were either native American species and their hybrids, or crosses between American vines and European species created earlier by colonists living on the East Coast hoping against hope to make American wine. Planchon also put together a catalog of phylloxera-resistant American vines. This listing, published in 1875, became a must-read for winegrowers, especially for believers in the North American solution: the Americanists.

Planchon brought home a number of vines—either native American hybrids or crosses between American plants and *Vitis vinifera*—that he intended to try to introduce just as they were, without grafting. It was thought that these hybrids—like Noah, Isabelle, Clinton, Othello, Jacquez, and Herbemont—could rapidly fill the gaping holes left by phylloxera. But those hopes were dashed as these grapes made an inferior-tasting wine and were discovered to be susceptible to disease. The spread of grafting also braked the use of such hybrids as primary producers.

Upon Planchon's nevertheless phylloxera-tolerant American roots, then, scientists and nurserymen in France turned to grafting their time-tried European vines. Little by little the U.S. rootstocks that turned out to be less than reasonably resistant to phylloxera were eliminated. Those better able to put up with the insect—*Vitis rupestris* and *Vitis riparia*—rose up the rankings. A fair beginning was made against the American invader.

Given such evidence, the Bordeaux congress recommended grafting atop American plants as the best response to the crisis. Not to say that there wasn't resistance: many people believed the weird taste already known in wine from American grapes would emerge from the new root-stocks. Their fears took a while to go away. (It wasn't until 1888 that a High Commission on Phylloxera officially sanctioned grafting as the supreme solution. "The scion will be French, the root will be American," it pronounced.)

Meantime, the tearing out of sickly, dying vines and the planting of the newly grafted ones got under way in several regions during the 1880s. It wasn't exactly a boom start, though; many growers, faced with the extreme cost of replanting, waited as long as financially possible to get started, hoping against hope that their phylloxera-weakened vines would somehow survive incessant chemical treatments. It also took some time to set up a network of businesses to import rootstock cuttings from the United States. Techniques for grafting root and scion (the plant that rides above) had to be refined and then carefully taught to winegrowers, for it wasn't an easy process. Lastly, finding just the right rootstock—involving the creation of a lot of hybrids—with which to replant amounted to a vast experiment of hit-and-miss, some soils liking American roots better than others.

The Charente region joined the replanting wave hesitantly at best, mostly around Jarnac and Cognac, but no sooner were the much-smaller vineyards getting toward maturity than a new problem cropped up, rattling everyone. European plants growing on varieties of American roots were succumbing to an iron deficiency called chlorosis that yellows the leaves and sharply cuts productivity. Chlorosis is linked to highly chalky, alkaline soils that keep a plant from absorbing the iron it needs to produce chlorophyll. (*Vitis vinifera* had always been among the world's most chalk-tolerant grapevines; many of the American rootstocks being tested in Cognac country tended not to like the very alkaline soils often found south of the Charente, but they did all right in siliceous, lower-lime soils that are common north of the river. Grande Champagne and Petite Champagne, where the chlorosis problem was the most acute, paid the biggest price of all the Cognac growths.)

Suddenly it became urgent to find another American rootstock that was resistant to phylloxera but that didn't succumb to chlorosis. To get to the bottom of this new problem, a committee of phylloxera experts in Charente-Inférieure decided that a scientist armed with a geological map of America would surely be able to locate terrain with chalky soil "just like ours" and to spot indigenous vines resistant to phylloxera and chlorosis.

Dispatched to find these rootstocks was Pierre Viala, a twenty-seven-year-old viticulture professor at the Montpellier Agriculture School. The Viala mission, from June to December 1887, had all the trappings of an adventure in which the academic braved slogs through insecure areas where he ran into wild animals and hardship—and even the temporary loss of all his notes.

During the voyage he traveled with another plant expert, Frank Lamson-Scribner of the United States Department of Agriculture, named by the government to aid the mission. The duo made three "tours": first, between New York and Boston; the second took them down to the Washington area, then out to Ohio and back to New York. But finding healthy grapevines with their roots firmly growing in limestone terrain wasn't all that easy. Viala learned that he had to go west if he was going to find what he was looking for—vigorous native plants clearly tapped deep into chalky ground and yet not suffering from chlorosis.

Still accompanied by Lamson-Scribner, Viala headed out a third time in the fall. They visited North Carolina, then went to Kentucky, Tennessee, Missouri, and into Indian Territory, present-day Oklahoma. Viala wrote: "I have just spent eight days in Indian Territory among the Wyandottes, the Modocs, the Senecas and the Cherokees. Except for the lack of routes and food, one travels through this area just as safely as in France, and it would be very hard to find an Indian willing to scalp you."

At the Red River, Viala and Lamson-Scribner crossed on the weekly train into Texas, where they met the American half of this heroic tale: Thomas Volney Munson, a horticulturist and nurseryman crazy about grapes, "the most beautiful, most wholesome and nutritious, most certain and most profitable fruit that could be grown." Munson had traveled to and lived in many places, before settling in north Texas at Denison in 1876 after an offer from a brother living there, William Benjamin Munson, to come and visit.

The spot turned out to be just right for Munson's tastes, for along the bluffs of the Red River he found a "grape paradise"—a half dozen native species he'd never seen before. Setting up a lab, he crossed these grapes to develop superior varieties and also roamed Texas for other species. Munson, in association with another brother, Joseph Theodore, even made wine.

Munson's travels through a central strip of the state turned out to be key to Cognac's survival. It was there, in the woodsy stretches of river valleys, that he found a number of native grapes, the "best of the best," according to Roy Renfro, overseer of the T. V. Munson Viticulture and Enology Center in Denison, "so he could crossbreed them to come up with insect- and disease-resistant varieties," grapes that were less acidic and far more palatable than wild grapes. By crossbreeding what he found with *labrusca*, for example, as well as some *vinifera* and many others, Renfro says Munson was able to create "a large selection of grape varieties for farmers to grow that would be getting ripe in June, July, August, September, maybe even October, so they could have a market and make money selling fresh grapes."

Along the way, and quite incidentally, Munson came across *Vitis berlandieri*, growing with thick green leaves despite the highly chalky soil. *Berlandieri* was first catalogued by J. L. Berlandier, a Swiss botanist who worked in Mexico in the 1830s and also explored Texas, where he found his first *berlandieri* north of San Antonio in 1834. This is the heart of Texas, and it is stacked with shelves of limestone as old and often older than Cognac's foundation, meaning that the basements and the soil that eroded out of them of central Texas and the Charente River valley are very similar. Traveling widely, Munson gathered up as many grapevines as he could find, took them to north Texas, and grew cuttings.

Munson was not the only nurseryman interested in *berlandieri*; others in Texas and elsewhere in the South and Midwest had this species in their collections. *Berlandieri* seeds got to scientists in southern France who tried them out and made cuttings as early as 1874. One researcher interested in *berlandieri* was Alexis Millardet, a botanist at the University of Bordeaux, who noted that the species was practically unaffected by phylloxera. In parallel, another scientist saw that *berlandieri* did well in chalky soils where no other vine survived. Unfortunately, it was also found that *berlandieri* didn't easily make cuttings, limiting its propagation in the mid-1870s.

Planchon, meanwhile, touted *berlandieri* as a good rootstock with which to replant France's vineyards. Millardet and another expert viticulturist, Gustave Foëx, agreed with Planchon and made the connection, as others had, that this species would be good for chalky soil, but again ran into the problem of making *berlandieri* cuttings. This was when Millardet

It was in the limestone beds of central Texas that the right grapes were found to reconstitute Cognac's vineyards.

began to realize, in the early 1880s, that by crossing *berlandieri* with Europe's *vinifera* (*chasselas*, in this case), he could make a rootstock that was both resistant to phylloxera and easier to reproduce by cuttings.

It's important to note that most of Millardet's work here crossing native American vines (*berlandieri* and others) with *vinifera* was not directly focused on creating a rootstock that could survive in chalky soil—but instead on coming up with a vine that could be a good, phylloxera-free direct producer. It wasn't until 1886, the year before Viala's mission to America, that he announced to a viticulture congress in Bordeaux that crosses with *berlandieri* would be the ideal rootstock "for the Champagne of the Charentes, where so far no new vine has survived."

In September 1887, when Viala arrived at the Munson establishment in Denison, the already successful nurseryman showed the Frenchman the *berlandieri* samples he'd collected. Viala studied Munson's conclusions about the chlorosis-free varieties of Texas and was convinced that they just might save the day back in Cognac country. Viala and Lamson-Scribner then traveled to the places where Munson had spotted *berlandieri* so that Viala could see it growing in situ, mostly on hills and along river valleys (like the Lampasas) in south-central Texas. Some reports say that later that autumn, Munson himself went south to the area to supervise the collection of cuttings. These dormant rootstocks were bundled in straw and burlap, transported to Denison, put on boats to go down the Red River to the Mississippi and then to New Orleans, before being sent on steamships across the Atlantic to La Rochelle and other ports in France.

Viala and Lamson-Scribner then turned west at San Antonio and headed to El Paso, then across New Mexico and Arizona to California, reaching Los Angeles in mid-October and San Francisco by the end of the month. Much of that territory was *berlandieri* country. Viala was weary, but he knew he'd come upon the solution he had been seeking: "I have crossed, over the last month, the driest regions that you can imagine. But I also saw limestone, pure limestone—maybe too pure—horribly dry terrain, with Indians on it—and vines growing there, and not unhealthy ones."

He and Lamson-Scribner made the trip back to New York via Salt Lake City, Denver, and Chicago. "The Americans helped me with my research with a devotion that can't be over-praised," Viala later wrote. "Their hospitality and assistance was never lacking and inspired me through difficult times."

You might wonder why the Viala mission was even necessary, given that so many scientists and nurserymen had already seen the utility of *berlandieri,* especially in chalky areas. But while Millardet and others were creating hybrids like 41B—the *berlandieri-chasselas* cross that would be the most popular rootstock in Cognac country for decades—knowledge of this initial success was available to only a few and by no means to wine-growers at large. Viala's engaging adventure, then, helped above all to spread the grand news—people eagerly followed the whole saga in the newspapers—about *berlandieri* and its hopeful descendants. From the untamed wilds of Texas, the miracle solution for the resurrection of Cognac country was at hand.

In Cognac country's chalky Grande Champagne and Petite Champagne, *berlandieri* was manna from heaven, and the word spread rapidly over the next few years. A tide of requests for *berlandieri* cuttings kept not only Munson but many other nurserymen—notably Hermann Jaeger in Missouri who'd been sending thousands of vines to France—busier than they'd ever dreamed. *Berlandieri* rootstocks were popular for years, judging from the many ads for them in viticulture magazines and newspapers, and only gradually gave way to *berlandieri* crosses with *vinifera* or with U.S. vines like *rupestris* and *riparia,* all of which were better because they made cuttings easily.

As the vineyards of France began at last to reappear, a joyous nation rained honors upon the propagators. Munson was made, upon Viala's recommendation, a Chevalier du Mérite Agricole in the French Legion of Honor in 1888. A French delegation visited America to confer the award, and overnight Munson became the country's most famous nurseryman.

One hundred years later, Cognac and Denison held celebrations to commemorate the award and the saga linking their cities. Representatives of Denison visited Cognac and vice versa, plaques went up in both places, and talks began about formal ties. In 1992, the grapevine hothouse of Texas and the capital of the world's most famous spirit became Sister Cities.

That international link surely would have drawn a satisfied grin from Munson, as would the vineyard today near Denison on the west campus of Grayson County College, in which Munson's grape varieties have been growing since 1975. After starting with just a handful of cultivars, the vineyard has now revived several dozen of Munson's creations (he made something like three hundred, with such names as Ben Hur, Headlight, Live Oak, Mrs. Munson, and Texas Pure). The T.V. Munson Viticulture and Enology Center sits nearby, from whose history collection you can learn how this savvy horticulturist, after having saved Cognac's vineyards, dazzled horticulturists even further with his display of practically all of the species in the *Vitis* genus at the Columbian Exposition in 1893 in Chicago, and how he compiled his findings a few years later in *Foundations of American Grape Culture*, the most definitive book on the subject. Munson, who died in Denison in 1913, is remembered fondly in France with several statues.

For all his magnificent efforts, Viala became a bona fide hero. There is a Rue Pierre Viala in Segonzac, at the heart of Grande Champagne, a Place Viala in Montpellier, and many other signposts of gratitude scattered around France. The professor spent the rest of his life teaching viticulture, and above all writing up his scientific findings, dozens of titles in all that were translated and read by specialists around the world. He was made a Chevalier du Mérite Agricole in the French Legion of Honor in 1888, the same year as Munson, and received many other awards. By 1920, at sixty-one, he was inducted into the prestigious Academy of Sciences.

Jean Cazelles, head of the French Viticulture Society, said of Viala: "A great scientist, you have been a good worker for the fortune of France, which owes you more than anyone else for the rebirth of the nation's viticulture." Viala died in 1936 at seventy-six. Friends formed a group to honor his memory.

Because farmers got big tax breaks when they replanted their vineyards with the new rootstocks, and because a lot of these rootstocks were provided free, the process accelerated. From just 1,300 hectares of grafted American roots in all of France in 1878, there were 436,000 hectares in 1890.

In Cognac country, there were 12,000 hectares of grafted vines by 1895. The most common rootstock was Millardet's 41B, which would be the workhorse of the vineyard until the 1970s. (It has now ceded to a cross between *riparia* and *berlandieri* called RSB1 that is also tolerant of lime, puts up with rainy spring weather, and does well in drought. Another rootstock, called Fercal—which, in a mouthful, is a *berlandieri-colombard* crossed with a *berlandieri-cabernet sauvignon*—is also used and has the highest tolerance of lime of any rootstock.) In 1900 the whole Cognac vineyard amounted to only 55,000 hectares.

Much of the land in the north of the region, especially in Aunis, was turned over to cows and making butter, an industry for which the area is well known today. A lot of this stock farming was done by emigrants from the Vendée who found land there cheap and who were able to occupy the vacuum created when so many phylloxera-ruined winegrowers decamped.

If, as Gilles Bernard says, "many people thought the region was cursed," the Vendéens didn't share that view. On the contrary, these Catholics moved into this longtime Protestant zone with "missionary zeal," he adds, and carved out a profitable niche in what used to be France's biggest vineyard.

Cognac's recovery was never better than slow, however, and in the meantime another problem arose. Incredibly, once more it came from America: a fungus that rode in on new rootstocks. It was called downy mildew, and was first identified in France by Planchon and by Millardet, who called it *mildiou*. While American vines did indeed carry this fungus, it didn't hurt most. In France, on the other hand, downy mildew is a mean malady. At its worst it shrivels the grapes, but it doesn't spare any part of the plant above ground. Wine made from grapes hit by this mildew has an odd taste, won't age, and turns sour. It started striking everywhere in 1878.

It was Millardet who developed the solution with his *bouillie bordelaise*—a blue goop of water, copper sulfate, and lime that was sprayed on the leaves and in widespread use by the 1890s. This scientist had stumbled on the answer when he once saw a blue powder on vine leaves along a road in Médoc. An estate manager told him that the pigment had been sprayed on the plants to make people think it was poison and to keep them away. Millardet noticed how the powder appeared to be keeping the leaves healthy.

When it rains it pours, however, and along came yet another American fungus—this one aptly called black rot (in English and in French). It was spotted by Viala and by Louis Ravaz, head of the Station Viticole of Cognac (a body working to rebuild the region's vineyards using American rootstocks), who tracked its spread out of the southwest into the heart of the country in the 1880s. Black rot, like downy mildew, also shrivels grapes and can easily wipe out an entire wine crop. Once more copper-based chemicals were applied, and these worked if used early enough in the season.

The combined effect of these serious ailments—along with all the trial-and-error work on hybrids and such—was an even sharper drop in wine production across France. Demand, meantime, was rising. To meet it, imports from places yet to be hit by phylloxera, like Algeria, soared. These wines were poured into poor French wines to pump them up. Others added chemicals and coloring to "save" low-quality French wines that would normally have been used for vinegar. Yet others made a wine by dumping beet sugar and water onto the marc, or the residue of pressed grapes (after a first fermentation of wine had been completed), to make a drink of about 8 to 10 degrees alcohol in just over one week. Many people also resorted to creating ersatz wine by fermenting imported raisins in water for twelve days, creating a potion of 10 to 11 degrees alcohol. Millions of hectoliters of these elixirs were produced.

Cognac country suffered from this type of phenomenon when distillers in Italy and Germany began committing large-scale fraud during the late 1800s. At the end of the century Italy was exporting fifty times more fake Cognac than it was importing of the real thing. Likewise, Russia had Koniak and Spain had Coniac. Making the situation all the worse was the fact that authentic Cognac had become rather scarce now that the huge stocks accumulated during the 1860s had been sold off to keep many Cognac traders afloat through the industry's crises. And there were even "fake" Cognac traders: brandy producers who simply got a postal address in Cognac so they could slap a label on their bottles declaring it to be from there no matter where it was made. Purveyors of fraudulent brandy also did their deeds in Mexico, Chile, and Brazil, where shoe leather and semiburned sugar were used to "tint" alcohol to look like aged Cognac.

Faced with intense competition from fakes—and with the rising popularity of other drinks like cider, beer, and whiskey—Cognac's leaders finally went to work to protect their terrain.

To start with, larger Cognac traders invested much capital in building distilleries. Where for many years they had depended on small distillers—*bouilleurs de cru*, who had disappeared by the thousands during the phylloxera epidemic—to supply them with eau-de-vie, now the big houses made it themselves. To stock it they built grand warehouses like the ones in Cognac belonging to Hennessy and Martell that sit along the Charente today.

The traders also began to work on specialized blending of different qualities of eau-de-vie and giving the results special ranks. Martell, in 1907, offered no less than eight: X, XX, XXX, VO, VSO, VSOP, ESOP (aged more than forty years in the barrel), and Extra (aged fifty years). Hennessy gave its Cognacs star rankings: one, two, and three, and also used VO, VSOP, and XO.

A hierarchy of these kinds of designations—always with the accent on "very" or "extra"—is used today to classify Cognacs by length of sojourn in the barrel. To make a VS (Very Special), the youngest Cognac in the blend must be at least two and a half years old; the outcome is a Cognac averaging three to three and a half years old. For VSOP (Very Superior

Old Pale) the greenest Cognac has to be at least four and a half years old; a VSOP might contain an assembly of something like sixty Cognacs originating from one to all six growths, and the resulting Cognac, then, will be an average of six or so years old. The more ancient classes start at six and a half years for the youngest part of the mix: the XOs, Napoleons, and others. An XO (Extra Old) might be made of eighty Cognacs, including some old ones to give it aromatic depth; the average age of the Cognac in a bottle of XO is twelve years, usually higher. For all Cognacs above VSOP, however, the real age of the product is often murky—and the buyer is left to trust the house.

As the original growth is always extremely important, many connoisseurs will keep in mind that Cognacs from Grande and Petite Champagne don't get much better after forty years of aging, and that Cognacs from the Borderies or Fins Bois need at least twenty years in the barrel to come to full maturity. That special mouthful of flavor is called *rancio*, a rich, full-bodied taste that speaks of cheese, butter, mushrooms, walnuts, and raisins.

Bottle labels enjoyed an artistic heyday, getting elaborate and a bit wilder—the better to attract drinkers. An *étiquette* on a Prunier Cognac, for instance, depicts a giant cannon shooting out bottles of Cognac under the brand name "Salvation Brandy," the unsubtle message being "bomb the enemy with Cognac instead of shells." On a De la Lune Fils Cognac, a man sits on a horn of moon and toasts its smiling face with "Salud." A Murel & Fils Grande Fine Champagne features a long-haired, bare-breasted maiden standing, arms upraised, on a frozen landscape to vaunt a Cognac called "L'Etoile Polaire," or North Star brandy. Then there is the amusing "Cognac Fin de Siècle" by Mathusalem Cognac that shows bald old Methuselah sitting, knees comfortably crossed, on a cloud between the dates 1800 and 1900 while holding a scythe in one hand and a glass of Cognac in the other.

A key step taken to defend Cognac in the riotous market of unsavory "fake" drinks was a 1909 government decree defining the Cognac zone. This declaration said that an eau-de-vie couldn't be called Cognac (or eau-de-vie de Cognac or eau-de-vie des Charentes) unless distilled within the specific geographic area that it described. The map long used by Cognac traders that set the borders of the region was thus ratified by this ruling.

This early process of defining Cognac's region of origin was paralleled in other winegrowing areas, like Champagne, Armagnac, and Bordeaux. Among other things, rules coming into force specified that wine was to be made only from, of all things, freshly fermented grapes. The sugar business shuddered as the government clamped down with restrictions and taxes; makers of additives to save poor wines were barred from selling their wares.

Without a doubt, the old vineyard was dead, and a new one was coming into view. The output of genuine wine took off again at the end of the 1800s as the yields of France's new vines climbed sharply. Part of that new productivity, in Cognac country at least, had to do with the replanting of vines in strict rows on wires, this method having begun in the 1860s. Now more and more farmers could employ ever-more-modern plows to work the soil between the rows. With vines hung up in neat order, it was that much easier to apply chemicals to battle disease. Phylloxera hadn't disappeared; it was ever-present in the American roots, and tended to drain them of some of their vigor. Thus winegrowers had to fertilize their plants often to keep them in shape, which set off an explosion in the use of chemicals in the vineyard.

This period also marked the start of a shift away from the *folle blanche* vine of yore to a new variety called *ugni blanc* that dominates the vineyard today. *Folle blanche*, highly productive and long the valuable workhorse of the region, tended to suffer from rot when grafted onto American roots. Today *ugni blanc*, also known as Saint-Emilion des Charentes, is France's most widely grown white grape, with something like 90 percent of all of them cultivated within the Cognac *appellation*. It is far less likely to suffer from late spring frosts than *folle blanche*. But some call *ugni blanc* downright characterless, which may be true if its wine were the only thing being judged. What is certain is that most people who make Cognac don't want to start the process with a wine that is highly aromatic. They argue that to do so doesn't leave enough room, as it were, for the oak barrels to add their flavors to the aging Cognac. Better, these experts say, to start the aging with the more acidic wine that *ugni blanc* gives.

In order for a Cognac producer to be legally allowed to put the name of a *cru* on his bottle—Grande Champagne, Petite Champagne, and so on— a minimum of 90 percent of his *cépages* must be *ugni blanc, folle blanche,* or *colombard*, either singly or altogether. He can use these *cépages* to meet all his needs, in fact, or he can round out his mixture with any of a half-dozen other varieties—*blanc ramé, jurançon blanc, montils,* and so on—so long as these others don't total more than 10 percent of his vines. If a winegrower wants to, he can even elect to use second-tier *cépages* to his heart's content, the only restriction being that he wouldn't then be permitted to put the *cru* on the bottle, though he could still call it Cognac. Since growth names count for a lot, this practice isn't at all common.

So long as wine prices stayed up, as they did in the 1880s and 1890s when genuine wine was scarce, winegrowing remained profitable. Farmers could pay for all the chemicals, for machines to disperse them, and for workers to do the spraying. But then a big surplus of wine developed at the turn of the century, and prices crashed. Whereas in the 1880s a hectoliter of wine cost 40 francs, in 1901 the same 100 liters fetched only 8 francs.

Cognac producers didn't suffer from the fall in wine prices in 1900 like wine producers did. The Charente valley produced large amounts of distillery-bound wine (often well over 2 million hectoliters) in the century's early years, and these made excellent Cognacs, as from 1904 to 1907. Meantime, Cognac's vineyard expanded, reaching nearly 75,000 hectares by the start of World War I. All in all, the prewar years were profitable.

The domestic market did well, but the international scene was even more lucrative: Cognac extended its market to Mexico, across South America, and into southern Africa, China, and India. As the historian Robert Delamain wrote, "Cognac's range now stretched all the way around the globe." He also intoned: "It's often said that there isn't a place in the world where people haven't heard of two names associated with France: Paris and Cognac. But if they've heard of only one name having to do with France, it's Cognac."

THE GERMAN WHO
SAVED COGNAC

AR CAME OUT OF NOWHERE IN THE LATE summer of 1914, mobilization was ordered in August, and in Cognac country enthusiasm to go fight the enemy rose to a fever pitch. Town after town filled with soldiers preparing to head to the front. People poured into the cities with automobiles, horses, and mules to offer them to the authorities. Cafés were full, church bells rang, and crowds belted out patriotic songs as trains packed with recruits pulled out.

Everyone thought it would all be over by the fall. Every son of Cognac believed he would be home harvesting grapes that October. Instead, the war bogged down and thousands of refugees poured into the Charente region.

It so happens that 1914 was an exceptional wine year, even as Europe was plunging into one of its darkest periods of killing. Cognac country produced more than 150,000 hectoliters of pure alcohol (a standard measure of output amounting to 28 centiliters in

Soldiers in Cognac heading off to war in 1914, a great wine year,
when eau-de-vie output soared to over fifty million bottles.

a standard 70-centiliter bottle of 40-degree Cognac) that year, or about 54
million bottles. But then output dropped to just 38,000 hectoliters of
pure alcohol in 1915, or 14 million bottles, crawling back slowly from
that low point to 117,000 hectoliters, or 42 million bottles, by 1919.
Average yield per hectare also hit bottom at this time, largely because of a
severe labor shortage with so many men at war.

The wine glut in the early 1900s was largely absorbed at the front when
the war minister decided to distribute wine to the soldiers. Cognac,
among other spirits, also got handed out. Red wine and eau-de-vie were
welcome changes from beer or cider. At first the daily wine ration was a
quarter-liter; by 1916 this rose to half a liter. In 1917, 12 million hectoliters were shipped to the front in thousands of rail tankers. In 1918, 16
million hectoliters went down the hatch, as another quarter-liter per sol-
dier per day became optional and yet another quarter-liter was offered at
rock-bottom prices.

Despite the disappearance of the wine surplus, farmers and winegrowers lost heart as it became clear that the conflict was going to drag on.
Agriculture slowed further and food supplies fell, while a submarine war

off the coasts kept goods out of ports. Prices skyrocketed, and shortages became acute.

Heavy industry, on the other hand, did well, as makers of arms, gunpowder, and steel in the Angoumois went into high gear. On the coast, the Rochefort *arsenal* cranked out submarines and outfitted warships. Thousands of women, immigrants from French colonies, and prisoners of war worked these factories—and also neglected vineyards and fields.

Sagging spirits were bolstered in 1917 when the Americans landed at La Pallice, near La Rochelle, and began off-loading matériel. In all, 800,000 tons of war supplies and 175,000 horses and mules were put ashore between November 1917 and the end of 1919. Several hundred thousand U.S. troops heading to the war front also came through here. The locals celebrated the Americans at every turn, even organizing a baseball game between American soldiers at Niort. Every Fourth of July brought fetes.

When war lumbered to an end, there was only exhaustion and loss. Tens of thousands of Charentais had fallen, with death striking hard among farmworkers, of whom one in four died. All told, a million and a half French soldiers and civilians, out of a population of 40 million, were killed.

While Cognac the drink had had a fairly profitable ride through the war, new trouble struck when Prohibition shut down the American market at the start of 1920. The anti-alcohol movement had been building for years. State after state had outlawed drink; now even the U.S. Constitution made it illegal. Just like that, Cognac lost an entire market: something like 2.5 million bottles a year. While that was not a huge proportion of Cognac's total output, it nevertheless amounted to a big bite.

Naturally, many people worked out ways around the barrier. Traders stockpiled Cognac in Bermuda and at Saint-Pierre and Miquelon, off Newfoundland, from which it was shipped in boats plying the East Coast. These vessels stationed themselves just outside the three-mile limit of U.S. territorial jurisdiction, and smaller boats came to them at night to load up with Cognac and other spirits. The booze was hidden in burlap sacks, two cases to a bag, these being easy to handle quickly. An enterprising smuggler could haul in profits of 700 percent. So much money was made that there was a trafficking frenzy in these waters, dubbed Rum Row.

Hennessy, for its part, got some of its Cognac directly into the American market by vaunting its medicinal uses; only small amounts made it in, though, being in principle for use only in hospitals and for the ill. Later in the 1920s, Hennessy shipped more and more Cognac to Canada, where that country's own Prohibition movement was tapering off, and a lot of these shipments surely ended up in the United States via contraband routes.

Markets for Cognac closer to home foundered, meantime. In Germany, reeling from the costs of the war, import tariffs rose higher and higher, so that by the late 1920s, imports of Cognac fell through the floor. Sales certainly weren't helped by domestic advertising that urged consumers to eschew French Cognac for the German equivalent. This alarmed the powers that be in Cognac, who protested that Germany, under the 1919 Treaty of Versailles, was obliged to respect the French *appellation* system and stop marketing products like Kognak, which of course wasn't brewed in Cognac country at all. French alcohol exports to Germany rode a roller coaster, from 50,000 hectoliters in 1920 to less than half that in 1923, before soaring to 80,000 hectoliters in 1924 only to plunge to practically nothing by 1930.

High import tariffs and a protectionist mood walloped Cognac in war-drained Britain, too. Imports of French eau-de-vie, including Cognac, fell sharply in the early 1920s, stabilized for a while, then slipped again in 1929. Another interesting statistic tells much about British consumption: in 1900, a Briton drank on average half a liter of imported alcohol a year; in 1924, he drank only one-tenth that. Consumption went the way of industrial production as Britain struggled through dark, deflationary years.

France, meantime, strove to rebuild war-ruined towns and factories in the north, but staggered under the weight of debts and mounting budget deficits as the value of the franc plummeted. Cognac makers cried foul when the national legislature, desperately trying to make up budget shortfalls, imposed stiff luxury taxes on spirits like eau-de-vie.

Even when French industry finally began to enjoy a postwar rebound, Cognac, being a narrow-market specialty, wasn't so lucky. For one thing, there was an acute shortage of bottles, as local output could not come close to meeting needs and the glass factories in the north had been destroyed.

And so it went as times got tougher in Cognac country. Many traders went bankrupt and there was a lot of bloodletting in the industry. One person who didn't intend to let that happen to his own trading house was Jean Monnet, who in the 1950s would help put in motion a whole new idea of Europe. Monnet was working in the early 1920s at the League of Nations when he decided to return to Cognac to reorganize his family's eau-de-vie business. One of the first things he realized was that Cognac— if it was to survive—needed a makeover. Now was the time, he fervently argued, for Cognac to cease being a luxury object and become a product affordable to all. His ideas marked the stirrings of mass-market thinking.

A devaluation of the French franc in 1926 did much to help Cognac's export markets, namely in Argentina, Venezuela, Colombia, and Mexico. It also gave Cognac a new push in the French colonies, especially Indochina. But then came the severe financial crisis of the late 1920s and 1930s. In Germany a banking crisis and soaring unemployment inspired a swing to the far right and the Nazis took power. In Britain dogged protectionism and soaring joblessness were the rule, while in the United States it was very much the same; both countries hoped that higher trade barriers would boost domestic consumption and raise much-needed revenue from tariffs. This only made the situation worse, however, as rising tariffs fed higher unemployment. All the major industrialized countries were affected, and every government went on the defensive.

It was no different in France, though the effects of the crash that began in America were rather slow to hit. While France had sparked some prosperity with its 1926 devaluation, devaluations of the British pound in 1931 and of the dollar in 1933 pushed the franc back up and braked exports again. As exports slowed, so did everything else, and food prices collapsed. Farmers were forced to destroy crops when they couldn't make a profit; many vineyards were torn out by government order because they produced far more wine than society could consume.

Cognac's troubles in the early 1930s mirrored those of its export markets. Production fell from 117,000 hectoliters of pure alcohol in 1930 to 68,000 in 1934; shipments fell in tandem.

It is perhaps surprising to learn that the 1933 repeal of Prohibition in the United States failed to light a giant fire under Cognac. Sales in newly imbibing America rose, but not wildly, and the explanation lies in the depths of the economic mess in which the United States found itself in the mid-1930s. Times were so hard overall that the lifting of the ban on alcohol didn't make a big difference in the spirits business: people had far less money to spend on such consumables. New Deal economics, on the other hand, did go a long way toward pulling the country out of its misery, as did a gearing up of industry as the prospect of war with Germany loomed large.

And yet Cognac managed a brisk domestic trade in the mid-1930s amid a "Buy French" campaign. This effort, which helped absorb some bumper crops of grapes, nevertheless provoked some frowns from the Cognac Chamber of Commerce, which pressed the government to fret less about domestic consumption and get to work on freeing up international trade. They would not get their way, as France's politicians and workers were focused on the home front, where the rallying cry of the Socialists and Communists for social change was rising ever louder. Joining together in a Popular Front, the left came to power in the spring of 1936 under the leadership of Léon Blum. In Charente-Inférieure, two-thirds of voters backed the Front in the first round of voting as the slogan of "Bread, Peace and Freedom" inspired many. Not only was the Front about leftism, it was about antifascism—and above all about economic recovery.

It turns out that 1936 wasn't a good year for wine, the crop amounting to just 43 million hectoliters. But with the rise in salaries (an average of 10 percent) produced by the Popular Front, workers had more money in their pockets—and wine consumption revived and wine surpluses declined. Another thing that the Socialists hoped would help the economy that autumn of 1936 was a new devaluation of the franc. But this move, intended to halt inflation, only propelled prices all the higher. Meantime, wine from North Africa and elsewhere kept pouring into France. Domestic sales of wine were moderate at best, export markets were still dead despite the devaluation, and once again millions of hectoliters of wine went unsold.

Amid these difficulties legislators finished work on defining Cognac's region of origin, or *appellation*, which they had begun in 1909. Now, by a decree issued in 1936, Cognac became a formal *Appellation d'Origine Contrôlée*. Two years later, a definitive map of Cognac became final as the authorities made official the regional *appellations*, namely Grande Champagne, Petite Champagne, Borderies, Fins Bois, and Bons Bois. This meant that a Cognac maker with a product exclusively from one of these regions could now legally put its *appellation* on his bottles, as in *Appellation Grande Champagne Contrôlée, Appellation Borderies Contrôlée*, and so on. Bois Ordinaires was the exception: this outlying zone, mostly close by the sea and which makes an inferior Cognac, was not blessed with a regional *appellation*, and even today you will not find a bottle marked *Appellation Bois Ordinaires Contrôlée*, even though this area is the sixth and last of the growths into which the Cognac region is subdivided. The 1938 decree also created a new *appellation*, though unlike the others this one wasn't based on *terroir*. Fine Champagne is a blend of Grande and Petite Champagne in which Grande Champagne constitutes at least half.

Protecting Cognac from fakes and wannabes was one thing, but when you draw lines in the dirt you can make enemies of neighbors. The outlines of the growths were of fundamental importance to everyone. Fortunes were made or lost according to the map, whose lines separated vineyards, villages, families. Feuds broke out the name of Cognac: to be in one growth area and not in another could make or unmake a winegrower. If you had a vineyard in the Borderies, for example, the future was bright; if your property lay in the Fins Bois, just steps away in the next, lesser growth, tomorrow was another story altogether. Though there was no outbreak of murder, many a bottom line and family history changed dramatically as these decrees were published.

Politicians played a founding role in defining the regional *appellations*: All of them thought first of protecting their own turf, be it a single farm, a town, or even a county. Such pressures had a direct effect on the outcome of the new look of Cognac's world.

To Gilles Bernard, with his eye for geology and the makeup of the basement of the region, the map is very debatable. "The lines showing the regional *appellations* of the region don't really correspond to the *terroir* of the region, with the exception, perhaps, of Grande Champagne," he asserts. To him, the very shape of the entire *appellation*—a bull's-eye of concentric circles with Cognac at its center—belies the artificiality of the concept. Within each zone there are pockets that ought to belong to another zone and so on, so that the notion of neatly expanding circles is really arbitrary—and in need of revision. He takes as an example the high-quality Cognacs produced in southern Cognac country along the Gironde all during the 1800s up to the phylloxera crisis; that wasn't Grande Champagne country and yet the Cognacs made there were long recognized as just as top-notch.

Another item putting pressure on Cognac was the soaring consumption of whiskey, an ever more popular product among the masses. The brandy of the Charente managed to resist that pressure, however, mainly on the strength of exports as the 1930s came to a close. Cognac shipments headed out pell-mell as state monopolies bought it up, especially in Sweden, and as traders moved precious stocks abroad because it was clear to all that war in Europe was coming—and soon.

This was the uncertain mood in which French viticulture found itself on the eve of the German invasion. Mayhem became a reality with the exodus of millions of people from the north to the south in May and June 1940. The population of La Rochelle swelled from 50,000 to 80,000 as refugees poured in; people camped out in the streets and on the squares. It was much the same all across the Charente as Frenchmen rushed into the region by the hundreds of thousands. There were many arriving Belgians, too, whose country had been overrun; now the government of Belgium briefly set up shop in Poitiers. The French government fled through Cognac country as well, after halting at Tours, then going on to Bordeaux and finally to Vichy.

By late June the Germans had overwhelmed the resisters and forced the French to sign an armistice. The occupied zone covered three-quarters of Cognac country, the dividing line running north-south to the east of Angoulême and putting a hefty slice of eastern Charente in the "free" zone where the Resistance set up bases from which to attack the enemy.

Right away the German-controlled Cognac market found itself cut off from its customers abroad and many a trader trembled as the occupiers began to pillage stocks. Would all the Cognac be hauled off?

Now comes the grand irony of the saga of World War II in Cognac country. But to tell it, you must go back in time to 1862 and the foundation of the Meukow trading house in Cognac by two Russian brothers. This company carved out a niche for itself by becoming a chief supplier to Czar Alexander II. Toward the end of the 1800s, Gustav Klaebisch took over the company from the Meukow brothers and enlarged its fortunes up to World War I. Because he was of German origin, Klaebisch was forced by the war to leave Cognac country, and his firm was seized by the state.

A quarter-century later, one of Klaebisch's sons, also named Gustav, was appointed to oversee the affairs of Cognac, namely it stocks. The younger Gustav Klaebisch had grown up in Cognac, gone to school there and in Angoulême, and after World War I had been a Cognac importer in Germany. The German foreign minister, Joachim von Ribbentrop, who himself had been a Champagne importer and a Cognac agent for Meukow, most probably had a big hand in getting Gustav Klaebisch named to watch over Cognac. That is partly because Gustav had a brother named Otto, a prosperous merchant in the sparkling wine business in Germany and also a major importer for Martell (since 1924), who happened to be Ribbentrop's brother-in-law. So while Gustav took power in Cognac, Otto was named to oversee Champagne. Suddenly the Cognac-born Klaebisch brothers found themselves in charge of two great stocks dear to the hearts of the French.

The brothers went about their new jobs with radically different zeal. Otto made himself a hated figure as he lorded it over Champagne's producers while carrying out his orders to requisition all the bubbly he could get his hands on, before sending it to Germany, after which it was sold for much more on the world market to help fund the war and for the pleasure of the armed forces. In so doing, Otto offended nearly everyone. Champagne's stocks were hit hard, and its producers were often ruined.

Gustav, by contrast, worked to protect Cognac for another day. Either he or someone higher in the chain of command—perhaps Ribbentrop— knew that by its nature Cognac would wither and die if all the stocks were hauled off. Let that happen and it would take at least a couple of decades to even begin to remake the body of reserves from which fine Cognac is blended. Preserving Cognac, then, was a major concern for the Germans, all the more because, before the Americans landed in Normandy, they were certain they would win the war and create a thriving export market, especially in the United States. For now, so Lieutenant Klaebisch's thinking went, the majority of the Cognac stocks needed to stay right where they were.

Bernard Hine, a sixth-generation scion of Hine Cognac in Jarnac, explains what the Germans had in mind from the start. "First, the Germans decided to put in some people who knew the trade," he says. "Their second thought was that the war was going to last just a couple of months, and we have here a mine of gold! So we've got to put people there to protect the stuff."

Key to the success of this plan was to control the military's thirst for grabbing it. "They didn't want the army and the commanders to come and just put their revolvers on the table and say, 'Monsieur Hine, or Monsieur Martell or Monsieur Hennessy, give me so much of your stock.'" One thing the German Army did take right away was aged stocks being blended before shipment to English customers, Hine says. They went through firms' records, and whenever they saw an English name next to an order they had those Cognacs pulled out of the warehouse. Hine, like other houses, had big stocks-in-waiting for English customers that were "taken away immediately."

But the pillaging stopped once Gustav Klaebisch got to work. Helping him to keep things within bounds, the heads of the major Cognac houses organized the trade. It was urgent to set limits on how much the German Army could requisition by creating a quota system to cap how much each military unit could demand. "Monsieur Klaebisch was very good at organizing all that," Hine notes, "because he spoke French, and because he was born here."

Klaebisch divided his time between sumptuous digs in the Hôtel George V in Paris and Cognac. When in Paris, he watched over shipments of Cognac to Germany that went through La-Plaine-Saint-Denis, a transport center north of the city; he kept in close touch with Martell, to the point of even advising the firm ahead of time of the risk of having some personnel sent to work camps in Germany. He also adjudicated matters whenever some other occupying authority, such as commanders in Bordeaux or Angoulême, demanded shipments of Cognac outside the requisitioning system.

Klaebisch was aided in his work by another German officer and wine importer, Gustav Schneider. "The two of them worked with the locals," Hine explains, to manage the quotas, regulate the size of each year's crop, and set taxes at various stages of production—all the basic aspects of the trade. Schneider was rather easygoing, says André Royer, head of the Royer Cognac house, whose father was mayor of Jarnac at the war's start. Workers who feared being sent off to labor camps in Germany approached the affable Schneider for help and often got themselves sent to work instead on the Atlantic Wall, an assignment that, while very hard, was much closer to home.

Quickly, leaders of the Cognac trade could rest easier. Instead of seeing their stocks drained away, they could expect to have enough Cognac left over each year to supply the domestic market and, in limited quantities, to export. The big Cognac houses reasoned that they could survive financially.

Compared with Champagne, Cognac had an easy ride of it. Champagne producers, under Otto Klaebisch, were barred from selling to French civilians and because of the war couldn't sell overseas; Champagne could only be sold to the Germans, who got millions of bottles on demand.

The close working relationship between Cognac makers and the German authorities led to the creation of a Bureau de Répartition—an official body to run the quota system—which in 1946 after the war became the Bureau National Interprofessionnel du Cognac. Today, the very powerful BNIC is financed by people employed in various sectors of the Cognac industry; its long-term mission is to defend and promote the business everywhere.

Maurice Hennessy is cited as recalling in the 1970s how the requisitioning by the Germans during the war amounted to a "tribute imposed by the occupying power." Clearly, it was a lot of Cognac: 27 million bottles for the entire war. Right from the first year of the occupation, 1941, the numbers staggered the leaders of the business when the Germans grabbed 8.5 million bottles, mostly younger Cognacs of lesser value. Thanks to the efforts of the big Cognac houses—and, it must be said, also Klaebisch and Schneider—the German take was never that big again.

This isn't to say, however, that the number of bottles going to the Germans plunged. On the contrary, in 1942 their take fell only slightly, to 6.5 million. To make matters worse, overall shipments of Cognac plummeted. As a result, the percentage of bottles for the Germans climbed to one-third of all output. That hit hard, especially as production was declining, too. The ranks of farmers and winegrowers were thinning out as more and more of them were held prisoner in camps in Germany or forced to work on farms or in factories there. And many of the materials of production, especially copper for making stills, just weren't to be had.

So while Klaebisch and the Cognac chiefs were able to save the house, a lot of furniture was still going out the door. And it only got worse, with the Germans getting 7.8 million bottles in 1943. This fell back to 3.8 million bottles in 1944, the last year of the war as concerns the Charente valley.

While many of the bigger houses worked closely with the Germans to "save" the industry—and they succeeded very well at it—others waged a resistance campaign. Some slowed down the filling of German orders by pretending to have run short of corks, labels, and such.

When smaller winegrowers and distillers weren't fighting back in this way, they made sure their stocks stayed safe. They also made certain that they got official notices from the Bureau de Répartition to post on their warehouses, signs in German and French warning everyone to keep out.

Jacques Fauré, former BNIC director, explains how the availability of these notices sparked a rush by winegrowers to tell the Bureau just what they possessed, the better to keep it from being hauled off. "All the winegrowers, even if they only had three barrels of Cognac in the cellar," he says, "came forward to get these notices so their stock would be protected. The big houses, meantime, already had such signs on their warehouses. The big surprise of all this, though, was that the big houses, who thought they held 90 percent of all the Cognac, discovered that they really had barely 60 percent, that out in the countryside there were huge holdings of Cognac."

At the opposite end of reaction to the occupation stands the infamous case of the Foucauld house, run by Marc Foucauld, which has the dubious honor of being the only firm to have sought a patent for a Cognac label bearing a swastika that was called "Svastika Brand." The Foucauld house and its stocks were acquired in the late 1970s by Michel Coste, as he formed the Compagnie de Guyenne in Cognac; another brand that Coste, himself formerly of the Otard house, brought into his group of houses was none other than Meukow, today a highly successful brand in many markets.

Between the two extremes were many houses that sold Cognac to the Germans above and beyond the quota system, given that some companies' stocks were climbing as cellars continued to be topped up with each new year's production.

"Certain houses, then," Royer recalls, "wanted to do a bit more business, and so they worked with the Germans" outside the requisitioning system. What made this very profitable was that these were often superior categories of Cognac: VSOP, XO, and older. Royer notes that his family's house didn't engage in this traffic. Most of this trading was managed by Schneider, he adds, who had deep ties to the Cognac business well before the war.

Hine also describes a significant "gray market" trade in which a few houses sought profit at the expense of fellow firms. "Some people made a pile of money during the war, by selling to anybody at very high prices," he says. Hine, though, did not, he adds. "The more reputable houses didn't do that, but smaller firms did, and they disappeared within the next few years."

Cognac houses came forward quickly to declare their stocks to the German authorities, the better to keep them from being pillaged.

To sum up the war years, Hine calls them "good and bad, all mixed together." He was too young to recall it all in detail, however, and his father, Robert, disdained talking about it. Still, Hine relates how his father and an uncle, François, joined the Resistance and worked to "pave the way south for American, Canadian, or English crew members whose planes had been shot down, to get them on the road to Spain." His uncle's secretive work, Hine says, aroused the suspicions of his wife, who was sure all during the war that her husband was having a love affair. François would go out at night and not come back until the next morning looking like he hadn't slept. The truth wasn't revealed until after the war out of fear that had he told his wife, she might have been tortured if arrested to unmask the Resistance.

As elsewhere in France, all of which was German-occupied by late 1942, the Resistance had its share of difficulties. It started out slowly, with anti-Nazi graffiti, attacks on telephone lines, and aid to escaped prisoners and Jews.

Royer recounts a particular episode regarding the Jews of Jarnac and environs who were saved from certain death in Germany by a secretary at the city hall. Royer's father, also named André, was mayor from 1937 to 1941, when he was tossed out after refusing to cooperate with the occupying authorities. He was replaced by a more pro-German individual who stayed in office until the departure of the Germans in 1944. Meantime, the secretary at city hall who had worked for André Royer the elder and now under a new boss continued to do the incredible thing she had been doing all along: hiding all the letters she received from various people denouncing Jews in the area. She ended up giving these terribly dangerous letters to André Royer, the son, who hid them in the organ at the local Protestant church. It was only in the early 1950s that Royer's wife went and fetched the packet of letters from the organ and, together with her husband, decided to destroy them, the better to spare descendants of these letter writers the awful news that their ancestors had tried to turn people over to the Germans during the war. (André Royer senior was returned to the mayor's office at war's end.)

In 1943 anti-Nazi forces began to work together, so that by the time the Allies landed in Normandy in June 1944, the Resistance took even more action, like blowing up German supply depots, closing off roads, derailing trains, and sabotaging locomotives. The objective was to keep German troops from going north to aid their fellow soldiers fighting the Allies.

The invasion force, for its part, was rapidly making its presence felt in the southwest, as Allied bombers struck military targets, especially switching yards and rail stations. Bombers hit Niort and Châtellerault in June, and also obliterated western Poitiers on June 13, killing 177 people, then attacked the rail station at Angoulême two days later, leaving 140 dead.

All at once, the war was very real for everyone in Cognac country. Bombs were exploding, and people were dying. The Germans replied to pressure from the Allies by striking the locals, and even massacred 642 villagers in Oradour-sur-Glane, at the edge of northeastern Charente.

But the German forces were either on the run or hunkering down for a final stand, as 20,000 did in the La Rochelle pocket, which included La Pallice, its submarine base, and also Ile de Ré; and as 9,000 did in the Royan pocket, farther south, including the Arvert Peninsula, which guards the entrance to the Gironde. During the fall and winter of 1944–1945, Resistance forces besieged these redoubts, and then Allied bombing intensified, including a strike by the Royal Air Force on Royan in January 1945 that killed hundreds and nearly destroyed the city. It was only three months later, in April, that 25,000 French troops were able to clear the Royan pocket. By the end of the month, Ile d'Oléron fell to the French. Not until the German surrender of May 8 were La Rochelle, La Pallice, and Ile de Ré finally freed. (Jarnac and Cognac had been liberated at the close of the previous summer, along with many other towns in the Charente valley.)

Few in Cognac country who still remember this period are comfortable with the subject, but it is plain to see that Klaebisch and his aides kept the Cognac industry from falling into the abyss. Here is where Cognac's often hermetic world becomes even more closed in. Many houses simply don't mention the war years in their publicity materials or on their Web sites. Others pass over World War II so quickly in their summary "histories" that you can barely tell there was a conflict at all. And many of the few remaining people in a position to know what happened frown at the whole notion of dragging that dark period up again—dark because so many people in the Cognac business worked with the enemy to ensure their future.

It's common knowledge that several of the biggest companies saw their profits climb during the war. It is also known that Cognac stocks not only did not decline during the war but rose. Once the houses had filled their quotas for the Germans, they sold only part of the rest to French customers and to a few others abroad—and then kept the rest locked up. They emerged from the occupation well positioned.

Gérard Jouannet, head of a historical society in the region, says some Cognac houses dress up their wartime doings as having been for the good of France. But what really occurred, he notes, is that many people put "business before patriotism" in their dealings with the Cognac-loving Nazis.

Disappearing into the prison in Cognac during a brief wave of reprisals at war's end were a number of Cognac traders seen by some as having been too friendly with the enemy. Among the most prominent were the mayor of Cognac and head of Martell, Paul Firino-Martell, and André Renaud of Rémy Martin. All told, sixty or so political detainees were held in the Cognac jail for a few days. With them was a literary light of Charente, Jacques Chardonne, assailed for having written and spoken too glowingly of the Germans. Chardonne had made the "mistake" of favoring a strong Franco-German alliance, which he perceived as being the only viable foundation for the affairs of Europe. With the prominent exception of Paul Firino-Martell, later condemned for complicity with the enemy but then soon pardoned by popular demand, these people were generally exonerated of wrongdoing.

Cognac emerged from the depths of World War II ready to seize its promising future. One trader who did well was Otto Klaebisch. Once he was cleared of any economic crimes in Champagne, he took up importing Martell when he got back home to Germany. He did so until 1973, when there was a parting of the ways because Martell didn't think the Klaebisch importing company was big enough to handle its affairs in Germany. In the meantime, however, Otto had done well for himself.

Schneider disappeared from the region in 1944, Royer recalls, and ended up turning himself in to the Americans. He was then trundled off to the United States, where he was imprisoned. Later, he returned to Germany, where he set up a business and became an importer and distributor in Germany for Rémy Martin.

Gustav, the conqueror who saved the day, appears to have worked with or advised his brother who was importing and distributing Martell. Cognac's wartime overlord died in 1962 from heart disease. Incredibly, certain people in Cognac wanted a square named after him. Even if Lieutenant Klaebisch hadn't been the devil, it's not surprising that no such square exists.

GLORY YEARS, WITH FEATHERS

THE COGNAC INDUSTRY WAS ONE OF THE lucky few to escape the ruinous destruction of the war, and chance once more held the key: had people like Klaebisch not been in place, had local Cognac makers not worked with him and his aides to protect the trade, had Cognac by its nature not been a product that had to stay stocked right where it was if there was to be an industry at all in the future, the system would certainly have collapsed. Instead, the first three postwar decades—a time of rising production and opening trade—came to be called *Les Trente Glorieuses.*

Cognac shipments in the Glorious Thirty shot up from 30 million bottles a year at the close of the war to 120 million in the early 1970s. At the same time, the Cognac country vineyard expanded from 62,000 hectares in 1945 to 110,000 in 1975.

Does that rise remind you of the Golden Age? It ought to, since in the commercial year ending in 1971 (August 31, though today Cognac country's statistics run from August 1 to July 31) Cognac

The first three postwar decades saw another huge explosion in the number
of hectares of vines for the white wine that goes into Cognac.

shipments surpassed the levels of the 1870s before phylloxera annihilated
the vineyard. What's more, with higher yields, the crop of 1970 was produced on far fewer hectares, about a third of the area growing grapes a
hundred years earlier.

Such numbers echo the industrial boom set off in Europe by vast infu-
sions of American reconstruction money under the Marshall Plan. They
also reflect the monetary devaluations in France and in other European
nations, which by spurring exports ratcheted up the Continent's economy.
Cognac profited as consumers' pocketbooks became fatter and people at all
levels of society downed ever more of the magical drink of Charente.

To drink Cognac became a mark of social standing. In many countries
to which the French brandy is exported, people were switching from
rum and whiskey to Cognac, even though it was a relatively expensive
product. "It's somewhat like when the French people went from drinking
low-quality wines to preferring good wines" in the happy postwar years,
recalls Jacques Fauré. Many people now had money to spend—and they
sought out the finesse of Cognac, a step up universally signifying "social
promotion."

As Cognac's star rose higher, its glory shone, especially over Europe.
The big houses—especially Hennessy and Martell—powered ahead, their
main markets being Britain and Germany. Now, for the first time, shipments headed to market in airplanes. Big-budget advertising became vital,

with the BNIC organizing publicity campaigns—especially in the United States, which had lagged since Prohibition—to inject much energy into the markets.

These years are often called Cognac's second heyday, and for the moment Europe was the center of its world. It was only natural, then, that Jean Monnet would reappear on the scene. As cofounder of the new Europe (along with Robert Schuman), he also had an intense interest in the number one business of his native region. Charles de Gaulle described Monnet, inspirer of the 1957 Treaty of Rome that created the European Economic Community of six nations, thus: "The inspirer of the European project is not a politician, a president or a minister, but the son of a Cognac merchant."

Amid the detailed negotiations following Europe's founding treaty, Cognac came to be classified not as an agricultural product but as an industrial one. This distinction, fervently sought by Cognac makers and traders, made all the difference. Now Cognac could take advantage of rules put into place to favor European industry, especially the lowering of tariffs within the Community and the suppression of production quotas. It would not, then, be subject to the rigors of the agricultural production rules being put into place, especially unloved output ceilings.

Again, numbers tell another success story, as Cognac exports to the other members of the group—Belgium, Germany, Italy, Luxembourg, and the Netherlands—exploded. About 40 million bottles were shipped out of Cognac country to the European Community (including France) by the end of the summer of 1972; that compares with fewer than 17 million in 1957. In just fifteen years, the market in just six countries (led by France and Germany) more than doubled to about a third of Cognac's total shipments.

The sky was the limit in Europe, it seemed. Jacques Chirac, as agriculture minister, even gave the green light for more planting for more wine to make more Cognac. Thousands of hectares were quickly added to the vineyard. All the economic signs were rosy, so why not?

But whatever goes up eventually comes down. This time, after the expansive 1960s when the industrialized nations whipped the world economy into a frenzy, it was a Middle East war in October 1973 that sank the show. The Arab-Israeli conflict inspired oil producers of the region to jack up their prices from $2 to as much as $5-plus a barrel. Then they decided to cut exports by 5 percent a month until the Israelis pulled out of Arab territory. Most dramatically, they imposed an oil embargo on the United States and several other nations. Finally, toward the end of 1973, the Organization of Petroleum Exporting Countries pulled out the stops and raised their prices to about $11 a barrel.

The economic world was shaken to its foundations that winter. Inflation punished the French economy, doubling in just two or three years to nearly 12 percent, and shipments of Cognac fell by 22 percent in just two years. If that wasn't bad enough, 1973–1974 was a record year for the production of Cognac after a bumper crop: 740,000 hectoliters of pure alcohol, nearly double the output of the year before, or about 265 million bottles.

Only 77 million bottles of the 1973 harvest got shipped abroad, owing to the conjunction of negative economic factors. And yet the surplus, as is always true, had to go somewhere. Cognac country found that it barely knew what to do with it all. From September 1973 to August 1974, stocks rose by 147 million bottles to 732 million bottles. That's the equivalent of 512 million liters—counting 70 centiliters a bottle, the industry standard—enough to fill about 160 Olympic swimming pools. (Thirty years later, in 2003, stocks are twice as voluminous, at a staggering 1.1 billion bottles.)

The BNIC figures that nearly seven years' worth of stocks lie sleeping in the *chais*, as of the summer of 2003. That's an average number; in reality there are only a couple of years' worth of young Cognacs in reserve but more than two decades of old Cognacs whiling away. In any case, it seems to be a tremendous volume of Cognac just sitting around doing nothing, and yet that's how it should be, more or less: you have to age Cognac to make Cognac and you have to have different ages to blend it into something wonderful. But there are rising voices—especially among traders and bankers who back the industry—who say surpluses have gotten out of hand.

A lot of things in regard to Cognac began to change in the 1970s. Besides the initial oil shock battering the industry, a battle with the United States was braking Cognac's dreams of making America its top market. This feud had come to be called *La Guerre du Poulet*, the Chicken War. As you might expect, it was fought over *La Taxe du Poulet*, a Chicken Tax.

Feathers began to fly in 1962, when the European Community raised its levy on imports of U.S. poultry by 180 percent per pound to spur its own poultry industry to self-sufficiency and to combat cheap American chickens; in response the United States declared that under the General

Agreement on Tariffs and Trade (GATT), it had the right to seek compensation for losses in the European market. The trade body agreed, saying the Americans had lost $26 million. The Americans chose to punish several products. One was brandies priced above $9 per gallon; they were hit with a 25 percent tariff increase.

Being the most expensive brandy around, Cognac was clearly the main target. Jean Vincent Coussié, who has written much about the Cognac business especially after World War II, says that historically the Americans have always been very "precise" in targeting certain industries whenever trade differences with Europe have arisen. "Of course they didn't say directly that it was Cognac they were after this time," he says. "Instead they targeted all brandies above a certain price. In the end, however, it was Cognac, and Armagnac, that suffered the bulk of the damage." Such tactics have usually worked, Coussié observes, since "targeting luxury products—the same thing happened with Roquefort cheese—causes a lot of pain, and that is the goal. And by creating so much pain, the pressure rises on the producer of that product to demand that his government back down."

Demands did rise and even more feathers flew, but nothing was done to stop the fiscal foxes in the yard, and more than a decade went by in this way until in 1974 the United States, in a peace gesture, raised the floor for the tax to $17. While still punishing costly Cognacs, this move helped to spur exports of cheaper ones to America. Two years later, however, despite conciliatory moves by the European Community to lower taxes on U.S. poultry, the Americans declared they would boost duties on bottled brandies priced at $13 to $17 per gallon and on bulk brandies priced at $9 to $17.

Europe cried foul, but Cognac traders didn't sit around waiting for the barnyard to calm: they sent as much as they could over the ocean ahead of the late December date for the new tax. Cognac exports to America in 1976—15 million bottles, double the year before—surpassed those of any other foreign market for the first time. (France, by the way, was Cognac's number one market overall, at 17 million bottles; this has declined steadily, however, to 6.5 million bottles in 2003, as consumers either drank less generally or drank more whiskey and vodka.) Britain moved into second place in 1976 among nations importing Cognac, with 14 million bottles, then came back into first place for the next three years, before losing its number one ranking for good in 1980 when the United States took in 25 million bottles and Britain 17.5 million. That was also the year the Americans decided they'd recovered enough money to cover their losses in the Chicken War—and called a truce.

Unfortunately, like many such international trade conflicts, this one went to sleep only for a while. In the late 1980s, another American argument with Europe would erupt over Spain, Portugal, corn, and Cognac.

In the meantime, Europe as a Community grew bigger, with the accession of Britain, Denmark, and Ireland in 1973 bringing the grouping to nine. Cognac exports to the Community (again, including France) survived the hardships of the first oil shock to climb more than 30 percent from 1974 to 1979. This was a good market that Cognac could count on. Taken together, sales to the nine countries had more than tripled since the 1950s.

Makers of Cognac are forward-looking. In their eyes, overproduction had become a time bomb ticking away under the industry as crops got bigger and unsold stocks rose. Notions that the Asian market was going to open up and absorb much of this Cognac lake proved overly optimistic.

By the mid-1970s, the BNIC took a look at the combination of 110,000 hectares of vines and nearly 1 billion surplus bottles of Cognac—and went into action. Backed by the French government, it began requiring winegrowers to observe caps on the production of pure alcohol for Cognac. The first of these distillation caps, in 1975, was set at four hectoliters of pure alcohol per hectare; in 2003 it stood at seven hectoliters of pure alcohol per hectare. (A hectare typically can produce ten hectoliters of pure alcohol, about three over the current limit; the winegrower will take his excess juice and sell it to firms making fruit juice or industrial alcohols.)

From the beginning, these distillation ceilings were obligatory, both under the auspices of the French government and, since 1982, under rules laid down by the European Community. The fixing of the ceiling, however, is a subject of intense discussion each year, with much input coming from the Cognac industry itself to guide the authorities in their decision.

To address the problem of an outsized vineyard in Cognac country, the European Community initiated programs starting in 1976 to tear out vines, earning the winegrower a premium per hectare and taking away his right to replant the plot. (The first premium amounted to only €2,000 per hectare, though this number has climbed over the years as the French state and the Cognac industry itself increased the offer from time to time to make it more appealing; some twenty-five years later, the premium is about €15,000.) This directive was expanded in 1979 to apply to other wine-producing regions of Europe where overproduction had created a fantastic glut. These downsizing efforts continue today, though the number of hectares of vines in the Cognac *appellation* declined by about one third between 1976 and 2003.

Such moves helped pull Cognac back from the brink. Exports to foreign markets in 1977–1978 surpassed the level of 1972–1973. But then an Islamic republic was born in Iran. This alone might not have been enough to change the economic course of the world had its radical nature not made other oil-producing countries nervous. These countries began raising prices and lowering output again so that the average price of oil in 1979 was more than $29 a barrel; in 1980 it climbed to $36 a barrel. The world's leading economies watched with fear, but this time they were fairly sure they could ride it out. Cognac exports sank nearly 7 percent from 1980 to 1983, edged back up in the following years, and fully emerged from the second oil shock in 1987. Petroleum prices came back down to earth, to about $14 to $18 a barrel, and the world economy exhaled and went back to work with high hopes.

All these events are interconnected in much the same way that the companies of the industrialized countries have come to be, their combined financial muscle building powerful multinational structures. Few industries of any weight have escaped this integrating revolution that has birthed the titans of today's corporate world. Cognac didn't leap into the mix as quickly as many would have suspected, owing largely to the cohesive, family-based nature of the business that for centuries held foreign capital (not foreign markets) at arm's length. But when the newly forming multinationals poked their noses over the vine-draped fence to look into Cognac's luxurious yard, they liked what they saw and, one way or another, invited themselves in.

Whereas Hennessy and Martell had been the Big Two, especially in the years since the war, they were joined in the 1970s by Rémy Martin and Courvoisier to round out what has become known as the Big Four, a status they all still enjoy. Courvoisier arrived in this hallowed group, though heavily in debt, after its purchase by Hiram Walker, the Canadian spirits giant, in 1964. Suddenly, foreign capital began pouring into the Cognac garden; Courvoisier, for one, did very well in the late 1960s in the United States and even dominated that market for a while.

The domino effect on ownership went into motion, so that by 1987 Hiram Walker was bought out by Allied Lyons of Britain, which in 1994 acquired a top spirits company in Mexico and Spain, Pedro Domecq, and became Allied Domecq. Courvoisier, the number three or number four Cognac company, now resides within the world's third-largest spirits empire, a company that also markets such brands as Ballantine's scotch and Beefeater gin.

Courvoisier's purchase began a slow but sure remixing of the Cognac vat. Another of the top ten Cognac companies, Bisquit, was bought out by the Ricard drinks company of France in 1966, and today belongs to Pernod Ricard, the world's number two spirits company. Hennessy joined with Moët & Chandon Champagne in 1971 to form Moët-Hennessy, a major wine and spirits group. Then, in 1988, Martell was snapped up by Seagram's of Canada, a relationship that lasted thirteen years before Pernod Ricard absorbed it at the end of 2001. (Seagram's drinks businesses were split up between Pernod Ricard and Diageo of Britain, the world's leading spirits company.) At the end of 1988, Suntory of Japan, now the number seven spirits company, took over the Royer Cognac house. And in 1991, Otard, of François I fame, which had already been bought out by Bass of Britain in 1987, changed hands once more, going to Martini & Rossi, which in turn was absorbed in 1992 by Bacardi of Bermuda, the number four spirits conglomerate.

Rounding out the changes, Rémy Martin fused with the Cointreau company to create Rémy Cointreau in 1991, specializing in Cognac, Champagne, and liqueurs. Rémy Cointreau remains a family-type business, however, and today is controlled by an old Cognac family, Hériard-Dubreuil. In this regard, Rémy Cointreau is the leading exception to the multinationalizing wave that rolled through the industry and carried decision making to boardrooms far away from Cognac. Camus, the number five Cognac house, has also remained a family affair; though well behind the Big Four in sales, it vaunts its self-styled niche as biggest of the small houses.

Cognac, already a globally known product, was thus well on the way to becoming a largely internationally owned one as well. Many smaller houses were mopped up by these large corporations, swelling the already considerable commercial power of the Big Four. In 2003, Hennessy sold 3.8 million cases of Cognac, Rémy Martin 1.7 million, Courvoisier 1.2 million, and Martell 1.2 million. (A case typically contains twelve bottles of seventy centiliters each.)

Concentration, globalization, diversification: this troika of philosophies has guided a directory of firms to reach into scores of markets and sell Cognacs of all ages and qualities for hundreds of millions of dollars a year.

Predictably, Cognac found itself in the thick of trouble again the next time swords were raised in the transatlantic duel. But it was a globalizing Cognac industry now, with interests ranging from drinks and perfumes to giant distribution networks and vineyards in foreign lands. Into this ever more tough and feisty sector, then, burst the Martini War of 1986–1987.

This gin-and-olives, Cognac-and-cheese clash was born of the accession of Spain and Portugal to the European Community, both big importers of U.S. farm products like sorghum and corn. (Now the Community counted twelve members, Greece having joined in 1981.) Under Community rules, Portugal and Spain were obliged to lift restrictions on imports from fellow nations in the bloc; likewise, they were allowed to set limits on imports from outside the group. The United States said the restrictions trampled international trade rules and would affect $1 billion in sales of American farm products a year.

Europe shrugged, and the two sides went onto war footing, with the United States declaring that if compensation for its losses wasn't made by July 1, 1986, then it would impose duties on $1 billion worth of European products, including cheese, wine, and the world's beloved brandy. Multiple skirmishes kept things hopping until midsummer, when a truce was reached that allowed the Americans to resume grain exports to Spain and Portugal.

The cease-fire called for a final accord by year-end, but when that pact didn't come together, the United States declared that it would impose a 200 percent duty on a variety of goods, including all white wines made in Europe, French brandy and cheeses, British gin, Belgian endives, Mediterranean olives, and so on. They said Europe had until January 30 to settle up or face the music.

Once more, the lieutenants of the Cognac division went into full export drive, scared stiff that they were about to lose 80 percent of the U.S. market, their largest over the last seven years. That January, strikes hit the French railroad, so Cognac traders put their bottles on trucks and hauled them to the ports; every boat they could come up with was filled to the brim to get several million more bottles of Cognac to America before war broke out.

Just as they did back in 1791 when fighting for Cognac's name, the industry's leaders proclaimed again, Enough is enough. The Bureau National rushed into the fight in the United States, where it formed a crisis group, the Free Trade Defense Association. Under the slogan "Trade War Is Hell," the group flooded U.S. newspapers, radio stations, and TV networks with appeals: The consumer is the first casualty! Talk before it's too late! One communiqué read in part: "We call upon the governments of both sides to return to negotiations, to explore all possible options, to reconcile their differences, to craft a reasonable and balanced settlement that will preserve fair trade. Innocent bystanders, businesses and consumers alike, deserve no less." A parallel blitz in the French media demanded to know of European businesses and consumers, Are you going to let this happen to you?

It worked. Or, more to the point, negotiators for both sides figured out what to do at the last minute. On the day before the deadline, the adversaries agreed on a formula for the United States to export grain to Spain at low tariffs and to enjoy reduced European tariffs on twenty-six U.S. industrial products, like cigars, bourbon, and whiskey. Many Europeans complained that the Community gave away too much, and yet they recognized that the price of a full-blown conflict would have been far higher.

Some people also called it the Yuppie Trade War, since this generation drank Cognac, ate fine cheese, and nibbled olives. In any case, the *New York Times* was relieved when the dust settled, though its editorial warned: "To be truthful about it, this was more like one battle; war danger endures."

While all that was going on, another important shift in Cognac's fortunes occurred in the Far East. Japan was beginning to cede to international pressure and lower tariffs protecting its own alcohol producers. The effect of these duties had made Cognac, among other goods, very high-priced; through the late 1980s it was subject to a 220 percent import tax.

Japan's imports of Cognac had never been spectacular, amounting to only half a million bottles in 1967 and just 12 million bottles by 1986. But then the GATT condemned its protectionist practices and Japan lowered its taxes and opened up. By 1990, 28 million bottles of Cognac went in. In 1991, Japan became the number one market for Cognac, just ahead of America.

It was still a very protected market, however, and while imports of Cognac stayed high for several years—25 million bottles in 1992, 22 million in 1993, and so on—they sank rapidly through the rest of the decade as the Japanese economy lay moribund following the dramatic decline of its stock markets. Many Cognac producers whose eyes had lit up at the prospect of making a fortune in Japan look back sadly upon that brief candle.

Through the 1980s and early 1990s, Hong Kong grew to become a key market for Cognac as Asia enjoyed an economic boom.

Hong Kong was more or less the same story. Once again, many restrictive taxes were in place in the 1980s and 1990s that braked imports or slowed the reexport of goods like Cognac, a trading role that Hong Kong had played for years. Still, Cognac got a formidable toehold in this high-rolling British colony, its exports soaring from 7 million bottles in 1980 to 13.5 million in 1990. In 1993 the number reached 18 million, so that for that year Hong Kong became Cognac's number two export market, after Japan. The United States was in third place. Other Asian markets skyrocketed. Taiwan went from 1.1 million bottles of Cognac in 1983 to 4.1 million in 1994; Singapore from 3 million in 1983 to nearly 7 million in 1995. Malaysia and Thailand also took off.

Cognac makers and traders rejoiced, since the bulk of this brandy was top-end stuff selling sometimes for thousands of dollars a bottle. But not all of them were positioned to play the game the same way. Among the Big Four, Hennessy seized the lion's share, its exports to Japan rising from about 5 million bottles in 1988 to 12 million in 1990. Rémy Martin also did well, climbing from under 1 million bottles to 3.6 million, while Courvoisier went from less than half a million bottles to nearly 2 million. Martell was the counterpoint: it advanced only slightly in Japan, preferring to focus on sales in Britain and America. Production of Cognac, meantime, hit a new record of 806,000 hectoliters in 1989–1990, followed by 799,000 in 1990–1991. (In 2003, production was about half that, just 391,000 hectoliters.)

While most of the big players were cashing in on Asia, another fire was smoldering under Europe-U.S. trade, again over subsidies and grains. This six-year-long argument emerged from the fog of the Chicken and Martini Wars after Europe began subsidizing production of oilseeds like soybeans and rapeseed, despite having agreed not to do so. America whipped out its big trade guns again and trained them on Europe, claiming that it was losing a fortune in soybean sales on the Continent because of this system. Once again, the GATT found that Europe was doing it all wrong, and yet the Community didn't budge in the face of American demands for compensation or cuts in the subsidies for oilseeds, which are used widely in animal feed.

Finally, in the summer of 1992, the United States announced that it intended to impose duties on $1 billion worth of European products. It's easy to guess what was in this largely French-made basket of goodies: Cognac and Roquefort. All over again, Cognac traders rushed to get their goods into America before any such tariffs were set. In just three months, from May to July, nearly 15 million bottles headed across the pond; the total for the year would be 32 million bottles, one of the highest levels ever.

The Soybean War came to a head in November 1992, when America said it would indeed put punitive tariffs in place starting December 6—200 percent on white wines, rapeseed oil, and wheat gluten—after which Europe said it would retaliate tit-for-tat, and so on. As if they just couldn't do without pushing themselves to the brink of trade slaughter, both sides sat arguing nose to nose at Blair House, the presidential guest house in Washington, in the run-up to the U.S. deadline. Somehow the negotiators got a deal by November 20, Europe agreeing to limit the number of hectares for oilseed production, but not to cap oilseed output, and pledging to cut subsidized farm exports. American farmers were happy, European farmers less so—and Cognac makers watched the clouds of war drifting away.

That made one real trade war, and two very near misses, enough for any generation of farmers to suffer, whether they produced wine, Cognac, olives, rapeseed, cheese, or soybeans. Shell-shocked and weary, the lieutenants of Cognac wondered what might be next in the great trading game.

What was next was now. The economies of the Western world had slowed sharply, even as fears of a third oil shock over the Gulf War receded, with both Europe and America forced to navigate a difficult, recessionist trough in the early 1990s. Cognac exports came down off their heights starting in 1991 and, by the fourth year of the crisis, had fallen one-fifth in volume. Afterward, they improved slightly, only to languish again through the late 1990s and then end up in 2003 about 17 percent lower than 1990, the peak year in the long postwar battle for markets.

In exact opposition fashion, Asia continued to enjoy its brisk rise at the start of the 1990s (Japan, though, was just starting to slip). The power-houses of South Korea, Hong Kong, Singapore, and Taiwan—joined by the emerging economies of Indonesia, Malaysia, Philippines, Thailand, and Vietnam—were largely responsible for keeping the Cognac industry above water during this difficult stretch when the rest of the financial world was floundering. But, again, it didn't last—and the Asian balloon burst as it had in Japan. Slowing exports in 1996, followed by currency turmoil and stock market crises in 1997, battered the region, ending the Far East boom.

The downfall was another rude shock to Cognac country, which had rubbed its hands together in joy while so much of its finest eau-de-vie was finding its way to the tables of high rollers on the other side of the world. But when times turn tough—and they often do in this business—the conventional wisdom is to find a profitable safe haven for exports and stay there as long as possible. It's a tactic bred into the genes of the Cognaçais.

The United States has been that harbor for a number of years as exports continued to rise steadily through both bad economic times and good. America took in 30 million bottles at the height of the Asian currency crisis in 1997, and in 2002–2003 absorbed 49 million, just six years later. Those 49 million bottles represent 41 percent of the value of all Cognac shipped out of France.

The United States remains a long-term sure bet for Cognac; it is now ranked as the seventh most-popular spirit in the country. Californians are the leading imbibers, followed by New Yorkers, Illinoisians, and Floridians. It's advertised to be drunk straight or mixed, especially as an *apéritif.* The number of cocktail ideas has exploded well beyond the already daring Cognac on ice and Cognac and tonic to include crazy constructions like Cognac-Cointreau-Malibu and orange juice, Cognac-Champagne and raspberry liqueur, Cognac-lemon and cane syrup. In this way, Cognac has transformed its image from a by-the-fireplace after-dinner drink into a lighter before-dinner pleasure with ice cubes bobbing in it. Or, more daringly, into a powerful concoction mixed with vodka and tropical fruit juices that has taken the American bar and nightclub scene by storm.

The Big Four houses are making a lot of young Cognacs especially for the barhopping evening crowd, which leads to some complaints by purists and other defenders of the finer side of the drink about a lowering of its longtime lofty taste. On the other hand, Cognac is selling in these kinds of markets like never before. A quarter of that is superior-quality eau-de-vie, and the remainder is VS (Very Special). Intense publicity drives by the Cognac industry—"The Art of Cognac" and "Around the World with Cognac"—are wooing over more and more Americans to this still rather expensive but classy drink.

Bernard Hine says Cognac could easily enjoy an even greater place among Americans' habits if they'd simply slow down. Americans usually down a lot of hard-liquor cocktails before dinner, drink very little wine with their meals, and often skip a *digestif*. If they would just switch that formula around, he says, and cut back on alcohol before the meal, they could still enjoy a Cognac afterward, best served in small doses, the better to get a taste of growths and ages, the better to unlock subtleties. "Cognac is for people who love life and good living," Hine extols. "It's a way of life. But, take your time. Taste it with your five senses. Look at it, take the glass in your hand and feel it, then smell it, then taste it, and then you clink your glass with your partner's and say 'Cheers!' It creates a perfect atmosphere."

There's much boosterism in that kind of talk, but the people who make and trade Cognac universally love their product and enjoy hailing its virtues. They believe firmly in its future, all the while giving ample vent to their worries. It's a delicate business, overall, constantly in need of fine-tuning.

Sébastien Dathané of the Centre International des Eaux-de-Vie in Segonzac puts it vividly: "The Cognac vineyard is like a high-performance car. You can hold it back a few years, easy on the pedal. But there's always a chance that one year you'll hit the pedal too hard and take off. With that kind of potential for sudden change, there's a huge risk of spinning out of control and production taking off like we saw back in 1990–1991."

Which is exactly what some people fear could happen with the U.S. market climbing so vigorously. Whereas the vineyard specifically producing wine for Cognac totals about 74,000 hectares, its ideal size, according to many, should be only 60,000 hectares: At that level, they argue, everyone could win and few would lose as supply and demand got into better balance. The concern at present is that, with demand rising in North America, winegrowers will start planting pell-mell, spurring another production crisis when there are still well over a billion bottles of Cognac stocked away.

That could very well occur, given the breakneck speed with which this industry flies when it does. But the difference this time is that the growing American market also looks durable. The Cognac companies are betting on that, at least, and placing a lot of money on the table in this high-stakes game, fairly certain that, come what may, demand in the United States won't plunge all of a sudden and leave them high and dry with their big stocks.

If that sounds like all the eggs have been placed pretty much in one basket for now, it's not that far off the mark. Then again, Cognac traders haven't forgotten about Asia, and especially about China, since the market there is rapidly opening, and millions of people coming into money for the first time will reach for the finest of everything when they buy.

America and Asia: two pillars that this industry can safely lean on today and in coming years without much fear—bogeys of trade wars and market crashes notwithstanding—as the Cognac saga rolls on, with no end in sight.

TALE OF A
BIG HOUSE

CHEZ HENNESSY, IT'S ALL ABOUT SIZE. Astronomical analogies are very appropriate, for this house is a giant star. It's not even a real contest anymore, though the other three houses in this four-star system do challenge the leader now and then. But Hennessy knows its reach and fills whatever place it wishes with more Cognac than you can imagine. Sales in 2003 amounted to 45.6 million bottles. That's 32 million liters, or the equivalent of all the water flowing over Niagara Falls in just ten seconds.

These days, Cognac's favorite planet with which to flood its bounty is the United States, and Hennessy is the leading brand there. Half of all the Cognac that Americans buy each year is made by Hennessy. Hennessy is so far ahead that Rémy Martin, Martell, and Courvoisier are left scrambling.

The secret to this commercial boom is the VS market. This is a young, vibrant Cognac that Hennessy has styled as an affordable mixer. Young people, especially blacks, are topmost in Hennessy's mind. The leader of the Cognac industry has turned up the power so high on these consumers that it has not only won them over but cornered the market: 80 percent of the Cognac bought in America is VS, and Hennessy has 68 percent of that.

Hennessy may shine as the biggest star among the Cognac Four, but it also glows brightly within the mega-luxury-goods company LVMH. Bernard Arnault's universe, with €12 billion in sales in 2003, includes Louis Vuitton leather goods, Moët & Chandon Champagne, and of course Hennessy. The Moët Hennessy part of the name (LVMH's wine & spirits sector) is the world leader in Champagne (besides Moët, add Dom Pérignon, Mercier, Ruinart, Veuve Clicquot, and Krug; LVMH's premier wine is Chateau d'Yquem, and it has wine interests in Argentina, Australia, California, and New Zealand). A cluster of LVMH names, from haute couture, perfumes, and cosmetics to watches and jewelry, rounds out the picture: Givenchy, Christian Lacroix, Thomas Pink, Pucci, Donna Karan, Fendi, Christian Dior, Guerlain, Tag Heuer, Zenith, Chaumet, Fred Paris, and De Beers.

Each part of LVMH strives to outshine the other, and Hennessy is no exception. It harbors a dream team of Cognac ambassadors. Christophe Navarre, for one, sits at the top of Moët Hennessy—an empire within an empire—which enjoyed sales of €2.1 billion in 2003, over a third of that Hennessy Cognac. For Navarre, Hennessy is only just beginning to realize its "colossal" U.S. potential. "We're on the verge of selling two million cases there a year. Why not, then, three million? There's no reason we can't. We have the quality of product, we have the investments, and we have a strong brand. It's Hennessy. By the way, it's Cognac. But it's Hennessy."

Navarre quickly turns the conversation to another giant market— China. "We have growth potential there that is phenomenal, and we are investing heavily in promotional efforts and in personnel. We have more than two hundred people working the market. But you have to give yourself the time to make it happen. Meanwhile, we're doing everything we can to encourage winegrowers to distill, to take part in this movement." Winning a market, he adds, is based on a simple idea: "To be there before the others."

He and Gilles Hennessy, vice president of Moët-Hennessy, also voice their hopes for Central and Eastern Europe, where the buying power of the middle class is rising. Again the secret is getting there first. Navarre says: "Central Europe is a marvelous opportunity. And we are already there, have been for a while. We cross our fingers, but everything is in position, our image and our brand. And as consumers gain more buying power, they will discover our products. They'll start out with our VS or VSOP, and then go to our XO, and later on they'll try our Paradis or Richard whenever they're ready to match an exceptional moment with an exceptional eau-de-vie."

Navarre is bullish about his product and reveres its heritage. "My role is that of the professional manager. But the thing that pleases me most is to play a role, however minor, in the long history of Cognac, in all the work done by so many men and women through the years. All this savoir-faire and tradition, and the good taste of Bernard Arnault and LVMH, come together as something very dynamic, very contemporary. And then there is the fundamental esprit of the company. At Hennessy, we never sleep. In the morning at the office you have calls coming in from Japan, China, Taiwan. In the afternoon, it's the United States. Very international. People who work for us love Hennessy. They have it in their soul. While the weight of history is important, you have to be careful not to live in the past." Gilles Hennessy adds: "I have a slogan in my office that says, 'Those who don't forget the past will be masters of the future.' Our job is to constantly reinterpret history. We've almost done everything as regards Cognac, and yet we have to keep it modern and competitive. Our role is to stay in front of the game."

Both admit that competition today is a different proposition from what it used to be. Whereas in yesterday's markets you could build up a faithful clientele, nowadays consumers "go from drink to drink, trying each one out," Navarre says, meaning high-end vodkas and whiskeys. This has made the "business game much more complicated today," he adds. "There are many, many new brands, new arrivals, and even if a lot of them don't last that long, competition is much more intense. You have to know how to stay the course, meantime, while the others come and go."

For Gilles Hennessy, the key to winning this battle is to continue to "recruit" new drinkers, to make every effort to draw them in. "It's a permanent fight, 365 days a year, 24 hours a day."

Pride is palpable at Hennessy, whether in the lofty spheres of the company or down below in the vineyards it owns in the heart of Cognac country. The man in charge of these is Alain Deret, who has worked on Hennessy's Tasting Committee since 1980. Deret supervises the technical aspects of winegrowing, equipment, and treatments, everything directly affecting 180 hectares of vines, almost all in Grande Champagne.

His work on the vineyards is done within a separate Hennessy-owned unit under orders from Yann Fillioux, Hennessy's cellar master; the unit also ages the eaux-de-vie from its wine until the time comes to sell them to the parent company. But for another idea of the scale of things: These sales amount to less than 1 percent of what Hennessy buys each year from the region's winegrowers.

"The 180 hectares aren't a strategic supply for Hennessy," Deret says. "Rather, Hennessy wants its vineyards to be a meeting ground with other winegrowers, a place where we can share our techniques, to enlarge the discussion so they, too, can profit from what we've learned."

The biggest single vineyard is called La Bataille, not far from Segonzac, comprising 65 hectares. The grape-processing facilities here are state-of-the-art, and Deret takes advantage of them by being sure, for starters, that the machine-harvested grapes get from the vineyard to the presses quickly to avoid oxidation that would cut the quality of the eau-de-vie. The grapes are weighed as they arrive, their sugar level is measured, then they are fed into pneumatic presses, big stainless steel tumblers in which an airbag-like device gently swells and crushes the grapes to extract the last juice. The juice is left to decant an hour or so before being fed into concrete cisterns for fermentation. Carefully selected yeasts are added to transform the sugar and, as Deret puts it, "make the best wine we possibly can." Measurements are taken often to check the density of sugar left to be changed into alcohol and to verify the temperature of the juice, which if it grows too warm will kill off the yeast and halt the fermentation. This step takes five to six days. A secondary fermentation usually follows soon after, bacteria this time transforming malic acid into lactic acid, lowering the acidity of the wine and thereby improving its flavor slightly; this step also lasts just a few days, and it is imperative that the distillation not begin while the secondary fermentation is still going. If it did, you'd get a rank, unstable eau-de-vie.

Distillation is the domain of Jean-Pierre Vidal, who has been on the Tasting Committee for twenty years and is the top lieutenant to Fillioux, who himself has been tasting Cognacs for Hennessy for thirty-seven years, since 1966. Along with Deret, the other senior tasters are Yves Tricoire, with twenty-nine years under his belt and who also manages Hennessy's contractual relations with its winegrowers, and Benoît Gindraud, with fifteen years' experience, who gauges the evolution of the stocks and barrels and refines the careful creation of the blends conceived by Fillioux. They are joined by three junior tasters who've sat in the inner sanctum a few years. According to Deret, it takes a decade of daily tasting to learn this special skill, to have enough knowledge to form and defend one's opinions. That's countless thousands of Cognacs that form a huge memory bank that can't be learned in any school.

What the committee tastes on any given day could be anything from freshly made eaux-de-vie to ancient stocks. It could be an eau-de-vie distilled by independent professionals—and there are twenty working for Hennessy in Grande Champagne, Petite Champagne, Borderies, and Fins Bois. It could also come from one of the three distilleries owned by Hennessy, like Le Peu, at Juillac-le-Coq in Grande Champagne.

Jean-Pierre Vidal supervises distillation at Le Peu and also carries out quality-control audits of Hennessy's 1,800 contracted winegrowers— 1,400 of whom supply their wine to the professional distillers working solely for Hennessy and 400 who distill their wine themselves before offering it to Hennessy. He chalks up the finesse of Hennessy Cognacs to considered choices made before distillation. Easily the most important part of the process is decanting the juice of the pressed grapes before fermentation begins in order to rid it of suspended matter that's thick and undesirable. This decanted juice, Vidal says, produces a wine that makes a light eau-de-vie that ages well.

A small amount of lees, the dead yeasts that remain from fermentation, are let into the distillation to add roundness and keep the eau-de-vie from being overly dry. On the other hand, Hennessy will snub an eau-de-vie distilled on an excess of lees, as this creates what Vidal calls an "extreme" overstrong eau-de-vie that turns cloudy when you add water to it. Other Cognac houses will prefer to distill by this method, but Hennessy says the result doesn't age all that well and is too *chargé*, heavy, for their tastes.

During the distillation season in midwinter, Vidal pays a visit to the highly polished Peu site at the end of every day. Putting his olfactory and tasting experience to work, he tests each batch of eau-de-vie made by the ten stills in operation round the clock. He can detect slight differences from day to day, and if something negative catches his attention, he will search out the origin of the problem by studying the production records of the vineyard. This doesn't happen often, but when it does, a visit to the winegrower is scheduled to correct the problem and ensure that it doesn't occur again. What excites Vidal is to detect the clear-cut benefit of having let a bit of lees into the process. First he'll do a nose test, and then a mouth taste. He most appreciates an eau-de-vie when it's especially floral. The daily samples for an entire week are then mixed together and sent to the Tasting Committee at Hennessy's headquarters in Cognac, which once a week during the distillation season will put these newborn eaux-de-vie to the same test as Vidal's. This will involve not only all the output of the Peu Distillery but of all the other professional distillers working for Hennessy. This way, each batch is checked and rechecked to assess its flavor and its potential for aging: whether it is destined to be blended into a lively VS or into a decades-old marvel like the Richard Hennessy.

Without a doubt, the Tasting Committee is the heart of the Hennessy affair. Each of its eight members leads a rather conservative lifestyle: none smokes, none drinks immoderately, and all keep themselves in shape for the job at hand. The group, which meets every workday of the year at 11 A.M. for an hour and a half, might test as many as 40 samples a session. Their lair is a clean, well-lighted place that resembles a laboratory, with numerous tiny bottles set all around.

Yann Fillioux, fifty-seven, seventh in a family line of *maîtres de chais* dating back to 1800, is the top scientist here, or high priest, since religious

Yann Fillioux, Hennessy's cellar master,
is revered for his singular talents in
shaping Cognacs, especially the
young and lively ones.

imagery comes to mind as you observe him leading these deliberations. But Fillioux, who is also managing director of Hennessy, is anything but dogmatic. He is self-effacing, even shy, and yet he's very personable and effusive when it comes to talking about Cognac and all that it can be.

"The Tasting Committee has two roles," he says. "One is to make good Cognac. The other is to preserve the company's long tradition for producing the exceptional. You have to have the means, the talent to make this work. Not all that many golden occasions come along, so you also have to know how to seize the moment. If you miss it, then it's definitively gone."

Improvisation isn't part of the formula, he notes. What really makes it all come together is solid, day-to-day work, that minimum ten-year learning experience that can't be rushed. "It's like being a writer. A person with that particular talent requires singular concentration. Some days it works well, some days it doesn't. Tasting Cognacs is much the same. In the end, I have to have confidence in my team, to trust its competence."

The tasters aren't fathers of Cognac, Fillioux says, but more like its baptizers. Meaning that their work isn't really art; what matters more is continuity. "What we're good at is making a good VS, and also making a good VSOP, which isn't just an older VS, and making a good XO, but which isn't just an older VSOP," and so on. "At each stage, we'll bring you just one part of our talent as a group. For sure, there are common points among all our Cognacs. But each quality, each type has a different concept behind it.

"And when it comes down to it, I'm simply concerned with quality. Not art. But quality. I'll know if something has potential."

How does he do this? "I'm not a distiller, so I couldn't go to a distiller and say, 'Do this or do that.' That, I wouldn't know how to do. But I do know this when I taste an eau-de-vie: 'This is all right, this should be a little better, this is better, this is good, this above average.' After that, I'll discuss these findings with the team working with me, and as for those eaux-de-vie that aren't good enough, we'll try to figure out how to correct that, and as for those that stand out, we'll preserve them and make them even better by proper aging. The ideal is to achieve elegance. I have tasted every kind of Cognac. But what gets my attention is elegance. That's the Holy Grail."

Elegance stands even above age. Whereas many drinkers will focus on the number of years behind a bottle, Fillioux would invite them to seek out that other quality: the quintessence of elegance, harder to pluck out of the continuum and pin down than the age of a Cognac, which is always striking.

And yet when it does come down to choices based on age, Fillioux will cite 1946 to 1961 as years that interest him. This period produced Cognacs with a "wonderful combination of elegance and age," a perfect balance that makes them exceptional. Occasionally, though, a year may not produce a notable result, and here he mentions 1981 and 1984: something was out of kilter, perhaps the weather was too humid that year, but the eau-de-vie wasn't right and not worth keeping, or maybe only a few barrels.

Fillioux speaks fondly of his uncle, Maurice, who preceded him as master taster until 1991, and also of his grandfather and great-grandfather, noting that they were specialists in selecting the eaux-de-vie that are now Hennessy's best. But today's master will concede that their talents aren't his, that what he excels at is making VS. "VS, that's me. And it's even harder to make than the others. Harder because you have to make a lot more of it. And while making a VS that is good, you have to be careful at the same time not to make it too good to the detriment of future higher qualities, and so on.

"Speaking of the exceptional old Cognacs we have in our stocks, our job is clear. We've been handed something precious. We have to maintain it, living off the interest it produces without damaging the principal, and then transfer it to the next generation. Making Cognac is straightforward. But if you take everything you've got and roll it out before it's really ready, then you won't have anything exceptional left for tomorrow."

Alain Deret is another Cognac master who knows the secrets of the different types of Hennessy and all the magic that went into them. Confidence is so high in Deret's savvy that the company has designated him manager of Hennessy's eau-de-vie stocks. He's not only in charge of buying them, he also makes sure that what shows up at the *chais* to be aged is what Hennessy had been expecting based on earlier tests; he keeps supplies of new eaux-de-vie at optimum levels, much as a chef will keep necessary ingredients on hand to make a great recipe. But to cook up a good Cognac, you have to know what you're aiming for. And so a survey of Deret's kitchen reveals much about what Hennessy has in mind.

First and foremost in the tasting process is to use tulip-shaped glasses; the balloon-shaped snifter exposes too much of the surface of the eau-de-vie to the air, changing its flavor. When testing a new eau-de-vie, Deret and his colleagues will first try it *sec*, dry, at about 70 degrees alcohol, and then add some water to bring it down to 50; by pouring in some water, any defects are amplified, and the sample can be eliminated for poor flavor due to some error that may have occurred during vinification or distillation.

Deret offers two examples to show basic differences of *terroirs*: a newborn Grande Champagne is powerful and will need time to age; a Fins Bois, on the other hand, is more floral and will need much less time in the barrel to become good. The Grande Champagne will usually end up in the XO-and-higher range of Cognacs; the Fins Bois will be a major component in VS and VSOP. Armed with the results of the tasting of a new eau-de-vie, specifically its potential for becoming one kind or another of Cognac, along with a judgment of the influence of its *terroir,* the Tasting Committee will then lay out an aging plan for it, a "primordial" decision that will set that Cognac's future. "Make an error at this point," Deret says, "like not aging an eau-de-vie in the right type of barrel, and there's no going back."

Hennessy's tasters definitely like to poke their noses deep into the glass. And no wonder: it's an exciting universe therein, whether it's a new Fins Bois that's redolent of white flowers or a Grande Champagne that's slightly buttery. After the nose test, you taste each on the front of your tongue, which in the Fins Bois reveals additional floral odors, young leaves, and some acidity, but much aromatic complexity; and which in the Grande Champagne unlocks even more of its buttery side and a subtle richness that fills the mouth and speaks of a future "on which we can gamble without fear."

The latter, if it is chosen, will almost always end up being aged in older barrels that will give less tannin to the Cognac as it develops and lend it the conditions it needs to mature slowly; a Fins Bois eau-de-vie, unless it is a startling exception, will go into newer barrels for a rapid infusion of wood as it is apt to age quickly and soon be ripe for inclusion in Hennessy's younger blends.

To show how oak colors and recharacterizes a young eau-de-vie, Deret offers two samples of Fins Bois from 2001: one has been aged in a new barrel for ten months, and the other in an old barrel for two years. The first is much darker in color, since the new wood tints the eau-de-vie quite sharply and has cinnamon flavors and hints of the toasted interior of a barrel, while the second remains much lighter in color and still very powerful in taste. It follows that putting an eau-de-vie with a lot of potential into a new barrel will "waste that potential." On the other hand, if you age an unpromising eau-de-vie in an old barrel, "because it's destined to be used when young, it won't have the time to develop the woody structure needed to go into a blend."

This choice is so important, Deret says, that Hennessy tastes samples of its unblended stocks every year, about 2,000 in all, from April to September, taken from the grand assembly of 220,000 barrels. The tasters learn how the eau-de-vie has developed and whether they made the right barrel choices; it might be switched to another barrel or it might be kept longer in the same one; also, each eau-de-vie is graded (12 out of 20, say) and its nuances catalogued (young, woody, and so on). Fillioux will use these results to pick Cognacs for "first blends," which are aged further and combined with others like them to make "final blends," which might be refined further before they are ready.

Besides the 2,000 samples tested in the annual inventory, the committee also passes judgment on 6,500 other samples of new and older eaux-de-vie proposed for sale in the course of a year.

For an idea of the range of Cognacs that Hennessy might include in a blend, take a 1983 Petite Champagne. At age twenty, this Cognac marks the passage to maturity; young aromas are left behind and older ones are now in view: dried apricots, grapefruit, underwood. Strong *rancio* signals are present, too: odors of old paper, a long-closed country house, even dry grass.

"It's a very good eau-de-vie," Deret says, "and soon it could go into an XO, without any problem. But it's not an exceptional Cognac, not one we consider to be among the very best."

Which ones, then, are the best? A 1956 Grande Champagne, for instance. Tasted by itself, before it joins a blend, an exceptional Cognac is likely to be at its peak between forty and sixty years, Deret says. Here, then, is a gem: harmonious, with long aromas, balanced, woody, and slightly acid.

"With this Cognac, we've left behind the very good and entered the world of the exceptional. We'd grade it 19 out of 20. There's still fifty or so barrels of this. It's an inestimable treasure."

Followed by a hundred-year-plus diamond: an 1893 Grande Champagne. Deret notes that this one represents the result of the concentration, via distillation, evaporation, and all those years, of three hundred liters of wine into one liter of Cognac. It stands on its own, though it could be seen as slightly inferior to the 1956. "This is much more concentrated. Old leather chairs, say. But what an explosion of aromas! Phenomenal power. What other product, a century after it was first made, gives this intensity of pleasure?"

So why not market the 1956 or the 1893? "This 1893 is quite remark-able, yes," Deret says, "but others of the same age maybe are different, their elegance dominated by age. By that I mean that if Hennessy simply began slicing up all of its stocks by year and selling them that way, we couldn't bring you the consistent product that we can make via blending."

Again, Cognacs hit their ideal between forty and sixty years. After sixty-something years you'll find less elegance and complexity and a more pow-erful flavor. On this scale, the 1956 is still a bit young: It has even more finesse to develop, probably over another ten to fifteen years. At the oppo-site extreme, a very old Cognac, one well past the century mark, might have "its beret on its ear," as the expression goes, meaning over the hill, too far gone: thickish and void of elegance. Which is to say there's a point at which every Cognac is ideally balanced, ready to join the perfect blend.

At XO-and-up levels, Hennessy has two styles: One that's rich and woody and that's a favorite among Asians, who like to drink it mixed with water (which is the way Cognac has mostly been drunk through history). This "traditional" XO is made from Cognacs from the four main growths. Hennessy also sells an XO Grande Champagne in duty-free shops or in its visitors' center in Cognac. This one is lighter in style and sits between the fine underwood aromas of the 1956 and the dry fruity flavors of the 1983.

One of the jewels of the Hennessy collection is the Paradis Extra, which contains more than one hundred Cognacs, the oldest of which dates to the second half of the 1800s, many from Grande Champagne. It recalls the 1956—rounded and elegant. Deret envisions Paradis Extra as part of an excellent meal: serve it straight out of the freezer with *foie gras.* This will highlight the Cognac's texture, its thick-sweet side, much like a good Sauternes will.

Lastly, he touts the Richard Hennessy, which echoes the 1893: concen-trated, woody, and spicy. Its oldest components date to the first half of the 1800s; and there are maybe 130 Cognacs in it. "This is the soul of Hen-nessy," Deret intones, a testament to all the people who selected Cognacs over the years and kept them under perfect conditions until they could become rarities like this one. "Not only are we making Cognacs today, but we are picking out the eaux-de-vie that will make the Cognacs of the future." He attributes the exquisiteness of the Richard Hennessy to the steady vision of the company's leaders and their trust in the Fillioux fam-ily to get it right.

Yann Fillioux echoes that, lauding the manner in which the company champions a "fundamental respect" for the quality of the Cognacs it produces. He is sure that while "what we're doing certainly isn't perfect, we're headed in the right direction—seeking quality, being perfectionist, finding elegance." He adds, "The company has a strong realistic streak, too. The product is there. The sales are there. In sum, Hennessy has a rare quality, one that puts it above and beyond the others, and that is its ability to make a very good VS and also a very good Paradis."

Not only good but in fantastic volumes, most of it put together at the Haut-Bagnolet production site north of Cognac where all the eaux-de-vie that Hennessy has purchased are brought in from distilleries and vineyards to be put into barrels and left to rest in the house's thirty warehouses. There they stay until it's time—maybe just a year for something destined to go into a young Cognac, or maybe twenty years for something much more special—to awaken them again and join them here as first blends, after which they are sent off to be aged a few months or years longer before they are pulled out of their slumber and put into final blends (such as an XO or Paradis Extra) before being aged for a number of months yet again.

Whenever these treasures are ready for prime time, they're sent over to the bottling plant south of Cognac. Here nine lines churn out tens of thousands of bottles a day, each of which has been either given a shot of compressed air to be sure no impurities remain inside or rinsed with

Stylish cartons of XO speed through Hennessy's ultramodern bottling and
packaging plant, which cranks out 46 million bottles of Cognac a year.

Cognac, before being filled, corked, capped, and labeled—all watched by cameras that check everything from the level of the Cognac to the depth of the cork. That's 46 million bottles, or 3.8 million cartons of 12, a year.

The house also has a well-appointed laboratory keeping an eye on hygiene and environmental security, carrying out chemical analyses of all the wine being offered to distillers working for Hennessy as well as of the eaux-de-vie that these distillers then cook up, and making sure that all parts of the Hennessy universe abide by the rules for the preparation of Cognac, which, after all, is destined to be drunk and so needs to be certified not only as safe for consumption but as the real thing and not a fraud.

This is the fiefdom of Jean Pineau. His lab's agents spend much time during the year talking with all the winegrowers and advising them on techniques, the better to make the wine Hennessy is hoping for to create its Cognacs. Pineau was working in other vineyards making wine before he came to Cognac country in 1991, where he was astonished to discover that Charente winegrowers spent much more time worrying about their vineyards than about winemaking. "They were vineyard men, not wine men. Since then, though, I've discovered that the hardest wine of all to make is the wine that goes into Cognac. That was a total surprise. In no enology school, mind you, do they teach the vinification of Cognac wine."

Why so difficult? "Because it's the only wine in which you don't add any antiseptic elements, like sulfur dioxide," he explains. "All the other wines use it, in the fermentation and to preserve it. That means it's not certain that you'll have good fermentation without it. You have to be very selective about the fermentation, then. What's more, it's a low-alcohol wine, and 8.5 to 9.5 percent is the ideal. This gives a frank, but not thick, taste. It won't be very aromatic, but it will express its origin very well, its *terroir*. It will have just the right acidity to preserve itself well if kept in the right conditions. These things are very important since distillation won't fix anything, won't repair things like when rot attacks the grapes during the growing season.

"In the end, Hennessy has had a real impact on the region by pushing winegrowers to make ever better wine. A lot of people laughed at us. At my first meeting with winegrowers they even wanted to throw me out. Now they know we're right. It's common sense. Hennessy is demanding about eau-de-vie, so it follows that it will be demanding about the wine that goes into it."

To keep the wine in good shape until it's distilled depends more on hygiene, in Pineau's book, than on its natural acidity. Top sanitary conditions, then, are another requirement that Hennessy tries to impress upon its winegrowers; Jean-Pierre Vidal, for example, might visit their *chais* and check out their equipment and give them advice on how to operate. "Over a three- or four-year period," Pineau says, "Vidal will have seen the ensemble of all our suppliers, to discuss with them everything from winegrowing to aging."

Pineau and a few select colleagues also do initial taste tests on new eaux-de-vie from Hennessy's artisanal distillers; the main tasting committee headed by Fillioux does the same with the eaux-de-vie from Hennessy's professional distillers. "We do this twice a week. The artisanal distillers bring us their product and we try it out to see if it conforms to what we're looking for. But whether it's my committee or Fillioux's, the results are the same. If you find that an eau-de-vie is not very good, you go back to the distiller to ask what happened and to try to understand what went wrong. We ask the distillers to keep a sample of each of their production cycles so that when we do have a problem we can go in and determine the cause—whether it was the wine or what. The work of these tasting committees lasts the whole distillation season, and it's complemented by chemical analyses that take the 'pulse' of the eau-de-vie that can reveal other errors, mistakes in fermentation or in the preservation of the wine. We can track these things and pinpoint the problem we discovered during the tasting session."

Another interesting activity is the deep analyses that the lab does on all Hennessy Cognacs, giving each what Pineau calls "an I.D. card" listing the sixty or so main elements of its chemical universe. This kind of statistical detail helps Hennessy not only to verify whether its qualities—VS, VSOP, and so on—are the same through time, but also to sniff out fakes. Pineau's team also does chemical analyses on many other spirits—whiskey, tequila, rum, brandy—to have a data bank to help it identify the alcohols (or whatever) that went into a bottle of fake Cognac. And because the lab has an I.D. card for each type of Cognac, then all it has to do is run an analysis of any drink to learn if, for example, the VS of another house has been substituted for a Hennessy VS. "Of course, they don't have the same profile."

Finally, the lab verifies that Cognacs heading out from Hennessy are perfectly stable and will be in good shape when they're poured maybe thousands of kilometers away. A big part of that work is filtering the Cognac at low temperatures just before it is bottled, to eliminate fatty acids that could destabilize the product. Pineau's team checks this process to be sure it doesn't "shock" the Cognac or rough it up. These technicians, stationed at each of Hennessy's sites, also certify that all the physical materials used in the manufacturing process comply with international food-safety norms: corks, joints, filters, bottles, anything coming into contact with the Cognac.

It's a huge job to keep an eye on all that, but part and parcel to Hennessy's efforts to hold the high ground. This makes for envious competitors who accuse it of doing unsavory things to make all Cognac the same. And yet Hennessy rules the roost because it puts out a good product.

Roland de Farcy, president of Hennessy, naturally has only good things to say about the company's huge size. "Hennessy has grown to be a behemoth—though historically it hasn't always been one—and I think that's because it has played the game pretty smartly. Product quality is clearly one aspect." Another part of its success is that "Hennessy understood the role of strong distribution and strong market presence" well ahead of its competitors. And "Hennessy started alliances before all the others, as with Moët-Hennessy and Diageo, which gave us the lead in terms of strength of distribution and in what you can do in terms of local presence and so on."

Working things at the local level, de Farcy insists, is the way to go. It's vital for distributors of Hennessy to roam the bars and restaurants and find out what people are drinking and why they like one thing more than another and be sure the right Cognacs are there in the right places for the potential customer. It's just as important to be in a market first, to have your brand linked with the very idea of Cognac before other brands pile in, as in Poland and Vietnam or any other emerging consumer society.

Above all, Hennessy should concentrate on making its Cognac "a more relevant brand to younger consumers," de Farcy says. In the United States, "we're there already" with young people, he notes. "But in some of the graying markets, in Asia, there are going to be big demographic shifts, and we need to be sure that we're relevant to twenty-five-to-thirty-year-olds." But getting young people not only to try Cognac but to turn away from the likes of whiskey is a "constant battle" and the biggest challenge of the future.

Hennessy's star is bright and getting brighter. It's a long and winding 240-year-old story so far—and one that may just be hitting its stride.

TALE OF A
LITTLE HOUSE

AT THE OPPOSITE END OF THE COGNAC universe glows a little star called Delamain, in a place called Jarnac, comfortably upriver from the bright giants. Everything is quieter here. Time runs languidly, as if to the rhythm of the river. You hear shoes clacking on cobblestones, and no street runs straight and true. Every nook and cranny of the place speaks of old secrets.

Delamain is one of the smallest Cognac houses around. And there are plenty of those. What makes all the difference, however, is that it is arguably the best one. For many it outshines even the giants downriver. All this from a small, two-story house jammed in among others along the winding rue Jacques and Robert Delamain, a couple of blocks north of the Charente. Everything here is white-shuttered. Only a small brass plaque by the door gives the place away. You have to go find Delamain, in other words.

Inside, Patrick Peyrelongue, managing director, and Charles Braastad-Delamain, sales director, work with their desks facing each

other, in what has been called a Dickensian setup. Of course the two gen-
tlemen, who age-wise could be father and son, wouldn't compare their
work to that of the great novelist, but the trappings of their lair do recall
a Victorian age: all in dark polished wood that creaks underfoot. Secre-
taries in the front office perch on stools at chest-high desks. The light of
the town and of gardens behind walls comes obliquely through windows,
only to disappear into the woodwork, as if sucked up by time itself. You
can't smell any Cognac here, but, better, you can see it in the reverence
everyone shows. It looks like a perfect spot to work, if you had treasure
making in mind, and they all do.

The genius of Delamain, in addition to its antiqueness, which is a rare
and seldom bona fide quality in this globalized era, is born in the tasting
room, four paces by four, with one window, one porcelain sink, a cabinet
of untouchably ancient Cognacs on the right, a countertop on the left for
today's work, and shelves above it lined with samples as in a lab. The ceiling is low, and the floor seems to sag a bit as the principals—Peyrelongue,
Braastad-Delamain, and Dominique Touteau, the cellar master—gather
at exactly 11 A.M. to check out the samples on offer. Maybe there are six,
or nine. All three men step forward to pour them into tulip glasses. Then
they step back, not saying much, though the dance of decision has definitely begun.

No music, no chitchat, just professional assessment at work here. The
stately Peyrelongue, perhaps because he's the boss, comes forward to go
first. He tries Sample 1, the youngest of the batch, though they don't have
numbers, and trying doesn't mean drinking. All nose here. He makes a
mental note, with no particular movement of the eyes to give it away, then
takes up the second sample, and so on, down the line, deeper through
time, the whole row done in thirty seconds. Then he steps away, and
Braastad-Delamain, towering, eases up to the offerings and does the
same. Lastly the cellar master, still sporting his leather jacket against
the autumn chill, slowly takes his turn, though he could just as well have
gone first.

No neophyte nor even an average connoisseur of Cognac could truly
plumb what these men share in this time-honored ritual. They learned
what they know from each other; Peyrelongue also learned it over the
years from his cousin Alain Braastad-Delamain, who led the company
from the 1970s to the end of the millennium and who also taught all
this to his son Charles. That's the way it's been done in this house since
the 1760s.

Charles Braastad-Delamain tests new eau-de-vie samples on offer
during the daily 11 A.M. ritual in Delamain's tasting room.

This relaxed, almost monastic tasting can't be done differently and
still be done right. Words finally emerge after a second pass through the
offerings. All these Cognacs are from Grande Champagne; Delamain
will consider no others. You can be sure these are among the finest examples around, too; Delamain pays a pretty penny to have the best. Color
doesn't count. In that way, they'll tell you, this work is not dissimilar to
the perfumer's.

You learn the vocabulary: woody, too woody, mushroom, banana,
mushroom again, caramel, cloves, moldy, even execrable. You discover
that they don't much abide eaux-de-vie distilled on lots of lees: faster to
age, these Cognacs end up having much less finesse in Delamain's books.
Some of the Cognacs on offer are thirty years old; others just five or so.
They might be judged for what they are now, or what they might become.
Or they could be imagined residing in a blend, a mixture to be made soon
for a new client, or to be brought forth a decade or two down the road.

The glasses remain lined up, the better for one taster not to prejudice
the next by shifting the poor ones aside. All at once they agree, shaking
their heads, that one offer is particularly unsavory; then they congregate
around another glass, as around a pretty girl at the dance, and whisper
compliments: fruity, cinnamon, long. It's like poets writing a collective
paean to perfection. Maybe two of the nine are worthy at this point.

Then they pour everything back into the bottles and step back, savoring, complexly, the moment. But this is no academic exercise. This is about interpretation, judgment, and prediction—and many other concerns besides, investment not being the least. Any errors noted in the first round get verbally reviewed now: faults of distillation or of aging, goof-ups that bring out flavors like, say, grass, a very base and un-noble aroma for a Cognac. There are others, old butter and worse, on down the scale to one that is so bad Touteau wants to enshrine it somewhere to be the quintessential Awful Cognac. But that kind of offering doesn't pop up often around here; send in one particularly bad sample to be tested by Delamain, and you probably won't even get a hearing next time around. Not that this is a mafia of taste. These fellows just don't have time to be filtering out trashy Cognacs.

The empty glasses are put to a final nose test. This round is very important, because a drained glass can give forth odors—the air and the glass are both warmer now, freeing up more aromas, like cigar tobacco—that were hidden when the Cognac was still in the glass. Sometimes a Cognac will be eliminated solely on its uninteresting after-aromas.

In the end, one or two samples get the nod. One lot might end up in a supple blend called Vesper, Delamain's second-youngest, about thirty-five years old (like Braastad-Delamain). Another might be a gem worthy of the title Réserve de la Famille: unblended, from one barrel, a sixty-something scintillating diamond in the rough (like Peyrelongue) at a natural 43 degrees alcohol. Peyrelongue has striking words for this Cognac: *vif et sauvage* (lively and wild). One should take an hour to fully appreciate a glass of it.

Over the course of a year of doing this, only one in ten samples gets through. That's not much: just a drop within a drop in the sea of Grande Champagne out there on offer, and a speck within a drop within a drop in the wide ocean of Cognac. You have to focus that finely if you're going to find the absolute best, they'll tell you. And to do that it takes these three noses working every day, all through the calendar, all their lives in fact, to even begin to know what they're doing, and none of them will claim to know enough or it all. That's plain old modesty, though: they know very well what they're up to. It's called making magic, otherwise known as Cognac, using time-honored methods and a dose of daring, and always with quiet confidence, discretion, and a particular gentlemanly savoir-faire.

To visit Delamain is to spend a day with a family that couldn't be more generous, as if time had ceased to matter here, or never did if it meant rushing for profits, which is exactly what this Cognac house isn't about. Being family, though, doesn't mean all things are forever settled and locked in stone; hence the formal entry a few years ago of the Bollinger Champagne company, now holder of 34 percent of Delamain. Distribution synergies are management bywords now, Bollinger getting Delamain into even more markets as the two companies row in the same direction.

Welcome dose of outside capital aside, this is still no gung ho outfit. At most twenty people work here, but you won't see more than four or five together, and so it's as if there are not enough bodies around, or as if the place runs itself. No one raises his or her voice. They don't whisper, either, and yet this old Cognac house is definitely like a library filled with ancient casks of time.

And you don't see distillers standing around in the foyer for their offerings to be received in the inner sanctum; it's as if the samples had been left at the door like milk bottles. But once these lots do pass the test and make the grade, Delamain takes over the final stages of their transformation. That will involve more aging, always in Limousin oak for its vanilla aromas; reducing too-powerful eaux-de-vie with a 15-degrees-alcohol mixture of demineralized water and old Cognac; and blending Cognacs from different years to strike a balance. Some lots come from vineyards that have had contracts with Delamain for more than a century.

Delamain also works closely with winegrower/distillers in assessing brand-new eau-de-vie just after it has been made, and by dispensing custom advice on how to age it and pamper it through the years, often in the winegrowers' own cellars. This works not with Delamain simply telling them what to do, Braastad-Delamain explains, "but through an exchange of ideas," the better to age each new eau-de-vie in a way that brings out its specific potential for a sale to Delamain that could come years later.

Delamain owns no vineyards of its own. It's like a little warehouse, in this respect, with its purchases stocked away in different sheds and cellars in Jarnac, never far from the humidity of the river, that velvety air so necessary to proper aging. That and the original *terroir* go hand in hand in bringing forth the Delamain specialty: the lightest of Cognacs. They couldn't do that with anything but Grande Champagne's primary matter. It takes just the right barrels, too, older ones, known as *fûts roux*, that have ceased to sharply color the eau-de-vie like young barrels do and that infuse it with less tannin.

Pale & Dry XO is Delamain's opening gambit: limpid, full of golden reflections, aromas of lemon and grapefruit and flowers, with flavors of

Once it buys a Cognac, Delamain directs the final stages of its creation: aging it,
reducing it, and blending different years for a fine balance.

licorice and vanilla. This is a blend with an average age of twenty-five years reduced to 40 degrees alcohol and allowed to settle down for eighteen to twenty-four months before being filtered and bottled. Noted for its extreme freshness and lightness despite its impressive age, Pale & Dry has a unique grip on certain ranks of Cognac lovers who savor fruity mellowness. Vesper and Très Vénérable climb through the ages of thirty-five and fifty-five, progressively superior blends with steadily more length, as well as floral and spicy scents and notes of raisins and honey. Naturally these three "styles," as Braastad-Delamain describes them, are followed by the Réserve de la Famille in all its single-cask glory.

And then there is the unequaled surprise of the vintage Cognacs, recently the 1973 and 1969. These are just as old as their labels say they are (and none bottled before it is at least thirty years old), which is no mean miracle considering how difficult it is to know the age of a Cognac. In that regard, fraud got so out of hand by the early 1960s that the industry decided to stop allowing the sale of vintage Cognacs. Thinking ahead, Delamain began putting some of its barrels of Cognac behind lock, key, and seal in a special cellar that can be entered only with a fraud official from the BNIC. Setting that Cognac aside proved very insightful when the industry lifted the interdiction on vintages in 1989. Now, when Delamain rolls out a barrel to bottle it as a 1973 or whatever, the drinker can be sure the Cognac hails from that year alone.

The 1973 comes from a winegrower/distiller near Saint-Même-les-Carrières; by naming its geographic origin, Delamain stresses the special *micro-terroir* that went into this Cognac. Having been only slightly adjusted to 40 degrees alcohol, it's a typical thirty-year-old Grande Champagne, pale gold, with hints of forest undergrowth and toasted almonds. The 1969 comes from a vineyard at La Nérolle, a village near Segonzac, and is similar in style but with ripe fruit flavors. (Peyrelongue's favorite Cognac ever is a 1947 that Delamain has in its cellar: light, floral, Grande Champagne at its finest. Braastad-Delamain's most memorable is the 1965.)

By the way, Delamain has a number of demijohns of pre-phylloxera Cognacs in its oldest reserves—but these treasures aren't for sale. "You couldn't put a price on them anyway," Peyrelongue notes, "because they are totally irreplaceable. And we can't sell them as vintages, either," since they couldn't prove the age of the Cognac if they had to. So these marvels out of the past—all full of the wonders of the *folle blanche* or *colombard* grapes that went into them—remain in the cellars.

Delamain doesn't bring forth that many bottles of vintages, and at times they're sold so fast it's as if they barely existed. (It has only three hundred barrels of vintage Cognacs-in-waiting in this special cellar.) On a recent afternoon, Touteau and Braastad-Delamain oversaw the bottling of a single cask of 1964, just 320 bottles, sold in no time just days before to two clients (one in Russia and the other in Switzerland). Nowadays, these barrels are so rare as to be practically impossible to find; one with a bona fide confirmed age is a miracle. It took half an afternoon for the bottling team to enshrine that 1964 elixir in straight, clear bottles; everyone wore gloves; the treasures were carried like newborns, encased in wooden boxes, wax-sealed, and stamped with the year. Jokes about not dropping one of these got no laughter from this reverential crew of women and men. Not that it would be impossible to come up with the €250 or so; Cognac this good simply can't end up on the floor. Each bottle was first rinsed with Cognac; each cork carefully reexamined for the slightest faults; each filled bottle held up against a bright light and pored over for the slightest defect. No one spoke, or just barely, as the bottling machine whirred and clicked and Touteau and Braastad-Delamain hovered near like fathers-to-be in the waiting room.

On almost any other day the little production line on the second floor of an old convent near the main house would be cranking out bottles of

Pale & Dry or Vesper—Delamain's mainstays. These are top-notch Cognacs destined, as Peyrelongue notes, for a "niche" of drinkers. Delamain's youngest Cognac is already an XO, meaning that, age-wise, it stands above and beyond 85 to 90 percent of the entire Cognac market, "making our Cognacs a niche within a niche since we work only with Grande Champagne Cognacs and very old ones at that. That's what makes our products more expensive. And we can't sell them cheaply." He adds: "Our typical client, then, is a confirmed lover of Cognac, an *amateur*. And in each of our markets, there's always a small but definite group of Cognac lovers who appreciate fine things and who have the means to buy our product."

All told, Delamain sells about 30,000 cases of Cognac a year, in sixty countries as far-flung as Ecuador and Sri Lanka; just 4,000 bottles, or the equivalent of 335 cases, come out as vintages. You'd think that, with such tiny numbers, Delamain would hardly get noticed. But what it puts out there in bars, stores, and restaurants is so exceptional it seizes a premium ranking and holds on to it. That's surely a testament to the consistent work of the team in Jarnac and of the efficiency of the 11 A.M. ritual through the years. Variance and drift are just not part of the formula as this company gleans the finest barrels of eau-de-vie from the Grande Champagne countryside.

Delamain is firmly planted in the French market, where it is very visible and popular, to the tune of 4,500 cases a year. (The other 85 percent or so of Delamain's annual sales occur outside France.) The cheapest bottle of Delamain is very expensive compared with many other Cognacs. Peyrelongue says that although Delamain can't possibly compete with the giants who mass-produce and sell for less, there's "no way we will 'give away' our Cognacs like a lot of the big companies do just to reach sales targets." That market-grabbing philosophy is alien to Delamain and an unthinkable way to do business and stay true to itself.

Delamain's biggest export market is the United States, where it sells 4,000 cases a year. While the U.S. market for all kinds of Cognac is about 4 million cases a year, according to Peyrelongue only 100,000 cases of that are very old, highest-quality Cognacs, or just 2.5 percent of the market. You can see, then, that Delamain's 4,000 cases amount to a tiny slice— only 4 percent—of that potential market of 100,000. "We may not sell a lot in America, but we're definitely well known," Peyrelongue says. All told, the whole of North America gets about 8,500 cases of Delamain, or one-third of all that the house exports. Another third of its exports goes elsewhere in Europe, Italy being the principal market; and the final third goes off to Asia.

Scandinavia, especially Norway, excites Delamain as this market continues to expand at a steady pace and more and more young people try out top-notch Cognacs. A change of taste is under way in this region, as Scandinavians eschew the sweeter, heavier Cognacs they've long loved for a lighter, drier fare like that offered by Delamain. Russia is another important scene, where Peyrelongue himself spends much of his time seeking clients and tapping into a customer base that he says is potentially huge. Equally gigantic to him, at least someday, is India. Here, tens of millions of people already have the buying power to afford Delamain Cognacs; it's now only a matter of India opening the doors further to its market. For Peyrelongue, India's is even more hopeful a market than China's—in contrast to most conventional wisdom about the Cognac drinkers of tomorrow.

In this regard Delamain is as forward-looking as it is faithful to its past. And there is a palpable continuity of vision. Peyrelongue will retire in a decade or so and spend even more time doing what he likes to do when he's not buying or selling Cognac—riding his motorbike or working his garden (but no vines) or helping to look after his flock of grandchildren. But he will leave behind to Braastad-Delamain—lover of rowing, gardening, family, and home—much of everything he has learned about Cognac, just like each director before him, generation to generation in an unbroken sequence.

Don't look here for newfangled Cognacs with top-dollar names to be coming out every now and then. Expect solid tradition. Not tradition with the dark weight of history but with the light-filled beauty of a great confluence of the elements. "It's a great stroke of luck, but we have everything we need right here," Peyrelongue intones. "The sea is near. We have just the right ground. We have just the right grapes. All that comes together to let us make the best eau-de-vie in the world."

The Last of the
Mohicans

P AUL-JEAN GIRAUD IS A COGNAC MILITANT
who lives up where the flattish, river-hugging
ground of Grande Champagne wrinkles into
hefty hills. Here in summer vines plunge and
rise together like ocean waves. It's as if the entire countryside up
behind Segonzac were conspiring to draw you deeper into Cognac's
heart of hearts. You want to keep riding from place to place for hours
to take in this seascape of grapes, winegrowing farms, and *chais* in
which untold rows of Cognac casks lie waiting.

And yet no sooner have you taken in one vista than the road
plunges down again over a ridge into Bouteville. This is probably the
most photographed village of Cognac country, and rightly so: green
vine, white stone, and yellow-blue light swirl down into a basin over
which ruins of an ancient castle loom. There's the church, its
Romanesque countenance facing the light, all the neat, clay-tiled
houses gathered around it, and the tiny streets winding through and
around this perfect model of a Cognac village.

Of course you wouldn't know it unless you'd been following the occasional little road signs, but right down below is Giraud's lair. The big two-story family home of 1889 vintage rises over an array of buildings around the courtyard, domain of brightly colored but well-worn machinery and trucks for conquering the hills hereabouts.

Standing in the tall door of the house, Giraud looks like a priest waiting for his flock. But this smiling Bouteville man is anything but a passive player. Maybe he's a fighter because he inherited the big stock of Cognac that his winegrowing father put together starting back during World War II (working with his own father, who himself had put together a fair stock of Cognac). It's a big leg up to be handed such a prize—thousands of liters of aging Grande Champagne Cognac—and it's the kind of thing that doesn't happen to many, even if you are from here. But the young man handed this gift saw that the real challenge wasn't owning it but sharing it with the public.

It's taken Giraud, fifty-two, every day for the last twenty-eight years to get that done. That's how long he's been swinging and jabbing in the Cognac ring, starting with his poor luck in Round 1, back in 1976, when

Inheriting a trove of Cognac from his father,
Paul-Jean Giraud saw that the challenge wasn't
just owning it but sharing it with the public.

everything that was golden had turned black. The oil crisis of 1973, amid wild production and unbridled vine planting, had turned out the lights on the Cognac industry's second big show (after the 1860s). Piling on this disaster was the simmering game of chicken with the Americans. Worse still, Cognac reserves were closing in on the unholy mark of 1 billion bottles of stockpiled elixir. The powers that be reversed course and offered to pay winegrowers to pull out vines; and just to be sure the beast got reined in, they also slapped caps on distillation. No one, then, even in his wildest dreams, could have entertained the notion that this was a good time to attack the market, to roll out Father's collection and go for it.

Yet that's exactly what Giraud did. And ran straight into fifteen long years of uncertainty: through the little industry rebound in the late 1970s to a fresh oil crisis in 1980, to the export downturn of the early 1980s, to a rebound and then a repeat of feuds with America. It wasn't until the late 1980s and the opening up of Japan that Giraud began making a name for himself.

It's not just that Cognac country is lorded over by twenty companies controlling 98 percent of the market. It's not just that the same Top 20 sell millions of cases a year via high-dollar advertising. As daunting as these numbers are, as difficult as the combination of international trade disputes and an overpopulation of overproductive winegrowers proved to be, getting Cognac Paul Giraud into the best bars, restaurants, and stores around the world is nearly impossible. Describing his independent fight to his American interlocutor, Giraud proclaims with a wry smile, "I'm the last of the Mohicans."

Here's how crazily the odds are stacked against him: in the whole region, there are 6,400 working vineyards making white wine for Cognac. About 250 of the region's winegrowers are independents who sell directly to clients at least some of the Cognac they make; three fourths of those independents do their own distilling. This is the home turf of Paul-Jean Giraud. It's a territory he intends not only to expand but to defend to the very end, most recently as president of a federation of 75 independent winegrowers. Usually these independents won't take the sum of their output to the market themselves; instead, some off-load the lion's share to traders for the big houses. But that small piece of the pie they do sell directly on the world's markets is quite a slice—and outside control of the larger beasts in the forest. Meanwhile, their brand gets to be known far and wide.

Giraud's fighting spirit has got to be in his genes, for his is a family with roots grown deep into Cognac bedrock: nine generations of Girauds have lived here since the mid-1600s, farming, cultivating vineyards, and making Cognac since 1830. The same is true on his mother's side: a great-great-grandfather of Giraud's had a vineyard at Saint-Simon, north of here near the Charente, and styled himself on his letterhead not only as a winegrower but as a trader, since he bought and sold others' Cognacs in addition to selling his own. He was a typical kind of operator in the final decades of the nineteenth century, with direct access to the river to get his product down to the ocean in majestic *gabarres*, one of those determined winegrowers who somehow made it through the phylloxera crisis. "Some people thought they'd never be able to make Cognac again," Giraud says. "Naturally, however, those who held on to their stocks got rich, because all of a sudden Cognac was worth a fortune. How else to account for this big house built fifteen years after phylloxera struck? It wasn't a ruined family that built such a home."

Nor was it a family of little means that could accumulate the fine stocks that ended up in Giraud's hands. It's as if you can hear the family longbeards saying: protect this Cognac with your life. Giraud understands that but also knows the secret to fulfilling the promise of these old Cognacs: getting them out there with his name on them for the public to love.

It's no rush to the sacrificial altar, however. To do that would be to commit the same error many a strapped winegrower has made: desperately selling off the trove to buy the next meal or to get through another season.

But once you roll it out, you roll out the best. And here's where Giraud's methods stand well above the rest of the Cognac crowd: of his six qualities, he blends only one. All the others come from single years. The high end of his range of offerings starts with what he calls Vieille Réserve, which is at least twenty-five years old and which he places in the age group of a venerable XO. And not only are Giraud's Cognacs single-year, they're obviously single-growth, making them unique examples of the finest characteristics of Grande Champagne.

Thus the Giraud method: bring forth some of the best of the stock, stuff that's typical of the marvels that this *cru* can produce, but never run it down, and always renew it with each year's production—additions he's made for nearly thirty years and will continue for years to come. For Giraud is a patient man who knows he's creating a treasure even greater than the one left to him.

He does this annual miracle on 32 hectares around Bouteville and on 3 close to nearby Saint-Même-les-Carrières. This is Campanian and Santonian ground, full of crumbled limestone soft under the step, pure

Grande Champagne. It's the Cognac vineyard's third-largest growth (12,800 hectares making white wine for Cognac), after Fins Bois (30,900 hectares) and Petite Champagne (15,000 hectares). The Borderies, by contrast, harbors only 3,900 hectares of vines; Bons Bois 10,000; and Bois Ordinaires 1,100. All six growths add up to nearly 74,000 hectares.

Take a walk around Giraud's vineyard and you, like him, will have no trouble picking out fossils lying in the surface rubble: every shape you can think of, as warped as oysters have ever been, or smooth like clams, or so oddly convoluted it would take people with doctorates to name them. Back in the courtyard of the house he keeps a collection of them lined up like prizes. None are terribly old—just 75 to 85 million years, a mere scratch in the great scale of time. But this old sea-bottom around here is just right for vines: it will keep them flourishing up to four decades or more.

Giraud has all of his *parcelles* (sections of land) planted in *ugni blanc*, the post-phylloxera favorite of Cognac winegrowers for its vigor, resistance to disease, regular yield, and late maturity (early October in Cognac country), and because it makes the very acid, low-alcohol wine that distillers love to cook. The rootstock he uses is RSB1, a big favorite of his father, who had a lot to do with its accession to the hallowed ranks of officially approved *porte-greffes*. Practically all of his vines are planted in rows with aisles 3 meters wide, and each plant 1.2 meters apart, giving a census of 2,777 plants per hectare. Giraud prefers this density because it favors ample sun exposure on the grapes, makes for bountiful crops, and cuts down on rot-type diseases. A Cognac winegrower will want a lot of bunches of grapes from each plant, since the more grapes a plant produces, the lower the concentration of sugar and the lower the level of alcohol after fermentation—which is exactly what's desirable for making Cognac. Grapevines that are planted more densely (say, with aisles only 2 meters wide) will produce fewer grapes per plant but will have a higher concentration of sugar and so more alcohol in the wine.

It follows that if the density of the vines on a plot matters so much, then the choice of the number of buds to leave on the plants after winter trimming is where it all starts. A short trim (leaving just three or four buds on the pair of canes rising from the vinestock) will obviously lead to fewer grape bunches on the vine come harvest; but, as seen with the density of the plants, fewer bunches per plant means a stronger concentration of sugar in the grapes and a stronger wine. A longer trim (leaving eight buds, as Giraud does) will lead to many more bunches, lower sugar levels, and the desired weaker wine. So choices about trimming, begun toward the end of the year when the sap has dropped and carried out over several wet months, go hand in hand with decisions about plant density and, when done the optimal way, keep the vineyard on track to make wine of just the right power.

The weather is the other factor: very hot weeks can lift the sugar levels of the grapes dramatically; damp weather can keep them inordinately low. So, as ever, a middle ground is optimal, especially in Cognac country, which seeks the moderate sugar and alcohol levels that are best for fine distillation.

Other wintertime tasks in the vineyard include gathering and disposing of trimmed canes—which are good for lighting logs in the fireplace and for grinding up to make humus for the vineyard; the pair of branches remaining on the plant must be directed one to the left, the other to the right, and tied into position; support wires that have broken must be replaced and drawn tight; support posts (mostly acacia from the Dordogne) that have snapped or rotted have to be discarded and new ones pounded into the ground; the trimmed vines must be properly affixed to their wires again, wound around the support so the heavy grapes to come will be high up facing the sun, and a general tidying up of the vinestocks is done by eliminating wasteful suckers that emerged over the summer at the base of the plant.

The age of the vineyard is also important. A younger vineyard makes a better eau-de-vie because, as a vine ages, each year it produces slightly fewer grapes whose sugar content keeps rising, which in turn lifts the alcohol content of the resulting wine, making it less and less suited for turning into Cognac. Thus, whenever a plot of vines starts to get old (say, forty years) or to deteriorate (with 20 to 30 percent of the vinestocks dead or dying), the winegrower will pull everything up and start over.

But from winter sleep emerges the spring—and a flurry of winegrower activities that will last the entire March-to-October explosion of green. Since spring brings rain and rain brings fungi and since fungi like grapes, the main thing on everyone's mind at the outset of the season is disease.

One of the biggest headaches is eutypia dieback (*eutypiose* in France), caused by a fungus whose spores are emitted in winter and spread via raindrops. The plant actually buds out and makes leaves, but it grows poorly, its grapes hardly get going before drying out, and the vinestock trunk starts rotting from the inside. No cure has been devised, and no fungicide seems to work, though efforts are under way at the Station Viticole and elsewhere to find a solution. Meanwhile, the winegrower can only watch as this disease kills about 1.5 percent of the Cognac vineyard each year.

Another disease is called *esca* in France. One form attacks lightning-fast, drying out the vine in just days. The slower form gives the leaves a marble look as the fungi spread. Grapes struck by *esca* will have dark blue or black spots (rarely in France but more often in California), hence its nickname in America, black measles. As with eutypia dieback, the slow-moving type of *esca* will take several years to kill a vine, rotting it. Until recently, this scourge was treated in winter with a chemical containing arsenic. That practice was outlawed in 2001 by the European Union, and so the Cognac vineyard, untreated, now loses 3 percent of its plants each year to *esca*.

Powdery mildew, downy mildew, black rot, and gray rot—all of which can devastate the grape harvest—are treated with fungicides that seem to do the trick. The degree to which these fungi wreak havoc varies from year to year and has a lot to do with the weather: humidity is their preference.

Gray rot (*pourriture grise* or *botrytis* in France) has been a perennial at least since the Middle Ages. While fungicides help control it, the wine-grower is also encouraged to try natural methods. It is known, for instance, that gray rot especially likes strong vines; scientists found that if you could weaken the vine it would be less susceptible to this rot. To decrease the vigor of the vine, then, the winegrower uses less fertilizer and may even choose not to plow between the rows, the better to let a mat of grass grow that will draw away biological resources. Another method is to use rootstocks that do well in high-lime soils but don't overenergize the scion.

Giraud has to treat his grapes all through the growing season. He also battles red and yellow mites that congregate on the bottoms of leaves where their bites discolor and make the leaves fall off, moths whose eggs give rise to caterpillars that dig into the grapes for a sweet meal, as well as beetles, including the *gribouri*, also known as the *écrivain*, or writer, which appears to scrawl genuine notes on the leaves that the winegrower tries to interpret to know whether the harvest will be good or bad.

Additions of nutrients for the general health of the vine are required, too. These will sound familiar to any gardener: nitrogen, phosphorus, and potassium. Giraud has used natural, organic fertilizer for twenty years, mostly sheep manure, but will add chemical fertilizer to meet the vine-yard's needs when conditions call for it. All are incorporated into the soil in early spring. Magnesium also has to be added from time to time, either sprayed directly on the leaves or worked into the dirt. The level of iron is another concern in limestone-packed Cognac country. Usually there is enough iron in the soil, but because the calcium carbonate blocks the vine's uptake of iron, provoking devastating chlorosis, the winegrower has to put even more iron to the ground—the better to overwhelm the blocking action of the calcium carbonate. To help keep things in balance, then, the winegrower adds iron sulfate to his vineyard once a year in winter.

As the leaves on the vines grow thick during the warm months, the winegrower tractors through his vineyard several times each season with a large sort of vertical lawnmower to slice back the greenery. It's a two-fisted beast, one arm raised toward the face of the wall of the vine on one side and another arm lifted to get the other side. Shredded leaves fly fast and furious and the ripping sound of this shaving (called *faucillage*) is often the only one you'll hear out in the fields in summer. It is not the safest of techniques, mind you: There's the old story of the unthinking vineyard worker who gets down from his tractor for a smoke, forgetting to stop the spinning blades and . . .

Not that working out in the Cognac vineyards is really all that dangerous. The chemicals used these days for treatments have been vetted to eliminate human carcinogens or poisoners of the water table. All in all, it's a lot more secure out there among the growing grapes than it used to be.

And so it goes through summer when rain is rarer, the thermometer gets up into the 30s centigrade, and the vines are on their own: no irrigation here. That's all right, because the roots have dug deep to where the humidity lies.

Some winegrowers, Giraud included, choose to plow the aisles between their vines, the better to aerate the soil; another effect of this slicing through the surface soil is to cut the sidewise roots of the vines and force the plant to send its main roots down low. The pro-plowing crowd will tell you that their choice improves the Cognac on account of that deep fix of nutrients and other flavor-giving mysteries. The anti-plowing people, on the other hand, will vaunt improvements to the health of the vineyard their method brings.

By September the air takes on a brass color as the sun rides a more southerly arc and the ocean of vines seems to ebb and flow. These are usually the final days of heat, when the grapes are coaxed toward maturity, before the often rainy and damp days of October. Sometime in the first week or so of this gray month of autumn it used to be that you'd see armies of people out starting the harvest. These were folks from all over: foreigners from Spain or Portugal hoping to round out their winter finances, locals from various walks of life looking to do much the same, and even university students, who suffered the butt-end of jokes and bled the most from the fingers when the pruners got away from them in the thick of the work.

And work it was: for three long weeks, sunrise to sunset, and pretty much for peanuts. You got a good meal at lunchtime, though, well-watered with red wine and Cognac. And just in case someone began to flag under the back-splitting labor of the afternoon, an extra bottle of wine was usually kept on the tractor, up front by the radiator. Bucket after

At Chez Giraud, most of the grape harvest is carefully done by hand to keep the grapes in good shape until they get to the presses.

bucket of grapes got dumped into a bin that filled up fast and got trundled off to the farm and the presses. So went the handpicking, now a lost art—or just about.

Chez Giraud, however, real people with real hands and real backbones using real pruners harvest 25 hectares of his grapes. That's twenty-five people for two weeks of labor. Hardly anyone in the Cognac region does it with actual people anymore. Too expensive. And yet Giraud is convinced that handpicking makes his Cognac finer. "We respect the grapes, and baby them all the way to the presses." Others these days might roundly laugh him out of town, but then those people are probably mechanical-harvester folks who live by the machine, which despite its hefty price sharply lowers costs in the long term. Giraud spends €900 a hectare to have his grapes handpicked; a machine could do the job for €300. Giraud hires a guy who owns one of these upside-down-U monsters, but only to get in the harvest from the other 10 hectares whose wine he legally can't make into Cognac.

Not use all your wine to make all the Cognac you can? For centuries you could do what you wanted, but no more, not since the mid-1970s when major cutbacks in output were made. It works this way: today a winegrower produces an average of 100 hectoliters of grape juice per hectare, which, once made into wine and then distilled, gives 10 hectoliters of pure alcohol. Current European rules say that the maximum output of pure alcohol per hectare can't surpass 7 hectoliters. The other 3 hectoliters of pure alcohol are, in Giraud's words, "destroyed," meaning that the grape juice that would have been vinified and then distilled right there in Bouteville is shipped off to be made into things like grape juice or rubbing alcohol. Do the math in Giraud's case and you discover that the equivalent of 10 of his 35 hectares are producing grape juice that won't be permitted to go into making Cognac. Since there's obviously no point in handpicking those 10 surplus hectares, Giraud hires the mechanical harvester to run through them and ships off the juice as soon as possible.

It's not a pretty picture when you think of nearly 30 percent of the crop going nowhere special. And yet it doesn't take a genius to see that perhaps there's too much land in grape production—especially if the surplus harvest is destined only for making industrial alcohol and fruit juice. Giraud would personally like the vineyard to total 60,000 hectares, a level it hasn't seen since the 1950s, but which he figures would balance supply and demand. "At that level everyone could earn a living," he says. "It's enough to keep the trader supplied properly and keep the winegrowers in business."

With a sort of fascinated horror, Giraud recalls the incredible production boom of the 1970s, when the Cognac vineyard shot up to more than 110,000 hectares. "But as soon as the oil shocks came along, right when all those new vines started producing, suddenly you couldn't sell the Cognac." Or couldn't afford to, because the price was too low for the grower to accept. The resulting surplus that built up toward a billion bottles was practically unimaginable; even today the "extra" supply of Cognac still sits well above one billion bottles. "And the winegrowers got caught in the middle," Giraud laments, recalling how everyone had thought the sky was the limit and had gone way out on a limb to buy land for vines, cellars, and houses. Then the rug got pulled from underneath them. It added up to some miserable years.

That somber time was further darkened at the start of 1983 by a sharp increase in French state taxes on certain alcohols, Cognac included, which cut consumption of such high-end drinks in half. The heavier taxes didn't apply to beer and wine. Cognac sales in France bogged down as the price of each bottle soared. This made the product "even more elitist," in Giraud's view, than before—and out of the reach of more people. Even today the state tax on each bottle of Cognac amounts to 45 percent of its sale price, or €8 of a typical €18 bottle sold at the store. (Cognacs of higher quality, XO and up, start at around €50 in France, much more than an equivalent whiskey.)

The Cognac industry's bad mood lasted until the Asian miracle came along. Giraud started to see a light at the end of the tunnel. "It was a euphoric time, but also an unreasonable one," he recalls. "All of a sudden we had very high demand coming from a whole group of countries in Southeast Asia. Their economies were doing well, buying power was rising, and people felt more and more like giving themselves luxury products. Cognac, thanks to the excellent efforts of the big houses, suddenly exploded." More often than not, these newly rich consumers wanted a bottle of high-end Cognac. Demand was so strong that there was room not only for the giants of the industry, but also for small producers like Giraud, who stepped in to feed these markets nicely for several years with top-notch, hands-on Cognacs.

When the Asian miracle ended, however, Cognac was once again saddled with tough times. How to stay above water? "By stocking away more and more of your Cognac" until things get better again, Giraud says. "In the end, the Asian boom was a period where we all truly believed we'd emerged from the crisis of the years before. Everyone thought everything was going well. Everyone believed in Santa Claus. Prices here in the Cognac region climbed and climbed. It was crazy. The price of Cognac soared, so did the price of land. And yet it all came to an end in just a few short years. And then we were back where we were before. It was bad for everyone."

As for the years since, in Giraud's view a sort of "rot" has spread through the industry. "Only no one wants to take responsibility for it," he says. Which doesn't make sense to him since he believes that everyone in one way or another has had a hand in what he calls "the weak state of Cognac's affairs," and so "everyone should pitch in to help find solutions." He believes that when the Asian boom came to an end, everyone in the Cognac industry should have gotten together and agreed to cut production. And by that he means the winegrowers should have settled on a deal where everyone would take part of their vineyard out of production. Doing that, he says, would help get the vineyard back to 60,000 hectares. Everyone left would end up better off, he argues, even if each had fewer hectares.

It's important to note that, even as Giraud calls for more cuts, the overall size of the Cognac vineyard has shrunk by about one third since 1976. Since the 1997 Asian crash alone it has shrunk nearly 10 percent if you count the number of hectares devoted only to making wine for Cognac. Naturally, there also has been a deep drop in the number of Cognac-producing vineyards, from nearly 11,000 in 1993 to 6,400 in 2003; that's a fall of more than 40 percent. This shift masks, however, the increasing size of the surviving vineyards; holdings of 10 hectares or more today amount to nearly 80 percent of the vineyard. It also fails to highlight the declining number of people either managing or working the vineyard.

Bigger but fewer vineyards, and a shrinking population of workers are just what Giraud doesn't want to see. But these are trends he and like-minded colleagues can do little about. On the other hand, he can speak out against the rising ceiling on the maximum output of alcohol per hectare, which in 2003 climbed from six hectoliters to seven. Already, even at six hectoliters, the Cognac houses and distillers weren't buying up all the wine available at each harvest, Giraud contends; at a ceiling of seven hectoliters, he says, there will be even more of a surplus of production as some winegrowers reach higher. Meantime, those same winegrowers stand to get less for their product if the wholesale price doesn't hold up. This, in his view, isn't the way to go—a vicious circle from which no one can escape.

And yet Giraud isn't nervous. On the contrary, he tends to float above the scene, keeping watch like the hawks that soar over the vineyards on a hot day. He advocates his positions within the association of independent winegrowers, but above all he takes whatever time he needs to nurture his vines and harvest them with much care—these efforts ultimately paying off in the outstanding quality of the Cognac born on down the road. That kind of attention costs money, for Giraud €5,800 a hectare, or about a third more than it costs others who don't go to the trouble. "You could do it all for as little as €4,300 a hectare, but it certainly wouldn't be the same product, for the simple reason that the vineyard, by its nature, needs much hands-on labor."

It's typical of him to go that extra kilometer out in the vineyard, and it's got to be because he respects this age-old product just about as much as a person can. Giraud will go yet another kilometer when it comes to distilling, starting by leaving the lees in the starter wine, the better to extract all the high-quality bouquet from the Grande Champagne *terroir*. "Those lees are a very important component of the eau-de-vie. We use this method largely because Grande Champagne eau-de-vie has to be aged a long time, which is one of its faults, being slow to mature in the barrel. But by distilling on the lees we can make up for this problem by bringing in intense aromas. It improves the results of the aging process. Everything works together."

Giraud uses two medium-sized stills, one of 1,400 hectoliters and another of 1,800. By his own definition his methods are "classic," with the heart of the *bonne chauffe* emerging at 75 to 60 degrees alcohol, for an average of 70 or so. Making just the right decision on where to cut off the heart is crucial. It's not always at exactly 60 degrees alcohol; he'll also use his nose to tell him what to do, maybe adjust it to 59 degrees, or not; he'll also check its taste and examine its visual aspects. "Down to 60 degrees, you can plainly see that it's pure. But after that, it usually gets fatty." *Gras* is the word he uses in French. Think of old butter and how bad it smells. The very first seconds flowing out can be kept, if still agreeable in odor, since they contain ingredients that help in the aging and lend certain pleasant aromas. But the majority of the seconds, becoming increasingly smelly as the alcohol level declines, are not allowed into the eau-de-vie and instead are put into the next batch of wine at the start of a new round of distillation. (Putting them in the wine allows them to be distilled twice more, first to make a *brouillis* and then for a new *bonne chauffe*; those two steps get rid of the seconds' heaviness.) The tails, which come out at the end, are simply revolting. None of these gets anywhere near his Cognac barrels.

It sounds terribly complicated, but Giraud insists that it isn't really that hard. "It's like cooking. But it's a lot of hours. I work from 4:30 in the morning to 9:30 at night. This can last from three weeks to a month in some years, or a month to a month and a half in other years." And he does it by himself, without any help. "It's not all that physical. On the other hand, once all the distilling is done, I'm really quite happy to get some sleep."

Giraud has four spacious Cognac cellars to put his barrels of eau-de-vie to sleep in and a stock equal to about 715,000 bottles (nearly thirty years' worth of sales at 25,000 bottles a year). He needs to maintain that much slumbering inventory in order to offer a wide range of qualities. The Cognac Paul Giraud dance opens with a VS called Elégance that is a light amber in color, just six years old, and geared for cocktails. This is followed by his VSOP, eight years old, with a powerful grapey bouquet. Next is the Napoléon, fifteen years old, that speaks of vine and acacia blossoms. Then there's the Vieille Réserve, at twenty-five, with aromas of apricots, peaches, and plums. Leading to the Très Rare, from barrels of 1959, that remains fruity but joined by spices like cloves and pepper. The one blend that Giraud does put together is called Héritage, from a short range of years just after World War II.

Under current European rules concerning distillation, Giraud could produce a total of 245 hectoliters of pure alcohol per year, the equivalent of about 88,000 bottles of Cognac. In reality, over the last decade he's been producing only 180 hectoliters of pure alcohol, or about 64,000 bottles, per year. Sales amount to more than 25,000 bottles a year; evaporation from the ensemble of his stock eats up another 25,000 bottles or more; and the equivalent of 11,000 bottles goes to Hennessy and Rémy Martin.

Each year he loses to the angels as much as he sells? That doesn't sound like a good business proposition, but again that's the fact of life with Cognac: it has to be aged and that can't be done without the long exchanges between the liquid in the barrel and the air outside via the oak between.

That makes the angels his number one customer. Back in the real world, however, his number one market is Japan, where he sells 26 percent of his Cognac each year, or 6,500 bottles. France is his second-biggest zone, with another 20 percent of his sales, followed by the United States, with 16 percent. Those three make up nearly two-thirds of his customers, with the rest going to Hungary (14 percent, a big chunk for one country but which he says probably gets resold elsewhere in eastern Europe), Germany (8 percent), and the Netherlands (6), followed by several others for a total of twenty nations.

This diverse set of countries, Giraud says, "keeps me from being vulnerable if one market decides to go south." He recalls how before the crash in Japan he'd been selling one-third of his Cognac there; today, he keeps that percentage significantly lower for a safer bet in his book.

But how does he manage to stay alive in the still-moribund Japanese market? Giraud claims that it's because the customer base he built up during the 1990s is still there, that these fans have remained faithful. He even relates the story of a customer who came all the way from Japan and called him from the train station in Cognac when he arrived looking to buy some bottles. Granted, it's not easy to find Bouteville when you come from the other side of the world; but for Giraud, this type of dogged enthusiasm is typical of the Japanese. And despite the continuing malaise in their country, the Japanese still have a lot of buying power, Giraud says; what's more, they're curious by nature and anxious to acquire the finest products around.

"An independent like me is better adapted to surviving a crisis like the Asian crash than a big Cognac company," Giraud explains. That kind of resilience is vital, he quickly adds, if you're going to survive the Cognac game. You have to believe in it, too, because everything imaginable is stacked against the small player: the tax regime in France that taps the value of his aged stocks-in-waiting, the financial punishment on his export-driven bottom line when the dollar falls and the euro rises, and the impossibility of competing with the industry giants, to name three big problems. Given this, it's almost silly to ask: Doesn't it take an insane amount of courage to stay the course? "Courage? I don't know. But you do have to be a little crazy."

What's even crazier is that Giraud barely makes a living out of this. It's not voluntary pauperism, though, but rather the name of the game: "We don't make a profit because we are always investing in the stocks, in tomorrow. If you want to be in business 25 years from now, it's imperative to invest in your stocks today. And if you want to be able to hand your gift to the next generation, then it's very difficult to make much money in the short-term." But isn't that simply too difficult, year in, year out? He shakes his head no and intones, "My soul is in this."

He plows forward on the hope that the next Paul Giraud, his son of nineteen who is studying political science at a French university, just might take up the reins of the firm. His son is aware that his father is putting away huge stocks for the future, but he doesn't quite understand how it's possible to keep going year after year while making no profits. "My son's very knowledgeable about the product, and he's got a great nose for Cognac," Giraud says, but for the moment he appears to be more interested in doing "something else" besides taking up his father's business. "We'll see what he does. In the meantime, I'll keep going as if he were going to follow in the tradition. I want to leave behind the same thing that was left to me."

FROM THE NURSERY
TO THE GLASS

COGNAC ISN'T JUST GLORIOUS STUFF served in a glass, but the distillate of vast effort by thousands of people. The official numbers light a dim corner about all the "other people" who help make Cognac happen. Many will be surprised to learn, for example, that there are 650 people making bottles, 780 cranking out cartons, boxes, and labels, 630 crafting barrels, 110 perfecting corks and stoppers, 430 delivering Cognac or writing up insurance for it, 25 recycling industry waste products, 110 compiling data like this or perfecting the science of it all at the BNIC, and 335 either working as Cognac brokers or building stills or making harvesting machines. Add workers in associated industries and you get 3,500. Include the 2,500 people who distill Cognac or work in the trading houses, along with about 13,000 winegrowers (an average of 2 people per vineyard is the way it's officially counted), and you get a total of at least 19,000 people in the region laboring for Cognac.

It starts at ground level. Jean-Claude and Yves Sauvaget are master vinemakers north of Cognac in Nercillac, heartland of the nurseries from which many a young vine emerges. You don't have to have a lot of room to raise a lot of the little ones in just a few months. These brothers, allied as Sauvaget Frères, put together several hundred thousand vines each year, assembled from rootstocks and scions. They do it all on just nine hectares.

The rootstocks-in-making are the most unexpected sight. One cradle of these lies on a half-hectare field where vines grow across the ground pell-mell, a knee-deep quilt of green. From this one mat, the Sauvaget brothers can produce 100,000 cuttings, each of which will turn out to be the foundation of a new plant. In all, the Sauvagets have three and a half hectares planted in to-be rootstocks, naturally including some with *Vitis berlandieri* in them for Cognac vineyards. In parallel, the Sauvagets grow thousands of scions on five and a half hectares, comprising seven major varieties—*ugni blanc, folle blanche*, and such—and their clones for all sorts of wines.

The process starts in January or February, when six-meter rootstock cuttings are taken from the dormant mother vine. Then, in March and April, a team of workers is hired to graft freshly harvested scions of about three centimeters each onto 30-centimeter pieces of rootstock, using a machine that makes the splicing work easier, followed by the application of a wax to hold the parts together. By May, the joined plants, which have undergone heating to reactivate the sap to give the plant a starter boost, are put out in fields: as many as 250,000 of them to a hectare, up to 40 plants a meter.

If all goes well, these young plants grow stronger all summer—though a good one-half of them die—before being pulled up in late November when their leaves have dropped and the sap has sunk. Workers check each plant once more to see if the graft is still strong and if the roots are healthy; that done, they rewax the graft a last time, and tag and bundle the vines. The new plants are then stored in cold lockers at the Sauvaget farm until spring, when they are either shipped to distant points in refrigerated trucks or picked up at the source by clients. In any case, the plants are put into the ground by May.

The cycle has lasted fifteen months. Once the plant is growing in the vineyard, it will make grapes as early as its third season. Vines planted in the spring of 2005 will make ten bunches of grapes by the fall of 2007.

The Sauvagets also do a sort of speeded-up version of the normal genesis for pressed clients. The rootstock is harvested in January, grafted to the scion in March, and then sold in June after a sojourn as a potted plant in a hothouse. The process has a good success rate, but the plant is fragile, at least in its first months, though after that it is just as robust as any other.

A single plant made by the fifteen-month process costs the Sauvaget brothers 75 euro cents; they sell it for €1.20. Multiple treatments during the year keep the plants safe from *oïdium*, downy mildew, and black rot. The Sauvagets sell 400,000 vines a year in France, half of which have ended up in the Cognac vineyard. They also have joined with two associates to form Charentes Plantes that exports 2 million vines a year. These plants go to Spain, Italy, Morocco, Turkey, Hungary, England, and so on.

The vineyards of the Cognac region need 2.5 million to 3 million new plants each year as the old ones die or are pulled up for more productive replacements. That is enough plants for 800 to 1,000 hectares in a vineyard totaling nearly 74,000 hectares (including all white and red wine production). The rate of death of these yearling plants is only about 2 percent, or about 60 of the average 3,000 plants crowded onto one hectare.

There are about 120 *pépiniéristes* in the whole Cognac zone creating grafted plants. The Sauvagets situate themselves in the middle of that pack busily creating new generations out of snips of vines and dabs of wax.

When those plants grow up, they'll still get a lot of attention, but it probably won't be all hands-on. Nearly everyone in the Cognac dominion has cast aside the grape bucket and pruner and crossed over to the machines. Hollywood couldn't have scripted this better, for all up and down the hills in early fall, from Grande Champagne to the Atlantic, lumbering mechanical marvels bring in the crop with ridiculous efficiency, as if the entire vineyard were theirs and real pickers mere artifices left to scurry out of the way.

You can stand up inside the jaws of one of these self-propelled monsters and yet find no teeth. Rather, you encounter a tangle of hydraulic gizmos, tubes, and rods, perfected parts that will work together to rattle grapes right off the vine and down to catcher trays and conveyors that will carry the unblemished berries to bins riding on the high shoulders of the behemoth. It looks quite benign, when not working, but you don't want to be a grapevine when one of these very intent devices is coming down the row. There's a roar, a thundering, and above all a startling shaking that practically sets the support wires of the vine to humming an old harvest tune. And when the great yellow or blue or green mouth has passed, the vines look stunned for a while before they shake themselves out of their stupor and resume life as they knew it—only minus their summer children, their grapes.

But this isn't cruelty, mind you, it's the marketplace that wants it that way. Back when they first made these things, the vineyards were literally beaten to death and the havoc was intense as support poles snapped and flew, as mechanical joints popped and spewed oil, as wires got twisted up in the guts of the thing and brought it to repeated, costly halts day after day.

Now that kind of hassle is largely history, thanks to the likes of Gregoire, a Cognac outfit that is an international leader in the manufacture of mechanical grape harvesters. From its beginnings in 1972 under Edmond Gregoire as a maker and repairer of farm equipment, the company expanded in the early 1980s when it developed a pull-type harvester, followed by a self-driven model, which led to further perfections in its grape-picking machinery that sharply increased sales in the late 1980s. By the end of the millennium, Gregoire became part of the Kverneland Group of Norway, the world's number one agriculture implement maker, and now offers twenty-five grape harvesters, a half-dozen especially suited to the Cognac vineyard.

All fit right over the vine, and most are driven from a lofty cab where the winegrower can pilot his machine almost any way he wishes: to glide along higher or lower, lean this way or that, tackle the steep slopes, coast along on cruise control. Most models can be fitted with other contraptions to do other work, including spraying, fertilizing, plowing, and even pruning. A top-of-the-line Gregoire harvester will set you back €100,000.

Gregoire's 160 workers in Cognac roll out 350 to 400 harvesters a year, 200 of which will head into French vineyards. Some 20 of those 200 machines will harvest grapes in Cognac country, whose winegrowers buy only 30 machines a year to join the regional fleet of 1,600. The other 180 Gregoire machines sold in France go to the Loire valley, Alsace, and the Languedoc, amounting to a quarter or so of all harvesters sold domestically each year. As for exports, Gregoire leads in a world market that absorbs 1,300 new machines a year; it sells in the United States, Canada, Australia, New Zealand, South Africa, and in nearly a dozen countries in Europe.

Because the Gregoire-style machine can do its job in just about any vineyard in the world, the company has a strong reputation for versatility. Its directors won't insist that their product is better than another, but they will point out the technology's advantages: you can pick grapes when they

Michel Bonhomme selects a length of oak trunk, usually two to six meters long, from which plenty of barrel staves will be made.

are exactly mature, anytime, day or night, rain or shine, ahead of bad weather or in the throes of it. And it's three times cheaper than hand-harvesting, one machine replacing 80 to 100 people per harvest, saving thousands of euros. Enterprising winegrowers riding a yellow Gregoire monster like that very much as they advance—or are carried—smoothly into the future in a well-heated cab above the shake and tumble of the fray.

Slick harvests done, Cognac also needs a good walk in the woods. The first thing you notice visiting the forest with Michel Bonhomme is all the trees, which seems perfectly natural but is a surprise since clear-cutting is the exception. Instead, trees are grown—nurtured, thinned out from time to time, but largely left alone—and then selected for cutting, one by one, which is just what Bonhomme does. And though he knows every tree in the forest, he only has eyes for oaks, the ones that'll make good Cognac barrels.

First, you have to get your oaks straight. There are two main species: *Quercus pedunculata* and *Quercus sessiliflora*. Pedunculates, the most widely grown oaks in France, have sprawling branches, rough bark, and long acorns. Pedunculates account for 20 percent of all the trees in the nation. Sessiles are taller, more upright, with smooth bark and roundish acorns. These make up 15 percent of the forest. Five minutes into the woods east of Cognac country with Bonhomme, and you can single them out with no trouble.

Pedunculate oak is the big favorite for Cognac *fûts*, since it has a wide
grain, of three to four millimeters. This porous wood allows air to enter
the barrel and transform eau-de-vie into the drink everyone loves; it also
imparts a strong dose of tannin, a smoky-red color, and a vanilla taste.
Sessile oak is also used for Cognac (and many wine barrels) whenever a
fine grain—just one millimeter—is desired. This wood gives up its tannin
less easily, making for an amber eau-de-vie, and lends flavors of cloves and
coconut. Cognac houses pick one kind of oak over the other, depending
on customers' tastes.

Bonhomme has been buying trees for nearly thirty years, first for a
sawmill in central France, and over the last eight years for Taransaud,
a leader among Cognac country's barrel makers. For Cognac and wine
barrels, he buys only the first few meters of the base of the tree, a log called
a *grume*. Finding the right trunks is like shopping: Bonhomme receives
catalogs from the state forestry service, studies the lots being sold, visits
the section where the trees for sale are already marked, and does his magic.
This consists of a lot of looking at the oak in question, circling it, measuring it, poking it. Tiny defects in the bark called *picots* are simply indis-
tinguishable to the neophyte even when Bonhomme puts his finger
right on one. But buy a *grume* with *picots* and you'll later discover a dark
needle of a knot running to the middle of the trunk, spoiling the wood's
purity. A *grume* needs to be as near to perfect as possible; defective wood
won't pass for *douelles*, or staves: They'll either weaken the barrel or make
it ugly.

So Bonhomme stomps through the forest seeking ideal trees with very
straight bark, which is a window onto the alignment of the grain within.
There are many acceptable candidates, believe it or not. For most Cognac
barrels, you'll want a pedunculate oak about 12 meters tall and 50 centimeters in diameter at the base; that's a tree about 125 years old. For other
Cognac *fûts* and for wine barrels, of which Taransaud makes quite a few,
you'll find a sessile oak maybe 25 meters tall and, again, at least 50 centimeters across, a tree that will be more than two hundred years old. A length of
trunk at the bottom of the tree, from just a couple of meters to a half-
dozen, will split into plenty of nice staves; the rest of the tree goes to other
industries. Armed with a pocket computer, Bonhomme goes through the
woods calculating the total volume of wood he'd like. Then, on auction day,
he bids on specific tree trunks against a crowd of other log buyers.

Taransaud doesn't buy pedunculate oaks directly, but via another company that harvests and readies the wood; Bonhomme does, however, buy

plenty of sessile oaks for his company. All the trees, of either variety, are culled from sprawling forests in central France—in the Limousin, the Tronçais, and environs—the oakiest region of the country. Which means that Bonhomme drives around a lot—thousands of kilometers a year, from one forest to another, and walks around a lot, too, inspecting the army of silent gray-black trunks awaiting their noble fate.

The woods is obviously Bonhomme's favorite place, and he's never gotten lost. He knows his tree history, too, and will tell you that France's forests today cover as much territory as they did in the Middle Ages. That's because the forests have been respected and cared for as a valuable resource, except for a few hiccups, through the centuries since Colbert's time. Puffing on his pipe, this fortysomething who says he never worries about the weather but always takes his rubber boots, remarks, "Just like wine and Cognac have their story, the forest has its long story, too. It's unfortunate, but people don't really know much about the forest and how it works." Occasionally he'll take a group from the Taransaud barrel factory to the forest just to show them. They always come back fascinated, Bonhomme says, and spewing out *pédonculé* and *sessile* like they've always known.

Alain Dallier likes what Bonhomme does because he knows that the wood that shows up at the factory in Merpins, outside Cognac, has had his friend's expert eye upon it. It arrives as rough boards called *merrains* that were split vertically out of Bonhomme's *grumes* and that will dry outdoors, stacked up high all around the factory, for two to three years, to leach out the bitterest tannin. Once the *merrains* are ready, Dallier brings all his many years at Taransaud to bear, overseeing the quality of production from start to finish: as the *merrains* are trimmed and planed into *douelles*; as the 30 to 37 *douelles* of varying widths are laid out side by side until they make a neat ensemble (256 centimeters wide for a 350-liter Cognac barrel); as the set of *douelles* are stood up and fitted at the top end into metal rings, making a tight-waisted wooden skirt that is then put over a fire until the *douelles* soften enough to bend with the rings slipped over their lower ends; as the inside walls of the now fully shaped barrel are toasted by a second fire in a process called *bousinage*, the better to free up natural aromas in the wood; as the tops and bottoms of the barrels are put into place, the boards conjoined with rushes from the Netherlands and Portugal and the rims sealed to the barrel with flour dough; as each barrel is put through leakage tests, using both cold and hot water; and as the barrels are packaged in paper and plastic for shipping, but only after a last

An artisan places the oak staves into the first of a series of metal
rings as he begins forming a new Cognac barrel.

check to be sure the toasting was done like the client wanted and to be
certain there are absolutely no defects.

That's far more than enough for one worker to supervise, but Dallier
says he can count on each person on the line to be sharp. There's no doubt
each worker has just as much on his plate as Dallier does. The sweat-
covered laborer who toasts the barrels, for instance, cranks out 140 units
a day; the fire raging in his face all day is well over 500 degrees centigrade,
and each *fût* can weigh up to 70 kilograms. Dallier keeps his eye on every
link in the chain, since more often than not each worker knows just one
job; it takes an expert overseer to make a good barrel emerge from all this
hands-on action by 175 or so people shaping wood in a grand fury of
hammering and fire.

In the end, 45,000 oak barrels come out of the factory each year,
10,000 of those for Cognac (the majority going to Hennessy) and the rest
for wine. Sixty percent of production goes to Argentina, Australia, Chile,
Italy, New Zealand, South Africa, Spain, and the United States. In France,
its barrels are used for Bordeaux, Burgundy, and Côtes du Rhône. Annual
sales are about €30 million and have been rising steadily for years.

Dallier has years of top-notch work under his belt: in 2002 he was awarded a gold medal by the government after thirty-seven years of plying his trade. That followed his silver medal in 1985, after 20 years. He's hoping for the grand gold medal soon to mark four decades at Taransaud.

It's been a long road, and many things have changed, he'll tell you, especially as machines began doing a lot of the work, from shaping the staves to bending them into the desired form. The number of hand tools used in making or repairing a barrel has fallen from ten to three, Dallier says, since he began working there. But that doesn't mean the barrels aren't as good as they used to be; on the contrary, they're only getting better, in his view.

And that's a long view: He's been here since age fourteen, when he went to school part of the day and worked at his cooper's bench the rest of the time. There are other kids in the workshop today learning just like he did, repairing barrels, making new ones entirely by hand, getting a first taste of the trade. When Dallier was seventeen, he started getting paid by the piece, and he could make maybe three new barrels a day and also repair older ones, to earn the equivalent of just €50 a month. And yet he stuck it out, learning every position on the line. His favorite in winter was *bousinage*, the better to stay warm. In summer, few men here wear a shirt. A day in August easily makes it an inferno on the factory floor, and as soon as the seven-hour shift is done, the place empties out. Except for maybe Dallier, still scurrying around checking a chart, a tally, measuring tape and pencil in hand, eyes wide open for anything that might make a barrel anything less than oaken perfection.

"I've always heard," he says, "that the Cognac region produces the best barrels in the world." You have no doubt that it makes him happy to know this—rightfully so after watching over those very barrels since 1965.

But you wouldn't need the barrels if you didn't have the stills to make the eau-de-vie in the first place, and it's Chalvignac that makes most of the giants that make the Cognac: shiny copper machines that look so complex it's easy to imagine them hurtling through outer space. The brain watching over the production of these elegant contraptions is Olivier Desbrée. When this plant manager is not on his cell phone with a customer discussing some widget in need of fine-tuning, he's probably hurrying along between the two workshops where Chalvignac cranks out its reddish Verne-like moonships.

The facts: It takes a metric ton of copper to make a Charentais-type still. Four months will go by between your order and its delivery, after which it will take another month to set it up. The main pot where you put the starter wine, which has a volume of 3,000 liters but can't legally be filled beyond 2,500 liters at a time, weighs 500 kilograms; the towering wine-warmer another 350 kilograms. The sides of the central pot are 2.4 millimeters thick, while the bottom, closest to the gas burner, is 13 millimeters thick. The cooling coil winds down through 6,000 liters of water that ranges from 75 degrees centigrade at the top to 9 degrees centigrade at the bottom; if this curving pipe were stretched out it would be 75 meters long. The only part of a still that's not copper is the stainless steel basin that holds the cooling coil. You'll pay €50,000 to €60,000 for your unit, installed.

Desbrée has been in the thick of Chalvignac's business for eight years, the last few months as manager of its sites in Jarnac-Champagne, about 20 kilometers south of Cognac, and in Merpins, just southwest of the city. He'll graciously walk you through the process of making a still, and you'd understand it all if you could only hear him over the banging. Basically, the workers beat the hell out of the copper to shape it the way they want, leaving jillions of dimples to adorn the bulbous walls. To make a main pot, for instance, they put a flat sheet of copper over a big cement mold that looks like a gigantic soup bowl and then whack it into the shape of the container. The other big copper parts are fashioned in much the same way, and then they'll use buffers to get every surface clean inside and out. Copper is a lovely color when it's shiny; it's dull and dark when it's not. And if there's one thing that Desbrée really insists on, it's the look of his stills.

Visit a newly installed Chalvignac distillery and you'll observe Desbrée at his post-sale best: studying valves and meters, peering at display screens, looking into tubes, touching drainpipes to check temperatures, and gazing at steam rising out of mysterious pipes. It's not like the old days anymore, he'll tell you: these contraptions are nearly all computer controlled. You just have to tap in some basic data and the electronic brains of the thing will run the show, hour after hour, day after day. It takes the errors out of the process, especially as regards the timing of the various cuts that have to be made to shunt aside some emerging alcohols in favor of others.

Even better, a Chalvignac still almost lasts forever, or about thirty years at least, even if you use it every winter. How do you know if your still needs an overhaul? You call in Chalvignac to measure the thickness of the walls of your pot, for instance. If the ultrasonic device shows it's down to

1.5 millimeters (from the original 2.4), then the pot has to be remade entirely. This is where Chalvignac makes its money, too: repairing or refurbishing 400 to 450 units a year. That's a lot of fiddling around, but it's vital to the company, all the more because Chalvignac, given the labor involved, makes only 5 to 8 new stills in those same twelve months. Sales of both new and remade stills total 30 to 40 a year, with 80 percent remaining in France (mostly in Cognac country, where there are some 3,200 functioning stills), the rest going to Spain, Peru, the United States, Canada, Turkey, Thailand, Japan, and Russia.

To Desbrée, the only danger lurking in this neatly functioning system is the future. He's not so sure that the up-and-coming generation will learn the art of perfection as it has been taught for decades. Heating copper parts to shape and form them, after all, is anything but straightforward. It can't be taught in a few days, no more than a Cognac can be made overnight. Perhaps the modernization of the process—with all its bells and whistles, meters and valves—will draw in a new generation of curious artisans. In any case, Chalvignac will surely make it a point to invest the time it needs to pass on its traditions of hands-on precision to the next batch of still makers ready to take a bunch of copper and make beautiful spaceships.

Likewise, without a bottle to put it in, Cognac can't travel far in today's frenetic commercial universe, and it's quite fitting that a world-class glassmaker has one of its biggest plants sitting right on the edge of the city of Cognac. The Saint-Gobain facility, with its three smokestacks, automated machines, and sprawling storage parks, has been here since the 1960s. The history of glassmaking in Cognac, of course, goes back much farther.

When Cognac houses began using bottles to get their product to market, during the great Cognac boom of the mid-nineteenth century, they relied on artisans who blew each bottle. Then Claude Boucher's invention of a machine by which compressed air could be injected into the molten glass replaced the work of the glassblower. Thus mass-production bottlemaking was born in Cognac by the close of the nineteenth century.

Selling Cognac in a bottle has many advantages in addition to making it easy to ship. It's readily visible to the consumer, the Cognac maker's name is right there on the label, and the shape of the bottle can be made to fit the market: slender, feminine bottles, say, for clients who want a sweeter, lighter, and younger Cognac; stockier, heavier bottles for drinkers who want richness, *rancio*, and the sensation of age. The range of bottles is as varied as the shells upon the seashore as each glassmaker strives to win over customers' hearts and minds. It is no secret, for instance, that some people actually buy their Cognac because of the bottle, and not so much for what's in it. Women like elegant bottles, men pick up weightier ones; young people want flashy styles, older drinkers stick with tradition. Some consumers couldn't care less about the bottle yet want the finest Cognac: these people like a simple bottle with a simple label. Many drinkers, however, prefer the unique marriage of a great bottle and a great Cognac.

Saint-Gobain, which in the 1920s became a majority shareholder in the company run by Boucher's sons, replaced the old Boucher glassmaking facility with a modern one in the early 1960s. The factory consolidated the production of the Cognac site with two other glass facilities in the region. Cognac was chosen for the Saint-Gobain site because of the expertise of the workers there and its central location to serve markets all over western France. In addition, the basic element of glass—pure sand— is found nearby in the Landes, south of Bordeaux along the Atlantic, in vast quantities.

Myriam Maugin, plant manager of Saint-Gobain in Cognac, has a vigorous enthusiasm for the products that emerge from her factory. She has been in the glass business for a number of years, running at least one other plant before coming here, and since 2003 has been making her mark in Cognac. With her first breath, she explains how the star of the line is glass called *extra blanc*, and then lunges to a cabinet to pull out a sample bottle. She holds it up to the light to show its vaguely white sheen. "Look, no colors," she exudes. "The customers don't want that. They want it pure."

Here again, then, is another industry associated with Cognac doing precisely refined work to make the perfectly colorless bottle to go with the perfection of the drink. Saint-Gobain succeeds at it because there's so little iron in the sand it gets from the Landes. More iron, and you'd get gray, rose, and blue hues to the bottle, especially in its thicker parts, where the light refracts more. These are not colors that most masters of Cognac have in mind. Above all, they want the customer to see the true color of the eau-de-vie, untinted, unadulterated by the bottle. Saint-Gobain at Cognac devotes one of its three huge ovens to making the molten soup for this type of glass, which can be molded into just about any shape you can imagine.

Note that Rémy Martin is one of the prominent exceptions to the colorless rule: it has often preferred dark green bottles for its Cognac. And Rémy Martin isn't alone; there are other Cognac houses that want this style, which lends a certain eliteness to the bottle, gold lettering and all. But most Cognac makers have made the switch, since the mid-1990s, to high-end colorless glass. Before, most Cognac bottles were typically light green, sporting something called *la teinte Cognac*, the Cognac hue.

Other customers for Saint-Gobain's *extra blanc* include bottlers of *rosé* in southern France, of sweetish white Bordeaux, and of Pineau (a pleasant Charente specialty that mixes Cognac and *moût*—the must that otherwise would have been made into Cognac—for a red or white *apéritif* of 16 to 22 degrees alcohol drunk chilled or on ice). Makers of spirits like vodka and whiskey use these kinds of very clear, almost crystalline, bottles, too.

Two other elements that go into making a colorless bottle are chalk, which this factory gets from the Savoie region of eastern France, and sodium carbonate, imported from the United States, such that 70 percent of the mixture heading into the oven is sand, 15 percent is chalk, 12 percent is sodium carbonate, and the rest a few other chemicals. The other two ovens at Saint-Gobain's Cognac site produce green glass, and what is notable about these units is that 80 percent of the primary material consists of recycled glass, making this factory one of the largest recyclers around. Unlike plastic and similar manufactured items, glass can be melted and remade an infinite number of times. All told, the computer-operated production line at Saint-Gobain's Cognac factory marches out nearly 2 million bottles a day. Four hundred people work here, making 300,000 metric tons of glass a year.

This is more than enough for all the Cognac in the world, easily. But Maugin isn't resting on her company's laurels. As ever, shaping the product is everything. And that means shaping it to keep the Cognac houses happy, for no client is a permanent client. "Nothing in this business is a given," this young manager intones. "Not even being located right here in Cognac guarantees anything. You have to fight to keep all your business." Maugin seems like a fighter who'll go the distance to be sure that the hundreds of thousands of bottles emerging under her watchful eye are perfect enough to get filled up with the Cognac of Hennessy, Martell, or Camus and all the other outfits that bottle their liquid inventions in transparence.

Note that you won't find a screw cap on any one of them. Every bottle of Cognac has a cork, and it's likely that the one you pull out is made by Les Bouchages Delages. Made isn't the right word: *finished* is better. The Delages factory east of Cognac takes the basic cork stopper and dresses it up to be just as recognizable as the bottle of Cognac it goes into.

The raw material arrives from big-time suppliers in Portugal and Italy, in standard shape and size. Teams of workers verify each and every cork as it comes in, and it's not a few hundred but tens of thousands they check every day for the slightest faults. A cork must be smooth and have no dents or dimples. Then each is sealed with a coat of paraffin. Air-tightness is important to Cognac, if only to halt leakage and evaporation since the distilled contents of the bottle, once opened, don't change much, unlike wine. The cork can't impart a "corky" taste to a Cognac unless you leave the bottle lying down, which isn't the way to store Cognac.

Delages does much fine-tuned work: it takes these hundreds of thousands of carefully monitored corks and glues a graspable cap onto each one. The caps can be plastic, wood, glass, porcelain, metal, or combinations. Everything is in the final look. The metal ones, usually gold-colored, go mostly on high-end bottles for a luxurious look. Delages also makes plastic seals to decorate the fronts of some bottles, each shaped to look like wax and stamped with the type of Cognac: Napoleon, XO, VSOP. Some corks are retouched a final time to make light incisions wherever the surface isn't ultrasmooth to keep bits of cork from flaking off and getting into the drink.

In one year, the seventy-five employees of this small plant crank out 100 million stoppers. Sales amount to €10 million a year, with half of the factory's output going to the Cognac industry. The rest is for the whiskey, Armagnac, Calvados, rum, vodka, and wine businesses—and even some for the perfume world. About a quarter of all production is sold outside France. Delages's star customers include Camus, Allied Domecq (owner of Courvoisier), Diageo, Hennessy, Pernod Ricard, Rémy Cointreau—and Chanel.

Delages's survival amid the recent downturn in the Cognac market is a testament to the company's philosophy of diversified markets. The Cognac houses alone buy tens of millions of corks a year, but even when Cognac heads south, there are always the other drinks industries that will still need stoppers. In business for more than sixty years and a leader in its domain, Delages has a comfortable range of clients making all kinds of popular drinks, each bottle of which will always need someone to put a cork in it.

And slap a label on it, which leads to the observation that it's human nature to sometimes choose a bottle for whatever appears on the little piece of paper stuck on its front. Given that all Cognac is at least passable, you can't go too far wrong simply judging it on its *étiquette*. But Litho Bru, Cognac country's top printing company, doesn't leave such things to chance. It makes sure you'll fall for the look: for the simple elegance of a Hine label with its stark red lettering, say, or for the historically charming 1610 engraving of the town of Jarnac on a bottle of Delamain. It takes notions of luxury and art—resting stags, ancient castles, uplifted weapons, and so on—and turns them into silver and gold symbols of great Cognacs instantly recognized around the world. And it appeals to the sense of touch by embossing practically every label, be it a gold-and-red Rémy Martin XO Special, a gray-and-gold Ragnaud-Sabourin Cognac Premier Cru, or a yellow-and-blue Courvoisier VS. Everything Litho Bru does is fashioned to draw the eye and the hand to the bottle to caress it—and then take it home.

Of course, it isn't easy to make all that click. Above all, it takes time, and the savoir-faire of many generations of printers. The deepest foundations of Litho Bru go back to the Golden Age of Cognac, when Imprimerie Bru was founded in Jarnac in 1865; the other branch, Lithographie Nouvelle, was established in Cognac in 1936. The two came together in 1993 to form a company with three work sites, 140 employees, and €12 million in yearly sales. No one else in the region comes close to matching Litho Bru's size and expertise, and so it's natural that the big Cognac houses would turn to a prince of printers to make the blazon upon which the eye will first fall.

It follows that Hennessy is Litho Bru's number one client, which is just fine with François Berland, managing director and grandson of the man who founded Lithographie Nouvelle. Berland is even more proud of the fact that his printing company has the rest of the Top 10 as its clients, too, which means that just about any label you read on a bottle of Cognac was cranked out by Litho Bru. Working with market leaders, Berland says, isn't always a walk in the park, however; they can bring huge pressure to bear on the details of a print run, and they love to change their minds often. Color choices are always the hard part, he says, and you get the distinct feeling that he's been through many long meetings about tints. But in the next breath Berland will tell you that it's all part of the game: "Trying to find the right balance." That is, trying hard not to say no to the all-important client, but to adapt. "We're an industrial concern now, but our methods are artisanal. And if we're going to hold on to our clients, we have to remain a hands-on company."

Litho Bru has one hundred clients in the area: half of all the printing business with the Cognac houses, and a good chunk of the regional Pineau and wine business. Elsewhere, Litho Bru has a broad range of clients in Champagne—Piper-Heidsieck, Bollinger, Jeanmaire—and also works with Pernod Ricard, notably on labels for its anisette liqueur. It also focuses on whiskey and scotch labels: Knockando, Dunbar, Glen Turner, and the likes. In all, Litho Bru has two hundred clients in France, Ireland, Scotland, the United States, Spain, Belgium, and a handful of East European nations.

From its three plants, Litho Bru churns out 2 million labels a day, or about 500 million a year. The paper for all that comes from various international sources, to the tune of 500 to 1,000 metric tons a year. Labels range in price from one-quarter of one euro cent for the most basic, to €1 each for the middle range, to several euros for those that adorn big items, like the 15-liter Champagne bottles that celebrating Formula One victors like to pop. A label can be modern and self-adhesive, or it can be traditional, glued to the bottle by hand the old-fashioned way. A lot of Litho Bru's work, in fact, is manual, despite the opposite impression given by machine-filled factory floors; teams of people leaf constantly through piles of printed materials to check for defects: misalignments, color faults, absent elements.

While labels account for 70 percent of the company's production, Litho Bru devotes the rest of its printing to the paper boxes and tubes in which bottles are sold. Here, it shines best in Champagne: silver and gold foil covering the container are de rigueur, and the thicker the embossing the better. Everything is shaped for a feeling of uniqueness. Some Cognac houses will even number individual bottles to augment the effect of creating one-of-a-kind products in a special, limited series.

Of course, you need an actual box or tube for the bottle, and here's where Etuis Cognac comes in. This maker of paper containers, owned by the Otor group, a world leader in cardboard, is the principal supplier of boxes and tubes to Litho Bru and one of its major clients as well. Etuis Cognac will take high-tech printing by Litho Bru and literally wrap it around its own boxes, or *étuis*, like paper around a gift. Or it might simply make virgin boxes and tubes that Litho Bru will finish up itself. Like Litho Bru, Etuis Cognac works to guide the client's choices about the design of the box itself—from its cardboard foundation to its polyester, aluminum, or paper covering upon which all the information and design elements are printed.

Etuis Cognac is the number one maker in France of containers for wine and spirits, with the Cognac industry being its biggest client, followed by Champagne and whiskey. Orders can range from a tiny one hundred for some clients to as many as six million for others. Johan Levaufre, managing director, watches over all that production: 50 million units a year, 25 to 30 million of which are for Cognac. His clients include all the major Cognac houses, for a total of 20 million boxes each year, and a number of smaller ones as well.

It takes one hundred employees working on five production lines for Etuis Cognac to make that many containers. Sales amount to €14 million a year, the basic Cognac box going for 30 euro cents, and the container for a carafe-like XO bottle fetching 90 euro cents. The price depends on the number of operations each box requires: a Champagne box might have eleven mechanical steps in its production, a basic Cognac box only three. In all, Etuis Cognac uses something like 6,000 metric tons of cardboard a year. A sister company, Otor Godard, also located in Cognac, uses another 54,000 tons of cardboard a year making boxes for various industries, especially food. All of the cardboard comes from factories in the Otor group, which produces 600,000 metric tons of cardboard a year, of which about half go to units in the group like Etuis Cognac. The Otor group has twenty-seven production sites and annual sales of €400 million.

This is all, of course, a far cry from the days of yore when bottles of Cognac traveled in wooden crates. Now Cognac makes its way around the world in complex and often terribly fancy boxes put together by the likes of Levaufre, who gained his expertise over seven years as an officer in the French merchant marine. That might seem to have nothing to do with making a pretty box, but working on the high seas with intricate machinery and teaching other officers how to use and maintain all that hardware gave Levaufre the skills he needed to run the Etuis Cognac factory. And keep it cruising ahead, as across the high seas of commerce, he does—a million boxes a week, no less. That's nearly five hundred a minute, all coming out in a blur, but each one a work of art worthy of housing the finest eau-de-vie around.

If what goes on the outside is so important, the stuff on the inside counts for no less. The Pecner company cooks up a couple of ingredients you probably wouldn't have thought of as lurking in the bottle—and they're both sweet. Most people turn up their noses when they hear the word additive, but the all-natural caramel colorant and sugar syrup that Pecner makes are both as old as the hills. They've been going into Cognac for decades, and given the way masters shape the drink, they'll be around a long time.

Olivier Drounau, who runs Pecner with his brother, Charles-Emmanuel, proudly tells you how an ancestor, Georges Pecner, created the company in 1878 in Cognac. Today the factory is located in Merpins, where many Cognac-related firms operate, from barrel makers to shippers. Here, too, are many new Cognac warehouses, now that the big houses are having second thoughts about keeping their volatile stocks within Cognac. The industrial park at Merpins, far from dense urban housing, is surely safer.

But Pecner is no giant in the accessories park of the Cognac world. It's a quiet, not-so-large outfit with a devotion to time-tested traditional methods. No chemicals here, you find out quickly. One hundred percent artisanal methods, too. You almost expect to find a crowd of monks behind the factory door—and then you do, in a way. The factory seems far too big for the small group of workers watching over a few fat copper pots parked under dark vent hoods. Here, in a sort of caricature of the witches' brew, pure sugar—beet sugar or cane sugar—is being slowly cooked down into a thick, brown goo. The air reeks of burned sugar, and the floor is sticky with spilled blotches of caramel. Big, solemn men in blue overalls wield wooden spoons as tall as they are to turn the bubbling, darkening potion.

"The company got started," Drounau says, "while the Cognac industry was completing its switch from barrels to bottles for shipping eau-de-vie. Because Cognac is a blend, it's up to each cellar master to join eaux-de-vie of different ages and qualities to make a consistent product batch after batch. Everyone knows that the assembly of Cognacs focuses essentially on taste. But with the wide variety of eaux-de-vie going into any one Cognac in order to get that same taste every time, it's very difficult to make it come out the same color every time." Hence the need for a modern witches' brew: the colorant. Only this one won't kill you, or turn you into an ogre. What it will do is convince you, subconsciously, that the bottle you're taking down from the shelf at the store is the right choice. "We know today that the color of a product plays a primary role in the consumer's mind," Drounau explains. "You don't want the shopper to go into the store and find that the Cognac he bought the last time now has a different color! So Cognac firms use our additives, to get exactly the right tint, to create a visual consistency to go along with the consistency of the Cognac's taste."

Who would have thought Cognac had additives? And yet it does, if only in the smallest of ways. The dose of caramel is like a drop in the ocean of a bottle. And you can't taste it. Strict rules prevent a dose of caramel high enough that you could pick it out; and even if for some reason you did, it wouldn't be a sweet taste but a burned one, for this sugar has been well cooked. Thus there is a natural tendency, backed by law and common sense, that keeps the dosage of caramel in a bottle of Cognac to a minimum.

"Besides, you don't have the right by law to give another bouquet to an eau-de-vie," Drounau explains, "or to bring to it any other flavors than those which would arise in it naturally." It follows that additives can't be used to "repair" a Cognac: if it is no good because it came from a bad wine or was poorly distilled, then no amount of sugar or other additive can undo the damage. Winegrowers and distillers know this—and so make every effort to create their Cognac right the first time, since there is no going back.

Pecner sells 200,000 liters of caramel colorant a year. About three-quarters of that goes to the Cognac industry, where just about everyone uses it. "But it's vital to remember," Drounau adds, "that it's not our caramel that colors Cognac. It serves only to 'finish' the tint." The basic red-brown color of Cognac, of course, comes from the long aging process in barrels.

Pecner's highly concentrated caramel, which in its pure state looks a lot like molasses, has other uses, too. "It can go in any other spirits that age in barrels, like rum, Calvados, Armagnac, whiskey, brandies," Drounau notes. "These, and the Cognac houses, are our major clients. We also work with the food and pharmaceutical industries. We even once had a client who bought our colorant to use in perfume-making." Caramel is the most widely used food and drink colorant in the world. It's in almost every soda, for instance. But it's there strictly to color, not to sweeten.

Pecner's other big product, sugar syrup, is used by cellar masters to round off the alcoholic punch of Cognac during the assembly process, especially when younger Cognacs are dominant in the blend. (Most older Cognacs usually don't need any of this attenuating substance, being nearly perfect already.) Again, it's pure, natural sugar, with nothing else added but water. The doses of this additive are significantly higher than for caramel, and so the drinker will get a sensation (but not the taste) of sweetness, yet almost without really noticing it because the Cognac has been smoothed out, tamped down, and made all the more balanced.

Most of Pecner's clients prefer to use sugar syrup made from brown cane sugar. The firm also makes flavorings for other drink products, including the growing range of drinks that mix Cognac with fruit juices and such.

Caramel and sugar syrups, along with demineralized water to "reduce" Cognac to a lower alcohol level during the long march down from its birth at 72 degrees, are the three common substances that Cognac makers are allowed to add to their distilled eau-de-vie as they see fit. Another additive that is tolerated, and regulated by the industry watchdog, is an infusion of oak. Pecner uses oak chips from local barrel makers, the better to use exactly the wood in which the Cognac will be aged, that it steeps in hot water to get varying strengths of a potion called *boisé*. It sells 30,000 liters of it a year, mostly to houses in the Cognac zone but also to winemakers elsewhere. Added to a Cognac, *boisé* imparts extra tannin to the drink, giving it an "oakier," more aged taste. Again, this kind of additive is used to "finish" a Cognac, to shape it for the market; you wouldn't use an oak infusion to hurry up and "replace" the aging done in the barrel. Self-respecting Cognac houses wouldn't even think of doing that, in any case. Instead, they work hand-in-hand with the likes of Pecner to get the colors, tones, and aromas of their Cognacs just right, bottle after bottle, year after year.

Deep time is everything in this business, and so the industry can't rightly do without specialists like timekeepers, auditors of the past, present, and future. Francis Audemard is one of these Cognac broker-cum-professors who may be tacking toward retirement but only after earning the unofficial title of "best of the best" of the *courtiers*. If you wanted to know the ins and outs of the industry over the past forty years, Audemard is the expert. And no wonder: He's been at the top of his form all that time, passing judgment on Cognacs, pointing the way when it's not right, and teaching others what it means to be a master taster, expert buyer, or both.

Audemard works for no particular master, no one house, no one winegrower, but rather a tight galaxy of people in the business who need his expert nose or memory of certain stocks of Cognac. The person coming to see him might be a *bouilleur du cru* (a winegrower who distills his own production) looking to find a buyer for his eau-de-vie; or it might be a *négociant* seeking a certain Cognac, "for example, a 1914 Grande Champagne that a house was looking for and that I located for them" to include in a blend. In either case, Audemard plays the middleman role, "like a mailman, putting two people in contact with each other," but only after carefully verifying the quality of the message, the eau-de-vie.

Distillation is an intricate process, and distillers
will often call on experts like Francis Audemard
to help them get just the right results.

Audemard spends another good part of his time dispensing advice to a
few dozen clients. At a winegrower's *chai*, he is often present throughout
the distillation process, ready to help during this often delicate operation,
the better to capture the elusive heart of the eau-de-vie. Other times a distiller will drop off samples of his new eau-de-vie with Audemard—at the
tobacco shop next to his office in Cognac when he's not in—to get his
impressions.

There are two kinds of errors, in Audemard's view. One has its source
in the quality of the primary material: the wine. But once it's been distilled a first time, "You can't do anything about it because the next pass
through the still is only going to concentrate the error further. You can't
go backwards." The other type of error—such as overrich, highly aggressive tones that can crop up in the first pass through the still—is easier to
correct: "Here, you can adjust things, do the second pass differently, eliminate more of the heads or seconds or whatever. The goal is to create an
eau-de-vie that is perfect, error-free, and one that includes that widest
possible palette of flavors."

With a *négociant*, who could very well be from a big house and who just might be one of his former students, Audemard will try to work out the source of some problem with a Cognac, usually some taste that has cropped up in the distillation or even in the aging process. And because people know that Audemard is the man to see to get solutions, they will recommend his services to others and so on, allowing him to build up a sizable clientele.

Audemard the broker makes his living off the buyers of the eaux-de-vie he proposes (he will deal only with flawless stuff) as the middleman of the operation, and the higher the price he obtains from them, the more he earns. The sellers don't pay him a fee, and Audemard doesn't bill them either; instead, they might show their appreciation with a "little something" at year-end "if they like the work I did for them" selling their product.

Audemard might also be sought out by someone wishing to sell a vineyard and its stock of Cognac; in that case, he goes in, inventories the lot, and assesses its quality and value. That kind of advice is primary, both to the seller and the potential buyer of the farm and its old, treasured casks.

He also spends much of the year teaching professional tasters from Cognac houses of all sizes, as well as other *courtiers*, or young students of enology envisioning a career in the business.

With the professionals, Audemard helps fine-tune their sense of the errors that can creep into the distillation and teaches them how to rectify them with the distiller. To the younger crowd, he explains the aromas of each growth and of each stage of the distillation, as well as the subtleties of the extraction of tannin and vanillin from the oak barrels, the gradual digestion of these aromas by the eau-de-vie, and the slow oxidation of this maturing drink as it slowly develops its inimitable *rancio*.

In every instance, Audemard is the guide, the linchpin, and there are probably only fifty people in the whole region doing anything even closely related. And maybe only two or three in that little crowd have the years of experience to rise to the top of the class of *courtiers*. Of course, Audemard wouldn't admit that or vaunt his powers. Asked if he enjoys his job, he smiles and replies sidewise, "I never learned how to do anything else!"

Which is not true, of course, for Audemard is also a master yachtsman who plies the western coast of France. His office in Cognac has a case of trophies won racing with and against other lovers of yachting, including some big names in the Cognac business. But beyond the ebb and flow of the pleasant Atlantic, Audemard's soul is firmly anchored in the heart of

Cognac country. And when he has the chance to come across something like the 1914 Grande Champagne he found the other day for a client, he knows he's found the best. "I can't help but imagine the guy, some guy, back ninety years ago who was out in the field and cut the grapes that went into the bottle. It's thanks to him that I get to taste such a marvel. Pure pleasure. Perfection."

The taste of the drink finds a happy partner in the taste of food that accompanies it. Bringing the two together in high style is Françoise Barbin-Lecrevisse, by far the number one cookbook writer of Cognac country, with a half-dozen titles, including such popular tomes as *La Cuisine de Cognac et du Pineau* (published by L'Hydre, in Dordogne). Culinary marvels that include Cognac aren't so commonplace as that, but the first one that comes to Barbin-Lecrevisse's mind is a concoction called Brandy Butter. It's a soft butter whipped with sugar and Cognac and used in desserts, for example as a topping on apple pie or to accompany Christmas pudding. Another Cognac-based dish that Barbin-Lecrevisse loves to point out is her *Moules en Salade*, a plate of steamed mussels cooled and slathered in a Cognac-rich sauce. Or perhaps *Magret de Canard au Miel*, sliced duck breast mixed with pieces of cooked apple and served with a glazelike sauce of shallots, Cognac, orange juice, and honey. And then there is an American favorite: *Brownies aux Noix*, in which Barbin-Lecrevisse has found a good home for Cognac, a nut-filled dessert, adding the brandy to the melting chocolate at the start; she notes that a glass of old Cognac goes quite nicely with this.

Barbin-Lecrevisse, who has worked for years in and around the Cognac business, including a long stint at Courvoisier, has never wanted to be a professional chef, even though her appreciative dinner guests have often urged her to open a restaurant. Instead, this self-effacing culinary talent decided to be an ambassador for the many fine products from this part of France, especially for Cognac. "My books aren't really about what I've found, about my own views, but rather about the region, its products, and who's doing what. For instance, for *La Cuisine du Cognac et du Pineau*, I asked ten top restaurants in the area to give me a recipe with Cognac and one with Pineau to include in the book." Here, for instance, she lets the chef-owner of Le Vieux Logis, Joëlle Brard, one of the rare women running a top restaurant in the region, introduce *Oeufs au Lait Parfumés au Cognac*, an egg custard with a good dose of Cognac to round out an aromatic trio with caramel and vanilla for a sumptuous dessert.

Barbin-Lecrevisse's forthcoming cookbook will study the galaxy of fine regional products—from sea and land—that come together to make Charentais cuisine, like oysters, snails, veal, beef, onions, beans, truffles, foie gras, oils, and so on. It will include traditional recipes, including *Cagouilles à la Charentaise*, a time-honored dish of snails. She'll also tout recipes of her own, again including all the major regional ingredients, and lay out new ideas for cooking with Pineau, local wines, and Cognac.

One of her favorite restaurants in Cognac country is La Ribaudière, in Bourg-Charente, where Thierry Verrat presides over a one-star gem. Settled just east of Cognac since 1989, Verrat and his wife, Patricia, have turned this old 1902 riverside café into one of most prestigious tables in the region.

For Verrat, Cognac can be an exciting accompaniment to a meal, the trick being to bring together "certain qualities of Cognac with certain dishes." You wouldn't, in his view, serve the same Cognac with fish that you would with game. "The secret is to take the aromas of a Cognac and to mirror them in the dish." La Ribaudière features a Cognac-based menu (echoing a Fine Champagne menu by Rémy Martin) that includes five dishes and five qualities of Cognac, each eau-de-vie served differently, starting with ice-cold and progressing through lightly chilled, room temperature, and even slightly warmed. "It's vital to remember, though, that in meals like this Cognac shouldn't be considered a drink, but a seasoning. You taste only a little at a time, holding it in your mouth a few seconds, just long enough to awake the palate and bring out the Cognac's various flavors."

He usually opens the menu with a VS, but will sometimes dare the reverse to "break the mold" by beginning the meal with older qualities like XO and closing it out with the younger ones. The dishes on the year-round Cognac menu at La Ribaudière change from season to season, with fish and crustaceans in summer, mushrooms and game in winter, as do the Cognacs: lighter ones in the warm months; the robust ones on chilly nights. "We've designed the menu to allow people to discover the vast world of Cognac. People generally know whether they like a Cognac or not. But often they don't quite know why it is good or not. That's because Cognac has such an incredible range, from very young to very old. So to discover the differences between them, it's good to associate them with different dishes—a young Cognac will be best with this, a middle-aged one with that, and so on."

So which Cognac with which dish? With a VS, a small amount served straight out of the freezer, "We'll have something very fresh, very exciting, probably a fish, marinated or *tartare*, something light and delicate." It's interesting that Verrat serves the Cognac in tall, narrow flutes, the better to lift up the eau-de-vie and keep it at eye level; in fact all the Cognacs, irrespective of age or temperature, will be served this way during the meal, in small doses, high up and very visible. They're to be tasted with each course, not drunk, and probably not even finished.

With an XO, full of *rancio* and textures of honey, poured at about 8 or 10 degrees centigrade in the middle of the meal, Verrat will serve game, rabbit, or duck, often with mushrooms, truffles or chestnuts, earthy forest products. "This is by far the easiest Cognac of all to associate with a dish."

With older Cognacs, especially an Extra, that have mellowed into refined and elegant brandies full of spices like saffron and fruit like candied orange, "We'll bring out *Coquilles Saint-Jacques* to reflect the fineness of the Cognac. Or grilled lobster, topped with melted butter, which like the alcohol in Cognac helps to mark out and highlight the various flavors."

As for the cheese course, featuring Roquefort or Mimolette, Verrat calls for a VSOP. "Here the Cognac could be thought of as an adolescent, compared with a VS, which is like an infant. But not all cheese will go with Cognac. Mimolette is the best suited, especially for the way it melts in the mouth, just like Cognac does. Roquefort, too, is excellent with Cognac, even more powerful, more shocking and tumultuous, a bit like fireworks!"

The chef's art of finding just what food to go with which Cognac starts, however, with tasting the eau-de-vie. "It's up to the Cognac lover to take each quality of Cognac and verbalize what aromas he finds within. It doesn't matter which brand it is. What's important is that he sift through the flavors and name them. Does this one seem strong, even rude? Or is it rather fine and delicate? And with that, it's up to him to say, 'I can see this Cognac going very well with such and such dish.' It happens that way with me: When I taste a Cognac and I note an aroma of mushrooms, I know I'll create a dish full of mushrooms to go with it. Coming up with something that pleases the senses to the fullest is the most important thing of all."

AGENDAS FOR
TOMORROW

THE FUTURE LOOKS BRIGHT FROM ATOP the Cognac industry. Listening to four talented leaders who work at high altitudes in the top companies that run this business is to quickly understand how they intend above all to keep the success story rolling. These are the people whose decisions today will make the Cognacs of tomorrow. They could be called the gods, but they would wave that lofty title away. It's not hocus-pocus; it's pure flair. It's making savvy choices, bringing together the right elements, investing in the long-term—and having the patience to wait while never resting upon your laurels.

Vincent Géré, product manager for Rémy Martin, minces no words. A winemaker by trade, he has a clear idea of his adopted product: "The unique vision of Rémy Martin is the balance between intensity of flavor and richness of texture. If you don't have both, you can't reproduce a harmonious feeling."

That makes Géré something of a powerful creator, which he

defines as "dreaming, conceiving, writing down ideas, testing them, realizing those ideas, and having many planning sessions to get to the right result."

As product director, he oversees the "elaboration" of all of Rémy Martin's Cognacs—"everything that goes into the bottle," participating at all points in the process and watching over his lieutenants who direct the different stages, from distillation on the lees to aging in Limousin oak.

Géré's favorites are Rémy Martin's VS Grand Cru (a blend of three-to-ten-year-old Petite Champagne Cognacs), its VSOP Fine Champagne (grouping 240 Petite and Grande Champagne Cognacs between four and fourteen years of age), and of course anything from the Louis XIII collection (assemblages of over a thousand Grande Champagne Cognacs between forty and one hundred years in age).

With VS and VSOP qualities, Géré works hard to keep vibrancy in check, as these young eaux-de-vie can be aggressive; rapid aging attenuates them, obviously, but at the same time Géré says it's vital not to "over-oak" and kill the youth of the drink by shutting down the natural floral, fruity, and spicy flavors. As with many VS and VSOP Cognacs, these basic offerings from Rémy Martin are often good mixers. On the other hand, a Louis XIII—with its flavors of myrrh, candied fruit, passion fruit, and honey—is a delicacy to savor. For Géré, this kind of top-end, "ne plus ultra" Cognac mirrors his perfectionist work as an assembler of liquid time.

"You have all those gems that are set aside by generation after generation of your predecessors, and then you yourself come to the cream of the cream of the process of deciding what to put aside for the Louis XIII collection. It's a very special decision. It's not so much about what you yourself are going to like, but rather about imagining that in one hundred years' time some people are going to look back at what you set aside. That's a very different perspective. There are things you do in your own lifetime, like diverting Cognacs to various blends and so forth, but with this, with the Louis XIII, it's something else altogether. This Cognac represents a selection of the top 10 of 1,800 sections of vineyard. After it is put aside, it's only in fifty or sixty years' time that you will start to understand what it's going to become. Make a mistake, select something today that happens to stay lovely but turns out to be boring, then somebody someday will be quite right to look back at your work and say, 'This person just didn't get it.' That keeps you humble. That's really history. You live with it every day."

Out of that deep past emerge attitudes about tomorrow that Géré believes will depend on a widening education about Cognac and its uses, the many styles and ways in which it can be presented. "The question becomes whether you should cater for niche markets or whether you should have a more universal dream. Historically, Rémy Martin has always gravitated toward the second option. It's the right way to go. We will continue building on our diversity and complexity of styles and flavors within our range."

About half of Rémy Martin's sales occur in North America, with the rest split between Asia and Europe. For Géré, the key to tomorrow's success is "more about better explaining your product than anything to do with changing its basic structure." With the right effort, having a good Cognac with a meal can become a common but not commonplace event, "perhaps served chilled, with a sorbet at dessert, and in an elegant dining room." Setting that kind of scene, says Géré, is "our vision and mission."

"Who's going to say, 'Time out'? Who's going to say, 'It took fifty years to make this but only fifteen minutes to taste it'? Who's going to say, 'Look, there are commodities and then there are remarkable exceptions'? Who's going to say, 'You can get more than three impressions at the same time from this drink'? It's not all that complicated. You just have to get people to stop, slow down." He sums up: "Full pleasure. You never get tired of that."

Philippe Treutenaere, CEO of Courvoisier, knows there are 160 years of experience behind the Cognacs that his house makes, which is no small number of generations of dedicated families and no light weight of history upon his shoulders. But he has no trepidations about Cognac's longevity, because the industry is well founded upon a solid "culture of quality," the product of all the sophisticated savoir-faire and extreme care that the people of the region have lavished upon Cognac down through the centuries.

"Cognac has always been a high-end item because it costs a lot to make. And those production costs have always forced the houses to sell their Cognac at high prices. But the fact that Cognac is positioned where it is, at the top of the market, has led over the years to the development of a pure culture of quality. It involves everyone, from the winegrowers watching over their vines all the way to their maturity, to final and specific elaboration of each quality of Cognac for each of the houses. In my view, it's exactly this long-standing quality culture that guarantees a good future for Cognac."

For Treutenaere, Cognac is nothing less than a sort of cultural safe haven in a speeded-up world, a product and concept to which people can turn for respite. And that doesn't mean that he believes more and more people will be drinking Cognac; on the contrary, drinkers around the world are cutting back on their intake of all alcohols. But what is most hopeful for the Cognac industry, he says, is that drinkers are focused more and more these days on quality, specific flavors and sensations. "Cognac fills that bill nicely."

Courvoisier controls about 12 percent of the Cognac market, sells its brand in 160 countries, and is the leader or coleader in 37 of those nations. With that kind of presence on the world drinks scene, confidence in tomorrow comes fairly easily. "As communications keep improving and getting faster, and as markets keep opening up, there will be an ever-larger body of people who are eager, curious to discover a product like Courvoisier. I always remind the people I work with that while we are just one link in a long chain we can't just be content with that, that we must also add something to all this, make a contribution. We must take into account all the long history of Cognac, but at the same time we mustn't be satisfied with that alone. Each person in the company must bring something special to the product and the company and its image. Everyone must be able to look back and say that they added something to the life of the product, that they didn't just glide through their careers without making some concrete contribution. This is the philosophy I'm instilling at Courvoisier. Of course, that's very demanding of people. But the goal is to go further, to take our rich heritage and improve it, to leave a lasting mark and build up our own culture of quality even higher. All this is a constant search. I say to people that we should never be content to do today only what we did yesterday."

As for Cognac's renown around the world, Treutenaere has an answer as fine as the brand he sells: "I have never met a single person in all my travels who said to me, 'I don't like Cognac.' No one. Interesting, isn't it? Here you have a highly sophisticated product, but no matter what kind of consumer, what kind of culture he comes from, let him have a taste of Cognac and you'll never hear him say he doesn't like it. If you're a Chinese drinker in Singapore, or an American drinker in the middle of Oklahoma, or someone in England or in Scotland, you'll never find someone turning their nose up at it. All right, sometimes they might not like the price! But they love Cognac. Which just goes to show you: all that quality is fundamentally attractive."

Courvoisier has historically focused on Anglo-Saxon markets like the United States and Britain. But like many other Cognac houses it is also thinking of China these days. "The Chinese people love Cognac. And when they make some money or have something special to celebrate, they often will do that with a bottle of Cognac, with family and friends." Another big market Treutenaere has his eyes on is Russia, where the people behind the rising new economy are drawn to high-class products like Cognac to "show they have arrived." He adds: "We follow the economic opening of countries very carefully to get into as many new markets as we can, and I have the impression there are many new markets coming our way."

Lionel Breton, chairman and CEO of Martell, notes straightaway that his house, in business nearly three hundred years, is the oldest of the Big Four. And one reason it has lasted so long and done so well, he says, has to do with the nature of Cognac. Breton, who came to Martell after twenty years of managing parts of the Pernod Ricard empire, believes that Cognac the drink is the "ultimate level" to which you can take the fruit of a vineyard—nothing less than the summum bonum of the venerable grape, he intones—lifted aloft by careful distillation, patient aging, and creative blending.

At Martell, creative blending is one of the secrets
to success—the work of artisans lifting the
product of the vineyard to its highest level.

For Breton, "Cognac is a mixture of three parts: a vibrant spirits industry, a concept of luxury, and the artisan's craft." Given that rounded cocktail of expertise, this CEO is sanguine about Cognac's prospects. "The
Cognac market is a mature market that will grow 1, 2, or 3 percent a year,
depending on world economic conditions and on investments by the Big
Four. There are many reasons to be hopeful, especially the fact that even
though Cognac is a niche item, its market isn't shrinking.

"I would even add that, in my view, the quality of the Cognacs being
sold around the world is on the rise, and that those top-end type Cognacs
will become more and more the norm. For that to happen, however, the
big houses are going to have to stay the course. One thing the powers that
be in the Cognac industry could do to help things along would be to
decide together to raise the average age of certain categories of Cognac.
That's of course a controversial subject, but I'm positive that I'm not alone
in the region to think that such a step is not only important but vital."

Martell's top three markets are Britain, the United States, and China—
one each in the big three geographic zones—with the United Kingdom
and the United States going for VS, and China preferring VSOP or better.

"The Cognac market is very healthy, and particularly so in the United
States, which accounts for nearly 40 percent of all Cognac consumed each
year in the world. And it's not a fad in America, either; it's a solid product with a solid position. Meanwhile, certain Asian countries are bounc-
ing back. Put all that together and, no, I'm not worried about the future
of Cognac."

Breton has one caveat, however: if the big Cognac houses make the
mistake of not defending the top-notch, classy nature of their product.
"Cognac is not just a spirit. It's a luxury product, and we have to be very
attentive to this. Take duty-free, for example. When a consumer is picking out a gift, he doesn't choose between a great bottle of Cognac and a
great bottle of whiskey. He chooses between a great bottle of Cognac and
a great watch. Of all the spirits in the world, Cognac is by far the most
luxurious. And that has to be safeguarded by everyone."

Martell's flagship Cordon Bleu, meanwhile, is Breton's favorite among
the house's many offerings, most of which are made from grapes grown in
the Borderies and all of which are aged in Tronçais oak for a light flavor.
Cordon Bleu, each bottle of which contains 150 eaux-de-vie, was created
in 1912 by Edouard Martell and remains a living legend—an "Old Classic Cognac" among the mellowest of all. For Breton, Cordon Bleu sets
Martell apart from the other big houses. "It's a unique product that exists

in its own right. The genius of Edouard Martell was in not putting XO on the label. This allowed Cordon Bleu to step outside the definition of XO-type Cognacs and find its own special position in the market. You know, if you asked people around here what two products they would take with them if they were going to go to a deserted island, you can be sure that one of them would be a bottle of Cordon Bleu." One of the silver-capped, blue-ribboned bottles sits in the window of Breton's office and he smiles admiringly at it, as at a beauty. There's no doubt that the other product he'd take with him to the far-off island would be a second bottle of Cordon Bleu.

Cyril Camus is a through-and-through Borderies man who follows his father, Jean-Paul, in a deep affection of Cognac, and who, at thirty-three, has now taken up the reins of the Camus company. It's not every house that can enjoy a smooth transition from father to son or daughter, given the complications of inheritance taxes, family rivalries, and so forth. So when it happens smoothly these days, it's almost an exception. Cyril Camus's older brother, Jean-Baptiste, decided to go into the professional hunting business, leaving Cyril as steward of the world's number five Cognac firm. It's a task as tough to tackle as that ranking has been diffi-cult to attain and keep.

Topmost in his mind these days is having a realistic perspective about Cognac. "We get very optimistic in this region as soon as we see one month better than the month before. Suddenly, everything is going all right. This points to one of the paradoxes of the region. While we live through long cycles, we also attach a lot of importance to the moment at hand, especially as regards sales. Likewise, we manage big stocks of Cognac, many years' worth, and make predictions about sales over the next five years. And yet we always look at the latest month. People in this region try hard to predict the future through what happened last month. Thankfully, there are a number of people in this business who are less impatient. And it's those people who are very optimistic about the future of Cognac. In fact it's essential to have a positive outlook in this business, especially over the long term."

With its XO and up, Camus focuses on a drinker who is forty years or older and wishes to offer himself something sophisticated. Half of its sales are via duty-free and the other half in Asia and Europe, with some inroads in North America and Africa. "We're rather pleased with the mar-kets we have, with the clients we have. But we think we could do much better by stressing more clearly the diversity and tastes of our Cognacs.

To Cyril Camus, Cognac is a "magical" drink that owes its powerful image
and its very existence to its long, unique history.

We also would like to recruit those drinkers in the 40-and-older group who've turned toward malt whiskeys, for example, and bring them back to Cognac, to authenticity, to *terroir*. Malt whiskey doesn't have a history—at least not like Cognac's."

Cognac's long history, for Cyril Camus, is "what gave it the strength it has today. Cognac is a product that was 'made' over several centuries, that has a very powerful image today. Cognac wouldn't be anything today if it weren't for that history. It's a magical product." The future of Cognac, in his view, will strongly resemble its lengthy history, enjoyed by many of the same people for the same age-old reasons. "But for that future to be assured it's going to be essential for some of our competitors to realize that the future of Cognac isn't in the nightclubs with the twenty-five-year-olds and to redirect their efforts to stress Cognac's superior qualities, traditions, and long history."

"Cognac is the only spirit that people actually take the time to inhale, to savor through the nose. Cognac is also a product that we always share; you never drink a Cognac alone. Cognac represents all that is best in *art-de-vivre* down through the centuries. It was always there at the key moments of history, at great junctures of human cultural development."

Between the depth of Cognac's past and the vista of its future is Cyril the married man and father. Because he has so many things on his plate—a family, children, and all that comes with that—he'll usually eschew a Cognac after dinner and instead have one before the meal: a VSOP as an *apéritif,* which he'll savor for a half-hour. To him, this is the perfect update of the old story, an ideal moment of *détente* in the life of modern man. And what's he thinking about while he's savoring his drink? Probably China, India, and South America, the highly hopeful markets to come: Cyril Camus's next Cognac stories, the ones that, if he has his way, will turn out just right.

THE SPIRIT FLOWS ON

IT'S FACILE TO SAY THAT COGNAC HAS COME a long way—and yet it truly has crossed deep dark oceans and scaled the highest jagged peaks of commerce, conquering markets the world over with its singular taste. This isn't a monetary success on the order of whiskey's or vodka's, and yet it is a shining victory nonetheless, a tale worth telling not just across two wingback chairs by the fireplace, glasses of the elixir in hand, but across a shiny bar in a skyscraper with a long view out over Tokyo or New York.

The clearest note of that victory is how special Cognac has come to be. From its humble beginnings more than four centuries ago as a raw eau-de-vie that substituted for water on sea voyages, today this drink is probably the most exquisite one available anywhere. And the Cognaçais know it: give them a few minutes and sure enough they'll whisper that while it's easy to turn grain into drinkable alcohol, seizing the spirit of the noble grape is something else—and only when they do get hold of it do they call it Cognac.

It seems to follow that where there's Cognac, there's culture. At least that's what a trader like Jacques Rivière, head of A. E. Dor in Jarnac, will proudly tell you. Coming up on seventy, he's confident he knows how Cognac got to its hallowed heights: by following the spread of Western civilization around the world and becoming a basic element of its way of life. That's a bold claim, but would you quibble with a master of Cognac who not only knows the past but can even see the future and knows what *not* to do?

"Ours is a world that is changing faster and faster through time," Rivière says. "And because things are evolving so fast, it's imperative that Cognac cling to its timelessness and not fall into the cycle of modes that quickly go out of fashion. Cognac must hold on to its identity—and not out of pure nostalgia, but because as the world moves ahead people are going to need authenticity in the middle of inconstancy, to have faith in something real. Cognac is the prime link between past, present, and future."

That's quite a big role for a single drink, and yet there's no disputing the truth of Cognac's reach through time. Here is a drink that has adopted many styles over the centuries, and without changing its stripes along the way: whether mixed with water to make an ersatz wine, or mixed with nothing at all and drunk straight, or stirred up with every fruit juice and fizzy water you can think of to make cocktails full of ice cubes. No one way is right. What's important is that Cognac has always adapted to make new inroads and inspire new aficionados. And it has evolved without losing its soul.

Searching far and wide, always on the lookout for new markets and new customers on the venerable commercial seas: This is the mind-set of the successful Cognac trader, whether in the late 1500s when the port to get to was just up the coast in boisterous Flemish country, or in the early 2000s when the glass to fill with his drink is in a hopping bar in Beijing or Los Angeles. Ships, and then airplanes and trucks have gotten his product to the places he wanted it to be down through the years; today sales are often made over the Internet in an instant and production lines altered in a flash to meet demand. Countless millions of dollars are invested in this business each year and profits come out regularly at the other end of the system, so that a number of trading houses thrive, despite the swings of the almighty dollar.

Here in the early twenty-first century, then, Cognac is looking robust—and not just for the moment. There are fundamentals at work, deep constructions of history holding up the enterprise very well. Cognac country weather is fairly mild, and the air isn't at all poisoned. Children learn to swim in the tranquil currents of the Charente and the beefy yet fleet rugby teams hereabouts are damn good. Such strength is natural, if only because Cognac is a hardened survivor, one of the legends, an indisputable winner.

Cognac also owes its glory to the generations of men and women who kept this endearing region of France on its feet—or got it back up whenever the vicious mash of events battered the wills of its winegrowers, distillers, and traders. An incredible number of people have watched over the verdant domain of Cognac. Almost all were good at advancing its name.

Through the centuries countless barrels of Cognac came down the Charente, today a tranquil waterway where you can still catch a good fish.

A European Union of 25 nations is here, which will leave the newly expanded bloc as a major regional market for Cognac for a long time (it's now the second-largest in net value, after North America). Britain will likely dominate that group; France will compete strongly. In the East, China is awake but not fully so; when it does rouse itself, a fantastic explosion of consumption will occur. Some people are thinking India, too, will be a mega-opening someday soon. South America could well refind the suave glory it used to know. The United States, one way or another, will likely remain Cognac's premier port.

This isn't a frightening outlook at all, though Cognac makers often wring their hands about tomorrow. On the contrary, there's enough history behind this double-distilled wine to keep it flowing forward for as long as there are vines and people to tend them and for as long as there are stills percolating in December and filling the air with sweet aromas of Cognac being born.

It takes the tight community of the Cognaçais to make the miracle happen. They live in the low-lying valley of the Charente anywhere from La Rochelle to Angoulême. The rock beneath their feet is tens of millions of years old. The European vines they care for have thrived here a couple of thousand years, their American rootstocks more than a hundred. The tall, bulbous stills that clang and hiss and let forth streams of crystalline to-be-gold have run for a few centuries. And the apprentice learning his trade at one of the many barrel-making firms has lived just a decade and a half. He pedals his bike home from work lickety-split, the better to pull out a fishing pole and get to his favorite spot. For it is a fine, life-filled river that runs through Cognac country, a story streaming out of the past toward more rich adventures, told one and all with clinking, hearty toasts, and much cheer.

ACKNOWLEDGMENTS

All of the people quoted in this work have my deepest gratitude. The historians I've cited are the ones who did all the heavy lifting over the years to erect the pillars of knowledge upon which I have leaned in composing this book. I appreciate all the time they spent talking with me about Cognac country and its travails down through the centuries, and it is my hope that this work accurately brings together their knowledge into one story for all to read. The many busy geologists, paleontologists, and archaeologists who shared their sharp understanding of the region's past also have my heartfelt thanks. Likewise, I am very grateful for all my conversations with scores of people working in so many capacities in the great business of Cognac, whether in the finely managed vineyards or deep within the venerable old houses, who patiently suffered my questions. Numerous people at the industry oversight body, the BNIC, graciously provided rapid answers, loads of insightful statistics, and a clear vision of the legal doings of Cognac. The savvy experts at the Station Viticole, Cognac's science center, explained the sometimes difficult life of the grape and its vineyard. Sébastien Dathané at the Centre International des Eaux-de-Vie in Segonzac gave me much perspective on Cognac's tiny but powerful position in the spirits universe. And nearly every museum and archival repository in the whole region warmly opened its doors to its vast collections and provided me with many graphic elements to depict this old trade. Across the pond in America, Roy Renfro of the T. V. Munson School of Viticulture and Enology in Denison, Texas, merits a grateful nod, too, for filling out the U.S. side of the story of the vines that saved

France after the phylloxera disaster. Francis Hardy, ex-mayor of Cognac, also shared his enthusiasm with me about the strong and warm links between his city and Denison, its official American sister. Likewise, every Charentais I met and spoke with over the two years of writing this work had something unique to add to the story, no matter how small their role in the production of this inimitable product: from cork maker to vine trimmer, from glassmaker to master taster, one and all were passionate about Cognac, which is no less than their lifeline.

I also would like to thank my literary agent, Giles Anderson, for urging me to write this book, as well as my editor at John Wiley, Hana Lane, for bringing proportion to my enthusiastic scrawl. Above all, my heart goes out to my American-tolerant in-laws in Cognac country, and to my patient Charentaise wife and my children for having put up with a writer's schedule all these months and for not having foundered during my absences.

SOURCES

Albertini, Pierre. *La France du XIXeme Siècle*. Paris: Hachette, 2000.

Allmand, Christopher. *The Hundred Years War*. Cambridge: Cambridge University Press, 1989.

Blanning, T. C. W., ed. *Short Oxford History of Europe: The Nineteenth Century*. Oxford: Oxford University Press, 2000.

Bluche, François. *Louis XV*. Paris: Librairie Académique Perrin, 2000.

Boardman, John, Jasper Griffin, and Oswyn Murray. *The Oxford History of the Roman World*. Oxford: Oxford University Press, 1991.

Boulaine, Jean, and Jean-Paul Legros. *D'Olivier de Serres à René Dumont: Portraits d'Agronomes*. Paris: Lavoisier, 1998.

Braudel, Fernand. *Civilisation Matérielle, Economie et Capitalisme: XVe–XVIIIe Siècle*. Paris: Librairie Armand Colin, 1979.

Brun, Jean-Pierre, Fanette Laubenheimer, et al. *Gallia, Archéologie de la France Antique, Tome 58. (Dossier: La Viticulture en Gaule.)* Paris: CNRS Editions, 2001.

Butel, Paul, and Alain Huetz de Lemps. *Histoire de la Société et de la Famille Hennessy (1765–1990)*. Cognac: Hennessy in-house publication.

Combes, Jean, ed. *Histoire du Poitou et des Pays Charentais*. Clermont-Ferrand: De Borée, 2001.

Condie, Kent C., and Robert E. Sloan. *Origin and Evolution of Earth: Principles of Historical Geology*. Upper Saddle River, N.J.: Prentice-Hall, 1998.

Coquand, Henri. *Description Physique, Géologique, Paléontologique et Minéralogique du Département de la Charente*. Marseille: 1862.

Coste, Michel. Cognac: *Les Clés de la Fortune*. Cognac: Librairie du Chateau, 2001.

Coussié, Jean Vincent. *Le Cognac et Les Aléas de l'Histoire*. Cognac: BNIC, 1996.

Crook, Malcolm, ed. *Short Oxford History of France: Revolutionary France*. Oxford: Oxford University Press, 2002.

Cullen, Louis M., with translation by Catherine Simon-Goulletquer and Alain Braastad-Delamain. *Le Commerce des Eaux-de-vie Sous L'Ancien Régime*. Paris: Le Croît Vif, 2002.

Dassié, Jacques. *Archéologie Aérienne*. Joué-les-Tours: Editions Alan Sutton, 2001.

Davies, Norman. *Europe: A History*. New York: HarperCollins, 1998.

Debenath, André, and Jean-François Tournepiche. *Préhistoire de la Charente*. Angoulême: Germa, 1996.

Delafosse, Marcel, ed. *Histoire de La Rochelle*. Toulouse: Editions Privat, 2002.

Delamain, Robert. *Histoire du Cognac*. 1935.

Delayant, L. *Histoire du Département de la Charente-Inférieure*. Saintes: Les Chemins de la Mémoire.

Delos, Gilbert. *Le Monde du Cognac*. Paris: Hatier, 1997.

Dion, Roger. *Histoire de la Vigne et du Vin en France*. Paris: Flammarion, 1977.

Doyle, William, ed. Short *Oxford History of France: Old Regime France*. Oxford: Oxford University Press, 2001.

Dubourg-Noves, Pierre, ed. *Histoire d'Angoulême et de ses Alentours*. Toulouse: Editions Privat, 1989.

Duby, Georges. *Le Dimanche de Bouvines*. Paris: Editions Gallimard, 1973.

———. *Grand Atlas Historique*. Paris: Larousse, 2001.

Duby, Georges, and Armand Wallon, eds. *Histoire de la France Rurale*, Vols. 1–3. Paris: Editions du Seuil, 1975 and 1976.

Einhard, and Notker the Stammerer, with translation by Lewis Thorpe. *Two Lives of Charlemagne*. London: Penguin Books, 1969.

Etienne, Robert, and Charles Higounet, eds. *Histoire de Bordeaux*. Toulouse: Editions Privat, 2001.

Fagan, Brian. *The Little Ice Age*. New York: Basic Books, 2000.

Faith, Nicholas. *Classic Brandy*. London: Prion, 2000.

Ferro, Marc. *Histoire de France*. Paris: Editions Odile Jacob, 2001.

Fossier, Robert, ed. *The Cambridge Illustrated History of the Middle Ages*, Vols. 1–3. Cambridge: Cambridge University Press, 1986, 1989, and 1997.

Fourquin, Guy. *Histoire Economique de L'Occident Médiéval*. Paris: Librairie Armand Colin, 1979.

Froissart, with translation by Geoffrey Brereton. *Chronicles*. London: Penguin Books, 1978.

Gabilly, Jean, and Elie Cariou. *Guides Géologiques Régionaux: Poitou, Vendée, Charentes*. Paris: Masson, 1997.

Galet, Pierre. *Cépages et Vignobles de France, Tome I: Les Vignes Américaines*. Montpellier: 1988.

———. *Précis de Pathologie Viticole*. Saint-Jean-de-Védas: Imprimerie JF Impression, 1999.

Garrier, Gilbert. *Histoire Sociale et Culturelle du Vin*. Paris: Larousse, 2002.

———. *Le Phylloxéra*. Paris: Albin Michel, 1989.

Genet, Christian, and Louis Moreau. *Les Deux Charentes Sous l'Occupation et la Résistance*. Gémozac: La Caillerie, 1987.

Gibbon, Edward. *The Decline and Fall of the Roman Empire*. London: Penguin Books, 1985.

Glénisson, Jean, Marc Seguin, et al. *Charente-Maritime*. Paris: Editions Bonneton, 2001.

Gobry, Ivan. *Les Capétiens*. Paris: Editions Tallandier, 2001.

Gomez de Soto, José, et al. *Charente*. Paris: Editions Bonneton, 1992.

Gomez de Soto, José, and Stéphane Verger. *Le Casque Celtique de la Grotte d'Agris*. Angoulême: Germa, 1999.

Graves, John. *From a Limestone Ledge*. Houston: Gulf Publishing, 1980.

Gregory of Tours, with translation by Lewis Thorpe. *The History of the Franks*. London: Penguin Classics, 1974.

Gribbin, John and Mary. *Ice Age: How a Change of Climate Made Us Human*. London: Penguin Books, 2001.

Groupe de Recherches et d'Etudes Historiques de la Charente Saintongeaise. *Annales du GREH, Nos. 1, 3, 4–6, 9–12, 15, 17–21*. Segonzac: GREH, 1979 to 2000.

Guitard-Auviste, Ginette. *Chardonne*. Paris: Editions Olivier Orban, 1984.

Hibbert, Christopher. *The Days of the French Revolution*. New York: Harper-Perennial, 2002.

Holmes, George. *Europe: Hierarchy and Revolt, 1320–1450*. Glasgow: Fontana, 1981.

Holt, Mack P. *The French Wars of Religion: 1562–1629*. Cambridge: Cambridge University Press, 1995.

Horne, Alistair. *Seven Ages of Paris*. New York: Alfred A. Knopf, 2002.

Johnson, Hugh. *Wine*. London: Mitchell Beazley, 1974.

Jones, Colin. *The Cambridge Illustrated History of France*. Cambridge: Cambridge University Press, 1999.

Keegan, John. *The First World War*. New York: Vintage Books, 2000.

Kladstrup, Don and Petie. *Wine and War*. New York: Broadway Books, 2001.

Knecht, R. J. *The Rise and Fall of Renaissance France: 1483–1610*. Oxford: Blackwell Publishers, 2001.

Kohler, Pierre. *Le Poitou-Charentes*. Rennes: Editions Ouest-France, 2001.

Kurlansky, Mark. *The Basque History of the World*. New York: Penguin Books, 1999.

———. *Salt: A World History*. New York: Walker & Co., 2002.

Lachiver, Marcel. *Vins, Vignes et Vignerons*. Paris: Fayard, 1988.

Lampre, Caroline. *Cognac par ses Etiquettes*. Paris: Editions Herscher, 2002.

Lancaster, Bruce. *The American Revolution*. Boston: Houghton Mifflin, 1987.

Laurenceau, Thomas. *Rémy Martin: L'Esprit du Cognac*. Paris: Editions EPA, 1991.

Le Roy Ladurie, Emmanuel. *L'Etat Royal*. Paris: Hachette, 1987.

———. *Histoire du Climat Depuis L'An Mil (Deuxième Volume)*. Paris: Flammarion, 1983.

———. *Histoire des Paysans Français*. Paris: Editions du Seuil, 2002.

Leakey, Richard, and Roger Lewin. *Origins Reconsidered*. New York: Anchor Books, 1992.

Legros, Jean-Paul, and Jean Argeles. *L'Odyssée des Agronomes de Montpellier*. Paris: Editeur Editagro, 1997.

Leguay, Jean-Pierre. *L'Europe Carolingienne*. Paris: Editions Belin, 2002.

———. *L'Europe des Etats Barbares*. Paris: Editions Belin, 2002.

Levenson, Thomas. *Ice Time*. New York: Harper & Row, 1989.

Lewis, Bernard. *The Muslim Discovery of Europe*. New York: W. W. Norton, 2001.

Loubère, Leo A. *The Red and the White: The History of Wine in France and Italy in the Nineteenth Century*. Albany: State University of New York Press, 1978.

Luc, Jean-Noël, ed. *La Charente Maritime: L'Aunis et la Saintonge des Origines à Nos Jours*. Saint-Jean-d'Angély: Editions Bordessoules, 1981.

Maurin, Louis, and Marianne Thauré. *Guides Archéologiques de la France: Saintes Antique*. Paris: Imprimerie National Editions, 1994.

McGrew, J. R., J. Loenholdt, T. Zabadal, A. Hunt, and H. Amberg. *Growing Wine Grapes*. Ann Arbor, Mich.: G. W. Kent, 1993.

McLeRoy, Sherrie S., and Roy E. Renfro Jr. *Grape Man of Texas: The Life of T. V. Munson*. Austin, Tex.: Eakin Press, 2004.

McPhee, John. *Annals of the Former World.* New York: Farrar, Straus and Giroux, 1998.

Miquel, Pierre. *Histoire de la France.* Paris: Fayard, 1976.

Mitford, Nancy. *The Sun King.* London: Penguin Books, 1994.

Monnet, Jean. *Mémoires.* Paris: Fayard, 1976.

Munson, T. V. *Foundations of American Grape Culture.* Denison, Tex.: T. V. Munson & Son, 1909.

Neveu, Jean-Louis, et al. *Vigne et Cognac en Pays Charentais.* Mougon: Geste Editions, 1995. Originally published in 1872.

Paczensky, Gert V. *Le Grand Livre du Cognac.* Paris: Edition du Club France Loisirs, 1987.

Parvulesco, Constantin. *Saveurs du Terroir: Le Cognac.* Paris: Flammarion, 2002.

Pessey, Christian. *L'ABCdaire du Cognac.* Paris: Flammarion, 2002.

Phelan, Richard. *Texas Wild.* Excalibur Books, 1976.

Phillips, Rod. *A Short History of Wine.* London: Penguin Books, 2000.

Pomerol, Charles, ed. *Terroirs et Vins de France: Itinéraires Oenologiques et Géologiques.* Orléans: Editions de BRGM, 1984.

Pouget, Roger. *Histoire de la Lutte Contre le Phylloxéra de la Vigne en France.* Paris: Institut National de la Recherche Agronomique, 1990.

Prestwich, Michael. *The Three Edwards.* London: Routledge, 1980.

Ray, Cyril. *Cognac.* London: Peter Davies, 1973.

Renaud, Jean. *Les Vikings en France.* Rennes: Editions Ouest-France, 2000.

Ribéra-Pervillé, Claude, and Hubert Bonin. *Histoire de l'Aquitaine.* Rennes: Editions Ouest-France, 2002.

Rombough, Lon. *The Grape Grower: A Guide to Organic Viticulture.* White River Junction, Vt.: Chelsea Green Publishing, 2002.

Runciman, Steven. *A History of the Crusades, Vol. 3: The Kingdom of Acre and the Later Crusades.* Cambridge: Cambridge University Press, 1951.

Scarre, Chris. *Chronicle of the Roman Emperors.* London: Thames & Hudson, 1995.

Schama, Simon. *Citizens: A Chronicle of the French Revolution.* New York: Vintage, 1990.

———. *The Embarrassment of Riches: An Interpretation of Dutch Culture in the Golden Age.* New York: Vintage Books, 1997.

———. *A History of Britain.* New York: Hyperion, 2000.

Schom, Alan. *Napoleon Bonaparte.* New York: HarperPerennial, 1998.

Sepulchre, Bruno. *Le Livre du Cognac.* Paris: Hubschmid & Bouret, 1983.

Shakespeare, William. *William Shakespeare: The Complete Works.* Baltimore: Penguin Books, 1969.

Simon, Andre L. *The Noble Grapes and the Great Wines of France.* London: McGraw-Hill, 1957.

Spearing, Darwin. *Roadside Geology of Texas.* Missoula, Mont.: Mountain Press Publishing, 1991.

Tattersall, Ian. *Becoming Human: Evolution and Human Uniqueness.* New York: Harcourt Brace, 1998.

Texier, Henri. *Petite Histoire de Saintes.* La Crèche: Geste Editions, 2003.

Tournepiche, Jean-François. *Géologie de la Charente.* Angoulême: Germa, 1998.

Tout, T. F. *The History of England.* London: Longmans, Green & Co., 1905.

Trinkaus, Erik, and Pat Shipman. *The Neandertals.* New York: Vintage Books, 1994.

Tuchman, Barbara W. *A Distant Mirror: The Calamitous 14th Century.* New York: Ballantine Books, 1978.

———. *The First Salute.* New York: Ballantine Books, 1988.

Unwin, Tim. *Wine and the Vine.* New York: Routledge, 1996.

Vale, Malcolm. *The Origins of the Hundred Years War: The Angevin Legacy, 1250–1340.* Oxford: Clarendon Press, 1996.

Vernou, Christian. *Carte Archéologique de la Gaule: La Charente.* Paris: Editions de la Fondation Maison des Sciences de l'Homme, 1993.

Vernou, Christian, Jean-François Buisson, and Louis Maurin. *La Ferme Gallo-Romaine de la Haute-Sarrazine Cognac-Crouin.* Cognac: Musée de Cognac, 1990.

Warren, W. L. *King John.* Los Angeles: University of California Press, 1978.

Weir, Alison. *Eleanor of Aquitaine.* New York: Ballantine Books, 1999.

Wenzler, Claude. *Généalogie des Rois de France et Epouses Royales.* Rennes: Editions Ouest-France, 2001.

Picture Credits

INDEX